**Work-Based Learning**

Level 1

NVQ/SVQ
CERTIFICATE

# PERFORMING ENGINEERING OPERATIONS

Terry Grimwood

Stephen Scanlon

Mike Tooley

Richard Tooley

ALWAYS LEARNING

**PEARSON**

Published by Pearson Education Limited, a company incorporated in England and Wales, having its registered office at Edinburgh Gate, Harlow, Essex, CM20 2JE. Registered company number: 872828

www.pearsonschoolsandfecolleges.co.uk

Text © Terry Grimwood, Stephen Scanlon, Mike Tooley, Richard Tooley 2012
Typeset by Tek-Art, Crawley Down, West Sussex
Original illustrations © Pearson Education Ltd 2012
Illustrated by Tek-Art

The rights of Terry Grimwood, Mike Tooley, Richard Tooley and Stephen Scanlon to be identified as authors of this work have been asserted by them in accordance with the Copyright, Designs and Patents Act 1988.

First published 2012

15 14 13 12
10 9 8 7 6 5 4 3 2 1

**British Library Cataloguing in Publication Data**
A catalogue record for this book is available from the British Library

ISBN 978 0 435 07508 8

Printed and bound in Spain by Grafos

**Acknowledgements**
Pearson Education Ltd and Terry Grimwood would like to thank Ferlin Quantrill and the staff at Lowestoft College for their advice and support in completing Chapter 11 of this book and for their assistance in setting and running an additional photo shoot for this and other chapters.

Pearson Education Ltd would like to thank Simon Smith and the team at SOS Consultancy for their invaluable help in reviewing the technical content of this resource and the staff and students of Chichester College and Oaklands College for their patience and assistance in setting up the photo shoots for this book.

The author and publisher would like to thank the following individuals and organisations for permission to reproduce photographs:

(Key: b-bottom; c-centre; l-left; r-right; t-top)

**Alamy Images:** 57stock 121, Adrian Brockwell 47tr, Alamy Creativity 119, Conrad Elias 20bl, David J. Green 124t, 144bl, Gari Wyn Williams 37tr, HAWKEYE 3, Hemis 9, incamerastock 10t, metalpix 217, Nic Hamilton 17, Robert Wilkinson 146b, Science Photo Library / Adam Gault 160tl, Tony Rolls 1; **Deb Limited:** 14tl; **Digital Stock:** 151tr; **Digital Vision:** 11, 155 (2); **Fotolia.com:** david hughes 83, Igor Kovalchuk 127; **Getty Images:** Datacraft Co. Ltd 95; **Imagemore Co., Ltd:** 257br; **Imagestate Media:** John Foxx Collection 151tl; **Masterfile UK Ltd:** 10b, 27, 36, 199; **Pearson Education Ltd:** Clark Wiseman / Studio 8 13br, 14cl, 14cr, 14bl, 14br, 15b, 16t, 29, 71l/3, 71l/6, 71l/7, 71r/3, 71r/4, 117r, 118l/8, 118l/9, 118r/5, 122, 138/2, 142bl, 143/2, 179/4, 182/1, Coleman Yuen 77cl, David Sanderson 13cr, Gareth Boden 19tl, 19cl, 19cr, 19bl, 19br, 24, 25tl, 25l, 56, 71l/1, 71l/2, 71l/8, 71l/9, 71r/1, 71r/2, 71r/6, 72, 73t, 73b, 76, 78/3, 82t, 82b, 97l, 103, 108, 109t, 112, 117tl, 117bl, 117br, 118l/2, 118l/3, 118l/4, 118l/5, 118l/6, 118l/7, 118r/3, 130tl, 137/1, 146tl, 148t, 153cl, 153bl, 168/1, 168/8, 169/1, 178b/1, 179/1, 179/2, 233/4, 241/1, Naki Photography 22bl, 71l/5, 71r/8, 74b, 101r, 110, 117tr, 118r/2, 118r/6, 118r/7, 130c, 137/2, 137/3, 137/4, 138/1, 168/2, 257tl, Trevor Clifford 168/3, 168/5, 172, 174/1, 174/4, 174/6, 193, 233/1; **PhotoDisc:** 13cl, 77bl, 144tr; **Press Association Images:** AP / Kimimasa Mayama 50, Emppics Entertainment / Jason Sheldon 90; **Science Photo Library Ltd:** Dr P. Marazzi 13tr, GlPhotostock 77tr, Steve Allen 258, TEK Image 141; **Shutterstock.com:** 1000 Words 105, Andrew Bassett 229, Balefire 257tr, Baloncici 25bl, Blaz Kure 118r/4, 121l, 138/3, c. byatt-norman 74t, Cobalt88 149b, Dalibor Sevaljevic 15t, Dario Sabljak 47tl, Deymos 118l/1, Dragana Gerasimoski 22br, Elnur 16b, fasphotographic 115, Frances A. Miller 10l, Georgi Roshkev 163, gorsky 146tr, Harald Hølland Tjøstheim 18l, 20t, jennyt 22tl, Joachim Wendler 15r, jon le-bon 78/2, Kurhan 18r, magnola 143/4, Michael Shake 14c, mpanch 49, pryzmat 15l, .shock 126, TFoxFoto 124b, ULKASTUDIO 69, Winthrop Brookhouse 155/5; **SuperStock:** Glow Images 255

**Cover images:** *Front:* **Shutterstock.com:** YellowJ

All other images © Pearson Education Ltd / Jules Selmes

Pearson would like to thank Jules Selmes and Adam Giles from Jules Selmes Photographer for their hard work and dedication throughout the photo shoots for this book. Pearson would also like to thank Sam Bennett for his co-operation in modelling for a number of the photos in this book.

# Contents

# Introduction

Welcome to the exciting and challenging world of engineering!

The world that we live in and the machines and systems that we depend on were all designed, built and maintained by engineers. The cars, ships, trains and aircraft that we travel in and the phones that we rely on are all examples of the work of engineers. Think what life would be like without these things!

Engineers drive key technological change. They are in the front line in moving the UK, and other European countries, from a society dependent on high carbon, low security energy to a mix of wind, wave, nuclear, solar and carbon capture energy sources. We urgently need this change to be made, making engineers all the more important in the modern world.

Engineering is a thriving sector of UK industry. It offers a very wide range of employment opportunities and is one area where there is no shortage of jobs. As an aspiring engineer you should be constantly questioning how and why things work the way they do and how they could be improved. We hope that this book will become a key part in this process.

## About Performing Engineering Operations

Performing Engineering Operations (PEO) is an ideal first qualification in engineering that supports the delivery and assessment of the basic skills and knowledge required by a range of industries. PEO is available with qualifications at Levels 1 and 2 and leads to a variety of pathways in line with the specific requirements of industrial sectors. This includes aerospace, transportation, and general manufacturing.

PEO is part of a long-established and highly respected framework of National Vocational Qualifications (NVQ). Many young people enter employment each year having followed the NVQ route and employers recognise the value of these qualifications in providing them with a competent and effective workforce.

## About this book

This book has been produced to help you build a sound knowledge and understanding of all aspects of the NVQ in Performing Engineering Operations. The topics in this book cover all the information you will need to attain the three core Level 1 units together with eight of the most popular optional units. Each chapter of the book relates to a particular unit and provides the information needed to form the required knowledge and understanding of that area. It can be used for any awarding organisation's qualification including Edexcel, EAL and City & Guilds.

The book has been written by a team of experienced authors and trainers who have many years of experience within the engineering sector. They aim to provide you with all the necessary information you need to support your studies and to ensure that the information is presented in a way that makes it both relevant and accessible.

# About the authors

**Terry Grimwood** is a lecturer in electrical installation and technology at Oaklands College St Albans. He has taught PEO courses for many years and his Level 1 learner workbook earned him praise from both Ofsted and City & Guilds. Previously he worked for many years in the electrical industry, both for contracting companies and for BT. He is a published author of fiction, with three books and numerous short stories. His first novel *Bloody War* is available from Eibonvale Press.

**Mike Tooley** is a technical author and consultant. He was formerly Dean of the Faculty of Engineering and Vice Principle at Brooklands College in Surrey, where he was responsible for the delivery of learning to over 9000 further and higher education students. Originally trained as an electronic engineer, Mike is now the well-known author of several popular engineering and related text books, including widely adopted course texts for BTEC, A-Level, GCSE, Diploma and NVQ qualifications in Engineering.

**Richard Tooley** is a lecturer, Course leader and ILT Champion at Chichester College. He has taught engineering at all levels from Entry to Degree across a range of disciplines. Previous publications include resources to support BTEC Level 2 and 3 qualifications as well as articles in national engineering magazines. A keen innovator, his passion for engineering and education drives him to aim to create work that can truly inspire and enthuse today's young engineers.

**Stephen Scanlon** is a lecturer in Engineering at Chichester College and the Program Manager for the engineering apprentices there. He previously worked as a school teacher and in other further education establishments, teaching engineering since 1997, including NVQ, Technical Certificate, BTEC, GNVQ, Diploma, Foundation Degree and GCSE. He started his career as a production technician but has worked in prototype and small batch manufacture, machine tool repair and as a fabrication welder.

Stephen would like to thank his wife for her great support during this project.

# Qualification mapping grid

This table maps the content of this book to some of the most popular awarding organisations.

| Chapter | EAL | Edexcel | City & Guilds |
|---|---|---|---|
| 1. Working safely in an engineering environment | QPEO1/001 | L/600/5781 | 301 D/103/8765 |
| 2. Working efficiently and effectively in engineering | QPEO1/002 | M/600/5899 | 302 H/103/8766 |
| 3. Using and communicating technical information | QPEO1/003 | D/600/5901 | 303 K/103/8767 |
| 4. Wiring electrical equipment and circuits | QPEO1/020 | K/600/5769 | 320 K/103/8784 |
| 5. Assembling electrical wiring support systems | QPEO1/021 | T/600/5774 | 321 M/103/8785 |
| 6. Assembling and wiring electrical panels | QPEO1/022 | J/600/5777 | 322 T/103/8786 |
| 7. Assembling electronic circuits | QPEO1/023 | J/600/5780 | 323 A/103/8787 |
| 8. Making components using hand tools and fitting techniques | QPEO1/004 | H/600/5902 | 304 M/103/8768 |
| 9. Using lathes for turning operations | QPEO1/007 | L/600/5912 | 807 M/103/8771 |
| 10. Carrying out sheet metal cutting, forming and assembly activities | QPEO1/012 | R/600/5930 | 312 L/103/8776 |
| 11. Using manual metal arc and manual oxy-fuel gas welding equipment | QPEO1/015 QPEO1/018 | F/600/5938 T/600/5757 | 315 D/103/8779 318 D/103/8782 |

# Features of this book

This book has been fully illustrated with artworks and photographs. These will help to give you more information about a concept or a procedure as well as helping you to follow a step-by-step technical skills procedure or identify a particular tool or material.

This book also contains a number of different features to help your learning and development.

## Kitting up pages

These pages pick up the key health and safety areas you need to be aware of as you carry out the practical tasks the chapter contains. They also give information about the different tools you will use throughout the chapter and describe any important legislation or paperwork you will need to be familiar with.

## Technical skills

Throughout the book you will find step-by-step procedures to help you practise the technical skills you need to complete to be successful in your studies (see example opposite).

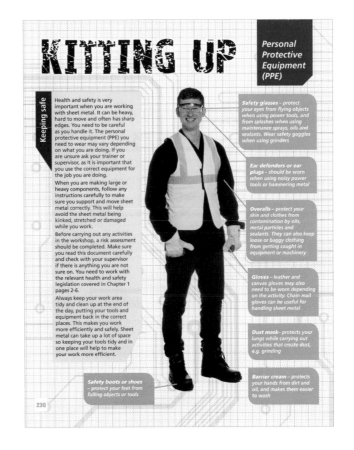

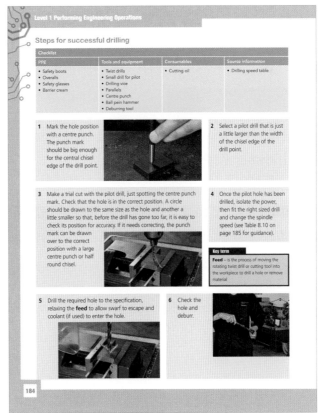

## Safety tips

These four features give you guidance for working safely with tools and equipment and in the workplace.

### Keep It Safe
Green safety tips provide useful information about SAFE conditions in emergency situations and your personal safety.

### Keep it safe
Red safety tips indicate a PROHIBITION (something you **must not** do).

### Keep It Safe
Blue safety tips indicate a MANDATORY instruction (something that you **must** do).

### Keep It Safe
Yellow safety tips indicate a WARNING (hazard or danger).

### Key terms
These are new or difficult words. They are picked out in **bold** in the text and then defined in the margin.

### Did You Know
This feature gives you interesting facts about the engineering sector.

### Quick Tip
These provide small suggestions and pieces of advice for practical work, suggesting possible tips for best practice.

### Hands On
These provide short activities or tasks to test your understanding of the subject.

### Case Study
This feature provides examples of real-life working practice for you to read about and discuss.

## Other features

### QUICK CHECK
These are questions that appear throughout the chapter, relating to the recent content of that chapter to see how you are getting along.

### CHECK YOUR KNOWLEDGE
This is a series of multiple choice questions at the end of each chapter, in the style of the end-of-unit tests used by some exam boards.

# 1 Working safely in an engineering environment

Being an engineer is a rewarding job and offers the chance to get involved in all sorts of exciting activities. However, you may be working with dangerous materials or tools and sometimes in a difficult working environment. You need to work safely, with thorough planning, carrying out the task correctly and clearing up afterwards. As an engineer, you must also know what to do in an emergency.

This chapter explores the essential working practices that will keep you and those around you safe. It also looks at the law and how it relates to your work.

In this chapter you will learn about:

- health and safety
- legislation and regulations
- risk assessment
- common hazards
- working safely
- personal protective equipment (PPE)

- warning signs
- manual handling
- fire
- emergency procedures
- first aid

# Health and safety

Working in engineering might involve carrying out some dangerous tasks and working with hazardous tools and materials. Health and safety is all about being able to do your job safely. It is a legal requirement for you and your employer to follow the rules and regulations on health and safety, making sure that whatever you do in your job, you can do it as safely as possible. It is just as important that *you* understand what working safely involves. After all, the results of something going wrong could be very severe.

# Legislation and regulations

There are lots of laws governing your work as an engineer. You don't need to know all the detail but you should be aware of the basic points of the main legislation.

Following the rules of health and safety is a legal requirement. If a company fails to follow these rules and regulations then those responsible could be prosecuted, fined or even imprisoned.

The Health and Safety Executive (HSE) is a government agency that designs, implements and monitors health and safety. A HSE inspector can visit a place of work at any time to check that all is well. They have the power to change the way things are done. If things are really bad they can completely close a company down if they feel that there is a severe threat to the health and safety of its staff. Inspectors would also be sent to a place of work to investigate the causes of a serious accident or if allegations have been made of unsafe practices.

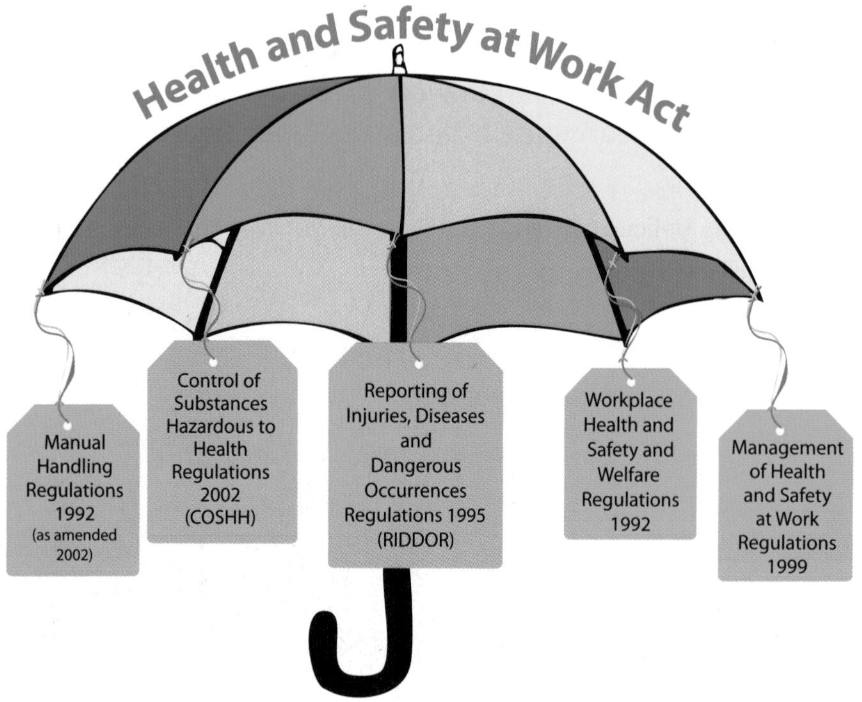

> **Key term**
>
> **Legislation** – a law passed by the Government that gives rules that must be followed

## The Health and Safety at Work Act (HASAWA) 1974

The Health and Safety at Work Act (HASAWA) 1974 is the main health and safety legislation in the UK and acts like an umbrella to cover all of the regulations that followed it.

HASAWA covers the main responsibilities of both employers and employees in terms of health and safety. A summary of these is shown in Table 1.01.

**Health and Safety at Work Act**

- Manual Handling Regulations 1992 (as amended 2002)
- Control of Substances Hazardous to Health Regulations 2002 (COSHH)
- Reporting of Injuries, Diseases and Dangerous Occurrences Regulations 1995 (RIDDOR)
- Workplace Health and Safety and Welfare Regulations 1992
- Management of Health and Safety at Work Regulations 1999

**Figure 1.01** Regulations covered by HASAWA

| Section 2: Employers | Section 7: Employees |
|---|---|
| All employers have a duty: | As an employee you have a duty: |
| • of care for the welfare, health and safety of their employees where it is practicable for them to do so | • to take reasonable care at work for the health and safety of yourself and others who may be affected by what you do or do not do |
| • to provide and maintain safe equipment, tools and plant within the workplace | • not to intentionally or recklessly interfere with or misuse anything provided for your health and safety |
| • to ensure working conditions are safe and hygienic | • to bring to your employer's attention any situation you consider dangerous |
| • to provide proper personal protective equipment (PPE) and make sure it is used correctly | • to use any PPE provided correctly |
| • to make sure items and substances are used, handled, stored and transported safely | • to help your employer to meet their **statutory** obligations |
| • to provide any necessary information, instruction, training and supervision to ensure the health and safety of employees | • to co-operate with your employer on health and safety matters |
| • to make sure everyone can get in and out of the workplace safely | • to bring to your employer's attention any weakness in their welfare, health and safety arrangements |
| • to provide adequate facilities and arrangements for welfare at work | |

**Table 1.01** Summary of the health and safety duties of employers and employees

## The Management of Health and Safety at Work Regulations 1999

The Management of Health and Safety at Work Regulations 1999 detail some of the employer responsibilities in terms of health and safety. This includes carrying out risk assessments (see pages 7–8) to identify hazards and help prevent accidents. They state that emergency procedures and health and safety policies must be well designed, properly documented and taught to all staff who, in turn, must follow them.

## The Workplace Health and Safety and Welfare Regulations 1992

The Workplace Health and Safety and Welfare Regulations 1992 cover the basic health and safety requirements of the working environment. For example, it says there should be a minimum working temperature of 16°C for desk work and 13°C for manual work (there are some exceptions such as freezer rooms or chilled processing environments). Employers must ensure the cleanliness of their facilities and provide toilets, drinking water, adequate ventilation, heating and lighting.

**Key term**

**Statutory** – something that must be done by law

**Figure 1.02** Facilities must be clean and well organised for employees

## The Personal Protective Equipment (PPE) at Work Regulations 2002

The Personal Protective Equipment (PPE) at Work Regulations 2002 describe the responsibilities of employers to provide and maintain appropriate PPE for the activities it carries out. For more information on PPE, see pages 13–17.

## The Manual Handling Operations Regulations 1992

The Manual Handling Operations Regulations 1992 cover the precautions and responsibilities of employers and employees when moving heavy loads. For more information on moving heavy loads safely, see pages 18–19.

## The Provision and Use of Work Equipment Regulations 1998

The Provision and Use of Work Equipment Regulations 1998 describe how all equipment used in a workplace must be fit for purpose, used properly and maintained. It states that equipment should display the right safety signs correctly (e.g. to identify any potential hazards and PPE requirements), have guards in place to protect workers, and be inspected regularly.

## The Display Screen Equipment Regulations 1992

This covers the safe use of visual display units such as computer/laptop screens as well as those on portable equipment and machinery. When working at a computer for a long time you are entitled to regular breaks and your employer may be required to pay for eye tests. Sitting in a bad position at a computer workstation while using a keyboard and mouse for long periods of time without a break can cause repetitive strain injuries.

**Hands On**

Ask a friend to take a photo of you when you are working at a computer workstation. Print out the picture and evaluate how you sit compared with the posture in Figure 1.03. What could you do to improve things?

**Figure 1.03** Correct posture for working at a computer workstation

## The Reporting of Injuries, Diseases and Dangerous Occurrences Regulations (RIDDOR) 1995

RIDDOR states that employers must keep a record of any accidents that occur as a result of their activities. It also states that any major accidents, diseases and dangerous occurrences must be reported to the Health and Safety Executive (HSE). This helps to see any potential trends developing as well as learning useful lessons from what has happened.

| Major injuries | Notifiable diseases | Dangerous occurrences |
|---|---|---|
| • Fracture or dislocation of main body parts (other than fingers or toes)<br>• Amputation<br>• Eye damage including burns (chemical or hot metal) and any penetrating eye wound<br>• Injury from electric shock causing unconsciousness<br>• Any injury which causes unconsciousness, requiring CPR or hospital admittance for more than 24 hours<br>• Unconsciousness caused by hazardous substance inhalation, ingestion or absorption through the skin<br>• Illness caused by biological hazards, toxins or infected material<br>• Injuries from any cause (however minor) that required the casualty to be away from work or incapable of fulfilling their full duties for a period of more than seven days | • Some types of poisoning<br>• Work-related skin conditions such as dermatitis, skin cancer, chrome ulcer, and oil folliculitis/acne<br>• Lung conditions including occupational asthma, farmer's lung, pneumoconiosis, asbestosis and mesothelioma<br>• Certain infections including leptospirosis, hepatitis, tuberculosis, anthrax, legionellosis and tetanus<br>• Other medical conditions caused as a result of work including occupational cancer, certain musculoskeletal disorders, decompression illness and hand-arm vibration syndrome | • Collapse of lifting equipment<br>• Explosion caused by damage to a pressurised vessel<br>• Explosions or collapse that extend beyond the boundary of company premises<br>• Accidents involving contact with overhead power lines<br>• Failure of radioactive equipment, e.g. X-ray machines<br>• Failure of breathing apparatus<br>• Accidental release of biological agents<br>• Accidents involving vehicles transporting hazardous materials<br>• Incidents at a well or pipeline |

**Table 1.02** Incidents that must be reported directly to the HSE under RIDDOR

Any accidents or dangerous occurences, however small, should be recorded by an employer in an accident book. This says the time and date of the accident, what happened and who it happened to, what injuries were caused and who witnessed it. Those considered serious (shown in Table 1.02) would also need to be reported to the HSE.

Figure 1.04 A fume cupboard used to extract potentially harmful fumes and gases

## The Control of Substances Hazardous to Health Regulations (COSHH) 2002

Engineers often use substances that have the potential to cause harm to themselves or others. COSHH sets down rules covering the safe handling, storage, use and disposal of such substances.

It states that correct PPE should be used when using hazardous substances (see pages 13–17) and that they are stored securely. Appropriate first aid and emergency equipment must also be available. Harmful waste products must be disposed of safely with consideration for the environment.

All materials must be clearly marked with their contents and the hazard that they present. A standard set of hazardous material symbols are shown in Figure 1.05.

**European symbols**

| Toxic | Harmful | Corrosive | Explosive | Highly flammable | Oxidising | Dangerous to the environment |

**New international symbols**

Figure 1.05 European and international hazardous substance labels

**Keep It Safe**

Always read the substance data sheet before working with any new hazardous materials.

**Keep It Safe**

Always check the regulations that relate to the kinds of activities that your job involves.

## Other relevant legislation

There are many additional pieces of health and safety legislation that might apply to you, depending on the area of engineering that you are involved in. These include:

- Electricity at Work Regulations 1989
- Control of Noise at Work Regulations 1995
- Confined Spaces Regulations 1997
- Lifting Operations and Lifting Equipment Regulations 1998
- Supply of Machinery (Safety) Regulations 2005
- Work at Height Regulations 2005

# Risk assessment

One of the key things that helps to ensure that whatever you do is done safely is a risk assessment. A risk assessment is carried out before an activity is started so that you can decide how safe it is and what you need to do to make it safer. Companies often have their own template for a risk assessment form but they generally all involve the following three basic steps:

1. **What are the hazards?** Look at any aspects of the activity that could potentially cause harm.

2. **What are the risks?** Once you know what the hazards are, you look at what these could cause to happen and how likely it is for this to happen.

   Who could potentially be harmed from aspects identified in points 1 and 2?

3. **What can we do to make it safer?** Decide what **control measures** you need to put in place to minimise the risks. This could be what PPE to wear, how to carry out the activity safely, what specialist equipment to use or what training is required before the task can be carried out.

A **risk factor** may also be calculated using the risk factor matrix. This takes into account how likely it is that something dangerous might happen and the seriousness of the injuries that may occur as a result.

**Key terms**

**Hazard** – anything that has the potential to cause harm to the engineers or anyone else around the activity area

**Risk** – what could happen as a result of the hazards identified

**Control measure** – action taken to try to reduce the risks involved in an activity

| LIKELIHOOD | |
|---|---|
| 1 | Unlikely |
| 2 | Possible |
| 3 | Probable |

| SEVERITY | |
|---|---|
| 1 | Minor |
| 2 | Serious |
| 3 | Critical |

| RISK FACTOR | |
|---|---|
| 1–3 | Low risk |
| 4–5 | Medium risk |
| 6–9 | High risk |

Score: [ ]  ✕  Score: [ ]  =  [ ]

Risk factor: [ ]

**Figure 1.06** Risk factor matrix

**Hands On**

Complete a risk assessment for an engineering activity that you are familiar with.

# Risk Assessment

## Details of assessor

| Name:<br>Gordon Jones | Signature:<br>GFJones | Date of assessment:<br>3rd September 2012 |
|---|---|---|

## Details of activity

| Activity name:<br>Circuit board assembly line | Activity location:<br>Spark Electronics - Workshops A & B |
|---|---|

Description of activity:
Assembly and hand soldering of consumer electronic products

## Hazard identification

| Hazards identified | Control measures in place to minimise |
|---|---|
| Fumes from solder flux could cause irritation and prolonged exposure is linked with occupation asthma. Aerosol flux cleaner is harmful if inhaled. | Permanent extraction system in place and inspected annually. |
| Electrical safety of portable equipment. | All equipment inspected before and after use. PAT testing carried out every six months. Broken or damaged equipment removed and logged. |
| Heat from soldering iron/solder could cause burns or start fire. | No flammable substances kept in vicinity. Soldering irons kept in stands when not in use. Equipment left to cool before storage. Lab coats worn to protect clothing and long hair tied back. |
| Trailing wires from equipment could cause trip hazard. | Dedicated bench-top power sockets used to minimise cable runs. |
| Sharp leads ejected during component trimming could cause eye damage if penetrating. | Safety spectacles worn by technicians. |

| Hazardous substances | Tools/equipment required | PPE required |
|---|---|---|
| Solder (containing flux)<br>De-flux aerosol spray | Hand soldering equipment (soldering iron, side cutters, long-nosed pliers etc.) | Safety spectacles<br>Lab coat<br>Extraction system<br>Anti-static wrist/leg strap |

## Risk factor assessment

| Likelihood: | Severity: | Risk Factor (Likelihood x severity): |
|---|---|---|
| *1 = unlikely to happen*<br>*2 = could possibly happen*<br>*3 = likely to happen* | *1 = minor injury*<br>*2 = serious injury*<br>*3 = life critical injury* | *1–3 = Low risk*<br>*4–5 = Medium risk*<br>*6–9 = High risk* |
| Score:<br>1 – unlikely to happen | Score:<br>1 – minor injury | Result:<br>2 x 1 = 2 – low risk |

**Figure 1.07** Example risk assessment

**Figure 1.08** Exposed belt drive on an antique combine harvester – this would never be allowed today!

# Common hazards

Hazards are everywhere in the engineering environment and when you carry out a risk assessment you will most likely notice lots of things that could cause you harm. Below are some common hazards in engineering:

## Tools and equipment

Even basic tools can be sharp or heavy with the potential to cause injury. Always handle and transport tools correctly. Never store tools in your pockets. Powered tools and machinery may present grab hazards that could catch clothing or hair and pull you in. Guards should be in place at all times to prevent this.

Figure 1.08 shows an exposed belt drive on an old piece of farming machinery. This would never be allowed today! It would be easy for a hand to get trapped in this machine.

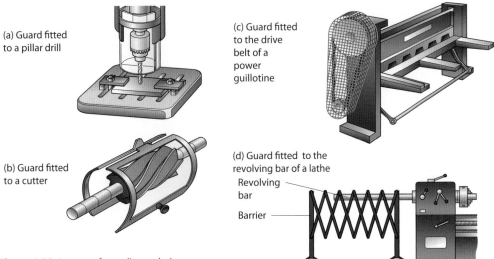

(a) Guard fitted to a pillar drill

(b) Guard fitted to a cutter

(c) Guard fitted to the drive belt of a power guillotine

(d) Guard fitted to the revolving bar of a lathe
Revolving bar
Barrier

**Figure 1.09** A range of guarding techniques

Figure 1.10 A PAT unit

Figure 1.11 Working at height on a building scaffold

## Electrical hazards

Electrical items have the potential to give lethal electric shocks. Equipment should be used according to the manufacturer's specifications, be maintained properly, with portable equipment **PAT tested** periodically. It is important to ensure that any test equipment used for PAT testing is also fully PAT tested.

## Hazardous materials

Engineers often have to use potentially dangerous materials in their work. These might present a risk of poisoning, physical damage, fire or explosion. Therefore you should always carefully follow the manufacturer's guidelines (found on the material data sheet) and store them appropriately (see also COSHH, page 6)

## Working at height

Injuries caused by someone falling or having objects dropped on them tend to be very serious so extra care should be taken when working at height. You may need extra training and need to use specialist equipment.

## Working in confined spaces

Cramped, hot or very cold conditions can take their toll on engineers. The build-up of gases can lead to explosions or suffocation (due to the lack of oxygen). Water hazards might also be present, for example in a sewer system. You may need to use ventilation systems or breathing apparatus.

Figure 1.12 Engineers inspecting a fuel tank in a confined space

## Hot work

Heat can have a big impact on the human body. You can easily become dehydrated or burn yourself if you don't take the necessary precautions. Make sure you are only in a hot environment for a safe, set period of time, take adequate breaks and drink regularly.

## Trip hazards

Many work-related accidents are caused by a slip or trip. These can be avoided if you make sure you always run cables safely by securing them or using cable runners, and avoid running them across gangways. Clear any spillages immediately and cone off areas that are unsafe. It is very important to keep to and practise the top tips described in Figure 1.14 at all times.

## Human error

We all make mistakes and knowingly or unknowingly do things incorrectly which could cause a hazard. The use of alcohol/drugs, stress and tiredness can affect our ability to work safely and make important decisions. Time pressure, laziness or ignorance might lead to 'cutting corners'. Failing to follow the correct procedures could be very dangerous.

**Keep It Safe**

Never work when you are under the influence of drugs or alcohol.

**Hands On**

Using the information covered so far as a guide, create a mind map of the types of hazards you might find in an engineering environment.

**Figure 1.13** A foundry is a very hot and dangerous working environment

Any risk of tripping up could be a BIG problem in the workplace

**TOP TIPS**
→ CLEAN SPILLAGES IMMEDIATELY
→ KEEP WALKWAYS CLEAR
→ TIDY UP AS YOU GO
→ REPORT LEAKS, OBSTRUCTIONS AND DAMAGED FLOORS
→ DON'T LEAVE IT TO OTHERS

DON'T JUST SEE IT, SORT IT.
visit www.watchyourstep.hse.gov.uk or call 0845 345 0055

HSE
Better health & safety benefits everyone

**Figure 1.14** HSE trip poster

# Working safely

All of the safety legislation looked at so far is really important for keeping you safe at work and everyone needs to play their part in following the rules. Below are some top tips on what to do and what not to do when working in engineering.

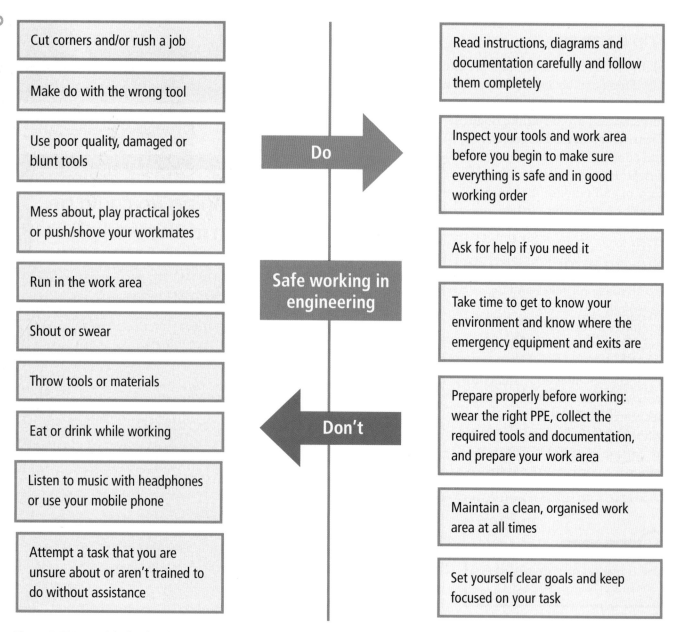

**Do**

**Safe working in engineering**

**Don't**

| Don't | Do |
|---|---|
| Cut corners and/or rush a job | Read instructions, diagrams and documentation carefully and follow them completely |
| Make do with the wrong tool | |
| Use poor quality, damaged or blunt tools | Inspect your tools and work area before you begin to make sure everything is safe and in good working order |
| Mess about, play practical jokes or push/shove your workmates | Ask for help if you need it |
| Run in the work area | Take time to get to know your environment and know where the emergency equipment and exits are |
| Shout or swear | |
| Throw tools or materials | Prepare properly before working: wear the right PPE, collect the required tools and documentation, and prepare your work area |
| Eat or drink while working | |
| Listen to music with headphones or use your mobile phone | Maintain a clean, organised work area at all times |
| Attempt a task that you are unsure about or aren't trained to do without assistance | Set yourself clear goals and keep focused on your task |

**Figure 1.15** Dos and don'ts of working safely in an engineering environment

**Hands On**

Use a video camera to record how you/your workmates work. At the end of the session review the footage and discuss how good your working practices were. Make a list of what you did well and not so well. Make three suggestions on how you could improve in the future.

# Personal protective equipment (PPE)

One of the most basic ways to protect yourself is by wearing the right PPE. The Personal Protective Equipment at Work Regulations 1992 state that employers must provide and maintain good quality PPE that is right for the job. Signs should also be clearly displayed to highlight what PPE needs to be used. A risk assessment (see page 7) will also state what PPE needs to be worn for a particular task.

PPE needs to be stored correctly and properly maintained to make sure that it always provides the best protection. The PPE that you use on a day-to-day basis will depend on the area of engineering that you are involved in and the type of activities that you carry out. PPE should be worn to provide protection to any part of the body that may be exposed to risk when doing a particular job, for example hands, eyes, ears, head, lungs and body.

## Hand protection

An engineer's hands often have to work very hard so it is really important that they are cleaned, protected and cared for properly. Wearing gloves, washing hands and using the correct barrier creams can help to prevent painful skin conditions such as dermatitis. This can be caused by coming into contact with industrial chemicals over time.

 **Keep It Safe**

Always wear the correct PPE for the job that you are carrying out.

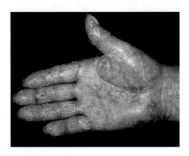

**Figure 1.16** Dermatitis is a very painful skin condition.

**Rigger gloves**

Tough fabric or leather gloves protect from physical damage. Rubber coatings can also help with grip and chemical/liquid protection. Used when handling large, heavy or rough objects

**Latex/plastic gloves**

Thin, often disposable gloves give protection from dirt and chemicals while allowing hands to move and feel easily

**Hand protection**

**Barrier creams**

Protect hands when gloves cannot be worn for safety reasons or when an engineer needs the freedom of bare hands

**Gauntlets**

Long, thick gloves protecting hands and lower arms from heat, e.g. when welding or brazing

**Figure 1.17** Ways to protect your hands

**Figure 1.18** A hand care station will help you to take care of your hands

After working always clean your hands thoroughly and use hand lotion to keep them in good condition. This will help to avoid long-term damage. Specialist soaps can help to remove oil and grease. Use a scrubbing brush to clean under finger nails. Take special care to clean your hands before eating or using the toilet; the consequences of not doing so could be highly undesirable!

## Eye and ear protection

Your eyes and ears are essential, very complex and fragile organs. Eyes can be easily damaged by things flying into them – both solids and liquids. Your hearing can be permanently damaged by even relatively low level noise over time. Therefore, you should always take care to protect them properly.

**Keep It Safe**

Never look at the welding with naked eyes – it can cause serious damage.

**Keep It Safe**

The light produced by welding contains harmful UV rays that can cause serious burns and skin damage.

**Safety glasses**

Used very often to give basic eye protection

**Welding mask**

Protects the eyes and face from the extreme light and heat of welding, and filters out harmful UV radiation

**Safety goggles**

Like safety glasses but seal around the face offering better protection from smaller particles and liquid splashes

**Eye and ear protection**

**Ear defenders**

Give greater noise reduction and can be more suited to outdoor work, where they also provide protection from the wind and cold

**Ear plugs**

Protect the ears from minor noise pollution. Often disposable for hygiene reasons and commonly provided in a dispenser for general workshop use

**Figure 1.19** Ways to protect your eyes and ears

## Head and breathing protection

You need to breathe to get oxygen in to your blood to keep your body running. If your ability to breathe properly is compromised you can become critically ill very rapidly. Your scull protects your brain inside it but its protection is limited and very serious injury can be caused by trauma to your head.

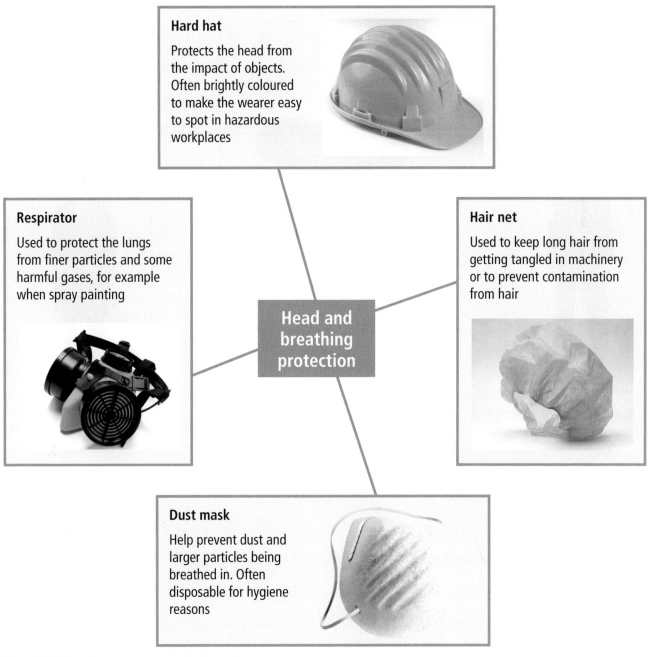

**Hard hat**

Protects the head from the impact of objects. Often brightly coloured to make the wearer easy to spot in hazardous workplaces

**Respirator**

Used to protect the lungs from finer particles and some harmful gases, for example when spray painting

**Hair net**

Used to keep long hair from getting tangled in machinery or to prevent contamination from hair

**Head and breathing protection**

**Dust mask**

Help prevent dust and larger particles being breathed in. Often disposable for hygiene reasons

**Figure 1.20** Ways of protecting your head and breathing

## Body protection

The environment an engineer has to work in is often dirty, unpleasant or dangerous and therefore you need to think about the clothes that you wear. Clothing might protect you from hazardous materials, temperatures or climate and sometimes it is also important that you are seen by others so they know where you are, for example when it is dark or very hard to see. Safety footwear is a basic an common requirement in case items are dropped as well as giving grip and chemical protection.

**Safety boots/shoes**

Have rigid metal or plastic toe-caps that provide protection to toes/feet

**Lab coat**

Suitable for light workshop activities protecting the upper body and arms from a dirty environment

**Overalls**

Provide whole body protection from a dirty environment

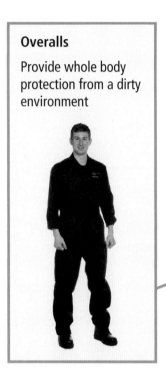

**Body protection**

**Hi-viz garments**

The luminescent colours make you stand out when it is important to be seen for safety reasons

**Figure 1.21** Ways of protecting your body

What type of PPE is necessary when:
1 working in a mine shaft?
2 carrying out a service on a sports car?
3 cutting metal with an oxy-acetylene torch?

## Warning signs

Signs are around you all of the time. Without knowing it you probably know the meaning of thousands of them. Signs tell you what to do, what not to do, when to be aware of something and how to get to safety in an emergency. They are especially important in engineering because of all the potentially dangerous things you do.

Companies are required by law to use signs properly. Good signage is especially important when people are visiting or are new to an area to make them aware of their surroundings. A good example of this is at the entrance to a construction site.

There are certain types of signs with specific meanings that have to be made to the right standards. These types are shown below.

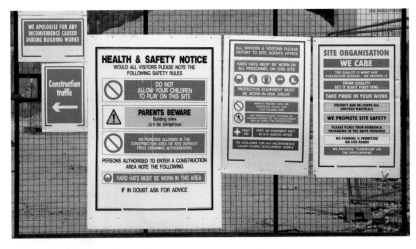

**Figure 1.22** Warning signs at the entrance to a construction site

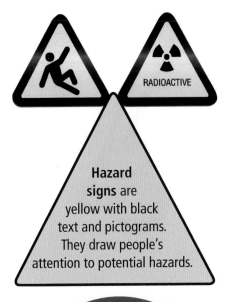

**Hazard signs** are yellow with black text and pictograms. They draw people's attention to potential hazards.

**Fire signs** are red with white text and pictograms. They are used to indicate fire equipment and devices such as fire alarms, fire extinguishers and hoses.

**Safe condition signs** are used to signpost anything to do with making safe, e.g fire exits, evacuation routes and first aid. They are green with white text and pictograms.

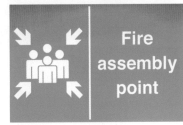

**Prohibition signs** tell you what you *must not* do. They have a distinctive red circle shape with a red line crossing through the middle.

**Mandatory signs** are blue with white text and pictograms. They tell you something that *must* be done. They are often used to tell you what PPE you have to wear.

**Key term**

**Pictogram** – a simple drawing used to represent text so that anyone can understand a sign without actually having to read any writing

**Hands On**

Design a sign of your own. It could have any meaning but it must follow the correct signage standards.

## Manual handling

Engineers often have to move around heavy and/or bulky items, such as tools, machinery, parts or materials. You can easily hurt yourself by not lifting them properly. It is therefore very important that you learn and practise safe handling techniques. People often try to lift/move things that they can't really do so safely. Therefore, as a general rule, always try to get help or consider using lifting aids, such as sack barrows or pallet trucks.

Figure 1.23 Pallet truck                    Figure 1.24 Sack barrow

When lifting alone, follow the steps in the safety guide opposite.

### Hands On

Practise your manual lifting technique with a range of light objects, such as empty cardboard boxes. You could get a friend to use a video camera to record you lifting. Watch the footage together to review your technique. How could you improve?

### Hands On

Create a workshop poster with a step-by-step guide to lifting a heavy object. Use page 19 as a guide. You could also take photographs of each stage to include in your poster.

**1** Always check the object before lifting it. Objects can be heavier than they appear. If you think lifting aids and/or assistance might be required, do not attempt to lift it by yourself.

**2** Clear your path to where the object needs to be moved to. Make sure that you have enough space to put it down. Stand with your legs either side of the object and shoulder-width apart.

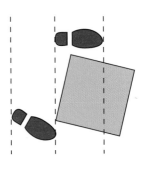

**3** Keeping your back straight, bend your legs and get a solid grip on the object with arms straight out.

**4** Begin to lift the object by straightening your legs and keeping your back straight.

**5** Move smoothly to your destination, keeping the object close to your body at waist height. Avoid jerky movements and never run.

**6** Put the object down steadily, bending your legs not your back. Remember that putting down can be as hazardous as lifting!

Figure 1.25 The frightening effects of fire

Figure 1.26 A fire triangle

Figure 1.27 A fire detector being tested

# Fire

Lots of things can start a fire in an engineering environment. It can spread quickly with devastating consequences. As an engineer, it is really important that you know how to prevent fire, deal with it and escape from it.

For fire to start you need three things: a source of fuel, something to ignite it and oxygen. These three things are often shown as 'the fire triangle' (see Figure 1.26). If you can prevent all three elements being together at the same time you can greatly reduce the chance of starting a fire. For example you should keep stocks of flammable liquids (fuel) away from areas where people are hot working (ignition). Remember that air contains oxygen so is present in nearly every situation that you might find the other two key elements in.

The 2005 Regulatory Reform (Fire Safety) Order are regulations that cover how a company must make proper provisions for fire.

By law an employer must:

- undertake fire risk assessments
- install, test and maintain appropriate fire alarm systems
- train staff on evacuation procedures and carry out fire drills
- have extra emergency plans for disabled workers
- provide the right type of firefighting equipment
- follow rules and regulations to keep their workplace safe in case of fire
- put up signage to signpost evacuation routes and safety equipment
- make fire exits accessible at all times.

## Fire extinguishers

Fire extinguishers come in a variety of different types. Your employer/training centre should make sure the most appropriate type of fire extinguisher is accessible in each area depending on what activities take place there. It's important to use the correct fire extinguisher as you could be seriously injured and/or make the fire worse if you get it wrong.

Ideally, only a trained person should use a fire extinguisher. You should never try to tackle anything other than a small fire that you can easily and safely put out.

Fire extinguishers should be checked regularly and never tampered with. Below is a description of some of the most common types of fire extinguisher.

**Keep It Safe**

The main purpose of fire extinguishers is not actually to put out fires – but to help you get to safety in the event of a fire! You should only attempt to put out the smallest of fires.

**Keep It Safe**

Using the wrong type of fire extinguisher can make the fire worse and cause serious injury.

**Water**

**Stripe colour:** Red
**Use on:** Solids, e.g. wood, paper and textiles
**Don't use on:**
Electricals – it can cause electric shock
Liquids/oils/fats – it can make the fire much worse
**How to use:** Aim at the base of the flames
Move it over the area of the fire

**Foam**

**Stripe colour:** White/cream
**Use on:** Solids, e.g. wood, paper and textiles, liquids
**Don't use on:**
Electricals – it cause electric shock
Oils/fats – it can spread the fire
**How to use:** For solids, aim at the base of the flames
For liquids, aim at the surface of the fluid

**Powder**

**Stripe colour:** Blue
**Use on:** Most types of fire (except those below)
**Don't use on:**
Electricals
Oils/fats
**How to use:** Aim at the base of the flames and sweep from side to side
Monitor in case of reignition

**CO$_2$**

**Stripe colour:** Black
**Use on:** Electricals and liquids
**Don't use on:**
Solids – the pressurised CO$_2$ can spread the materials out
Fires in confined spaces
**How to use:** Aim at the base of the flames and sweep from side to side
Never touch the horn as it gets very cold when in use

**Figure 1.28** Types of fire extinguisher

**QUICK CHECK**

What type of fire extinguisher should you use on:
1 an electrical fire?
2 a fire of wood and paper?

**Figure 1.29** A break glass point

# Emergency procedures

Sometimes things go wrong and accidents do happen, no matter how much you try to prevent it. As an engineer, you are often involved in more dangerous activities than in other jobs. The impact of an accident in an engineering workplace can be very severe. It is therefore very important to know how to deal with an emergency effectively.

It is everybody's responsibility to know what to do in an emergency – not just your managers' and safety officers'. Wherever you are you should know:

- what the emergency alarm sounds like
- the evacuation route, nearest exit(s) and evacuation point
- the location of safety and fire equipment
- where the nearest alarm call point is
- who to contact in an emergency.

If required to evacuate you should do so quickly but never run. If necessary, turn off any equipment, but do not delay your exit from the building.

Companies often have a procedure for raising the alarm and calling the emergency services rather than individuals calling 999 directly. This is so that they can:

- centrally control the incident
- send first-aiders and/or specially trained staff
- raise the alarm
- direct the emergency services to the accident site.

**Keep It Safe**

Always make sure that you know the nearest fire exit and evacuation route wherever you work.

**Hands On**

Draw a map of the evacuation route where you work/study. Walk through the route – checking for a clear path, correct signage and exits as you go. Are there any improvements that you could make?

**Figure 1.30** First aid box with contents

# First aid

It is a good idea for all engineers to have at least a basic knowledge of emergency first aid. You never know when someone might need your help, at work or at home. It could very well save a life one day. Some employers organise first aid training or you can get in touch with your local St John Ambulance centre to arrange some training. The Health and Safety (First Aid) Regulations 1981 state that any company must supply first aid materials and trained first aid staff. Companies often have designated first-aiders who are on call and have had approved first aid training that must be renewed periodically.

This section covers some basic first aid advice. However, this is in no way a substitute for formal first aid training.

**Keep It Safe**

First aid is an important life skill – it is well worth getting proper training.

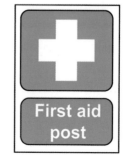

**Figure 1.31** First aid sign

## Wounds and bleeding

It is very important to stop a wound from bleeding quickly and effectively. Loss of blood can lead to someone quickly becoming critically ill. When dealing with cuts and grazes:

* clean small cuts and grazes and apply a clean dressing
* for larger cuts apply pressure to the wound and raise the bleeding body part above the heart (laying the victim down might help)
* never remove something that is sticking into a wound as it might be acting like a plug and stopping the flow of blood; instead, apply pressure around it
* if something has been cut off, wrap it in a clean cloth and pack ice around it to keep it cool (never place it directly on ice).

## Burns

Cool down burns as quickly as possible by running them under cold water for at least 10 minutes or until the burning stops. Severe burns should be dealt with by professionals. In which case, remove any jewellery near the burn. Wrap it in clean dressings (as burns are easily infected) or cover it in cling film and seek immediate medical attention.

## Broken bones

Signs of a broken bone include pain, swelling, deformity and loss of or unusual movement of a limb. Support the affected limb and stop it from moving then seek urgent medical attention. If in doubt about a broken bone, always seek specialist help as internal injuries can go unnoticed at first and be very dangerous.

## Eye damage

Your eyes are very sensitive and when damaged require specialist attention. Eyewash stations may be used to flush out liquids or very small particles. Anything larger than this should be left as it is, covered with an eye patch and seen by a specialist as soon as possible.

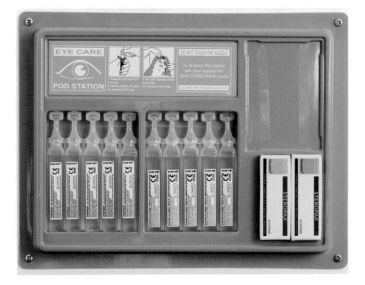

**Figure 1.32** An eyewash station

## Poisoning

Poisoning can occur if something is accidentally swallowed, inhaled or absorbed through the skin. What you should do in the event of poisoning depends on what substance is involved. Follow the advice on the substance data sheet and take it with you to hospital so that they can identify it. If the data sheet isn't available, take the bottle or container.

## Shock

Shock can be caused by many things including blood loss, heart attack, fluid loss and burns. Signs of someone going into shock include pale, cold, clammy skin and fast rapid breathing and/or pulse rate. When treating shock, look for what has caused the shock in the first place and deal with that as your first priority. Lay the victim down, reassure them, make them comfortable and seek urgent medical help.

## The recovery position

When someone is breathing but has fallen unconscious, it is best to put them in the recovery position. This is the safest way for them to be positioned while they recover and/or wait for medical help.

2. Gently roll person onto their side

4. Tilt head back and tuck hand under chin to keep mouth open

3. Bend leg to support position

1. Bend arm to stop person rolling over

5. Make sure someone is keeping an eye on the injured person

**Figure 1.33** Steps to the recovery position

## Cardiopulmonary resuscitation (CPR)

Cardiopulmonary resuscitation (CPR) is performed when a victim is unconscious and not breathing normally. It is always best to practise CPR using a model or mannequin with a trained first aid instructor. Never attempt to practise on another person!

Advice on how to carry out CPR effectively does change from time to time as new research on the subject comes to light. The following instructions are based on the Resuscitation Council UK 2010 resuscitation guidelines:

1. **Assess the scene** – ensure it is safe to approach them, remove any surrounding hazards and lay them flat on their back.

2. **Check their responsiveness** – talk to the casualty to see if they are unconscious. If so, **shout for help** and continue CPR. If you are in your workplace call for the duty first-aider urgently.

3. **Check breathing** – check that their airway is clear and free from blockages. Tilt their head back and open their mouth. Listen to their breathing and watch their chest to see if it rises/falls. If they are breathing put them into the recovery position. If not, continue CPR.

Figure 1.34 Opening the airway

4. **Call 999** – get someone to call 999 or follow your company's procedure for contacting the emergency services.

5. **Give 30 chest compressions** – kneel by the side of the casualty with arms locked straight and fingers interlocked. Push down firmly about 5–6 cm on the centre of the chest and release, at a rate of two a second.

7. **Give two rescue breaths** – open the airway wide, pinch the nose and give two slow steady breaths into the victim's mouth, allowing the breath to release between.

Figure 1.35 Chest compressions

8. **Repeat** – without any delay, return to your chest compressions, continuing in a ratio of 30 chest compressions to two rescue breaths, as before. Only stop if the casualty recovers, help arrives or you are exhausted.

Delivering CPR is hard work and you will tire easily. Therefore, if possible, work with another first-aider – switching every couple of minutes.

## Hands-only CPR

For untrained first-aiders, hands-only CPR (i.e. delivering only the chest compressions without the breaths) has been shown to be effective in itself. The British Heart Foundation has recently carried out a national advertising campaign supporting this with the strap line 'Call 999. Then press hard and fast to the beat of Stayin' Alive'. You can view the TV advert and find out more at their website www.bhf.org.uk. They also have an excellent free of charge CPR mobile phone app available for download.

**Hands On**

Ask your employer or contact St John Ambulance to book a formal first aid course. It is a vital life skill for engineers and looks great on your CV!

## Automated external defibrillators (AED)

Many public and workplaces now keep an automated external defibrillator (AED) which can be used during CPR. AEDs are computer-controlled devices that monitor a casualty's heart. They can deliver electric shocks to try to make the heart start beating normally again. AEDs give clear visual instructions and many speak instructions out loud when in use. They are designed to be used safely and effectively by an untrained person.

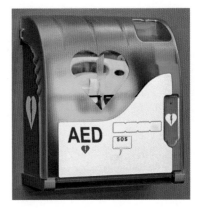
Figure 1.36 A typical AED

**QUICK CHECK**

1 What is the ratio of chest compressions to rescue breaths when undertaking CPR?
2 What should you do with a patient who is unconscious but breathing normally?
3 What are the signs of someone going into shock and what action should you take?

## CHECK YOUR KNOWLEDGE

1 RIDDOR stands for?

 a Reporting Infections Dermatitis Death Or Resuscitation

 b Reporting of Injuries, Diseases and Dangerous Occurrences Regulations

 c Regulations Involving Disease, Disorders and Occurrences Related to health

 d Reporting Internal Damage to Doctors Online Regulations

2 A control measure is:

 a something used to control the power in a workshop

 b the most important dimension in a diagram

 c something put in place to reduce risk

 d a type of accurate measuring device

3 According to the Workplace Health and Safety and Welfare Regulations the minimum temperature for working at a computer is:

 a 13 °C

 b 14 °C

 c 15 °C

 d 16 °C

4 The international symbol shown below means the substance is:

 a an irritant

 b oxidising

 c explosive

 d hazardous

5 A painful, itchy skin condition caused by exposure to industrial chemicals is called:

 a asphyxiation

 d dermatitis

 c asthma

 d repetitive strain injury

6 A fire exit sign is:

 a red with white text

 b blue and circular in shape

 c yellow with black text

 d green with white text

7 What are the three requirements to start a fire?

 a fuel, $CO_2$, ignition

 b fuel, oxygen, ignition

 c oxygen, $CO_2$, heat

 d fuel, oxygen, air

8 Which of the following fire extinguishers is best suited to tackling an electrical fire?

 a $CO_2$

 b powder

 c water

 d foam

9 When giving first aid for a severe cut which of the following should you **not** do?

 a Elevate the wound above the heart

 b Remove anything penetrating the skin

 c Apply pressure to the wound

 d Seek medical attention as soon as possible

10 In a workplace, who is responsible for maintaining health and safety?

 a the Health and Safety Executive

 b the employer

 c the employees

 d everyone

# 2 Working efficiently and effectively in engineering

Being effective at work involves recognising your strengths and weaknesses, and developing a broad range of skills that go beyond the basic skills an engineer needs to do their job. In other words, building on the things you are good at and improving the things you are not so good at.

There are many good reasons to be effective in your job. People who are effective often gain respect, quickly gain promotion and get involved in exciting projects.

This chapter explores how you can become more effective in your work and what you should focus on. It looks at the skills you can develop, and the strategies and resources you can use to increase your effectiveness. Knowing your own strengths and weaknesses is a good starting point and doing something about them is the next step!

In this chapter you will learn about:

- keeping safe at work
- planning
- job cards and work instructions
- preparation
- tools and equipment

- dealing with problems
- maintaining effective working relationships
- personal training and development
- completing the job
- improving working procedures

Figure 2.01 shows what is meant by 'being effective'. Can you think of anything that has been left out? Make a copy of the drawing and add at least three further ways in which you can be effective at work.

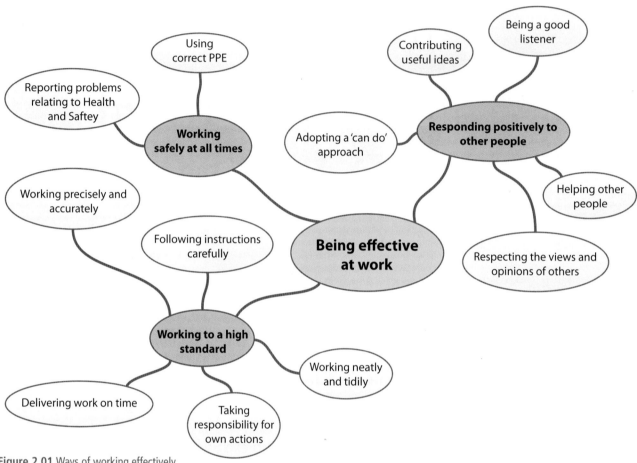

Figure 2.01 Ways of working effectively

## Keeping safe at work

As part of being effective at work it is important to keep yourself safe. You also need to make sure that *your* actions don't put *others* in danger! There can be many hazards in an engineering workplace (see Chapter 1 for more details) so it is very important to know about them and know how to avoid them.

### Personal protective equipment (PPE)

When working as an engineer you need to wear sensible clothing and have the right **personal protective equipment** (PPE) for the work that you do. The PPE might include:

- overalls – to protect you (and your clothing) against dirt, grease, oil and minor chemical spills

- safety glasses – to protect your eyes from dust, dirt and flying debris
- safety boots or shoes – to protect your feet from falling objects and chemicals
- gloves – to protect your hands from cuts and abrasions as well as dirt, grease, oil and chemicals
- masks – to protect your face and eyes when carrying out welding operations.

**Figure 2.02** Typical examples of PPE

### Hands On

List the particular hazards you would expect to find when carrying out each of the following engineering tasks:

1. cutting, milling and shaping
2. welding and joining
3. testing electrical and electronic equipment
4. transporting materials and equipment
5. maintaining engines and other heavy machinery.

Include at least three hazards for each of the tasks listed.

### Hands On

Being safe at work is so important that several laws, regulations and guidelines have been written. These protect you and those around you when carrying out engineering activities.

Take a look at your own work area. What laws and regulations apply to it? How could it be improved in order to make it a safer place to work in? (Hint: Take a look at the work in Chapter 1 relating to risk assessment and the control of substances hazardous to health).

### QUICK CHECK

List the PPE you would need when:
1 grinding the point of a chisel
2 soldering a connector onto a cable
3 removing the gearbox from a car
4 welding the seams of a box.

## Planning

Before you carry out an engineering task, you need to have a plan. Planning involves thinking about all the stages involved in completing a task. Your plan needs to be:

- **specific** – you need to be clear about what it is you want to achieve
- **realistic** – you need to be sure you can complete the task in time, using the resources, skills and manpower available
- **measurable** – you need to be able to measure the progress towards your final goal and know when you have reached it.

Planning is important because it will help you to ensure that:

- the work goes smoothly and is trouble-free from start to finish
- individual tasks are performed in the correct order
- the right tools and equipment are available (and that they are in a fit and safe condition for use)
- the time taken to perform the task is reduced and the cost of doing it is minimised
- the work is done safely and efficiently.

Now imagine your car has a flat tyre. You will need to remove the wheel and replace it with the spare. Think about the steps you need to take and the order you need to carry them out in.

First you will need to find a safe, level place to work in and firm ground to work on. If you have broken down on a motorway you will need to ensure your hazard lights are on and that you have put out a warning triangle. Ideally, you will also need a pair of gloves to protect your hands, safety boots or shoes to protect your feet, and overalls to protect your clothing.

Before you can remove the wheel, engage the handbrake and select and engage the lowest gear on a manual gearbox or select P for parked if an automatic. This will leave the wheel free to turn. However, the other wheels on the car will need to be blocked *before* the brakes are released to make sure the car won't move during the jacking process.

Next you need to remove the spare wheel from its storage place. Then you need to attach the jack at the recommended point closest to the wheel with the flat tyre. Use a wheel brace to slacken each of the wheel nuts before using the jack to carefully raise the wheel clear of the ground. You will need to raise the jack high enough to put the new inflated tyre on the car – remember it will be larger than the one you are replacing. Undo each of the wheel nuts in turn and remove the wheel, taking care not to disturb the jack in the process. Then locate and fit the replacement spare wheel. Use the wheel brace to tighten each of the nuts but not over-tighten them.

Release the jack slowly to lower the vehicle and then remove the jack. Tighten each of the wheel nuts with the wheel brace, applying torque to opposite pairs of nuts in turn. This helps to ensure that the wheel is seated correctly. Finally, check the torque on each nut is correct and inflate the tyre to the recommended pressure.

## Work plans

A work plan involves breaking down an engineering activity into a series of smaller **tasks**. Each task can then be described separately in a **job card** or **work instruction** (see page 32). Work plans can be

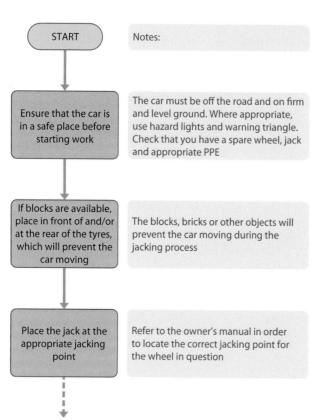

**Figure 2.03** Flow chart of first steps to changing a wheel on a car

extremely complex so sometimes computer software is used to make the process easier. Alternatively, you can use one or more flow charts (like the one for changing a wheel shown in Figure 2.03).

Work plans are particularly important when a team of people is working on a project together. This is because they show how each task relates to another, and the order tasks should be completed in. This way, everyone involved in the project follows the same plan and knows who should be doing what and when.

It is important to remember that a work plan is only as good as the thought that goes into it. Having a clear idea of what is involved is really important right from the start.

A work plan for the design, manufacture and installation of a pumping system is shown in Figure 2.04. Note how the work plan is broken down into a number of smaller tasks and how the sequence of tasks is clearly shown. The work plan relates to the supply of a pumping system. It starts with a **specification** that sets down the client's requirements and identifies the performance characteristics for the pump. No work can start until the specification is complete and has been fully agreed with the client.

For more information on specifications, see page 55.

When the specification has been finalised, the next three tasks can begin.

1. Manufacturing the pump itself.
2. Designing the enclosure for the pumping system.
3. Designing the electrical control system for the pump.

All of these tasks take time. Manufacturing the pump takes two days. Design work on the enclosure and control system will each take one day. When these jobs have been completed three further tasks can start.

> **Key term**
>
> **Specification** – a detailed and comprehensive description of a product or service. It is important for a specification to be precise and complete because it often forms the basis of a contract between a customer or client and a manufacturer or supplier. Specifications are therefore usually made up of written documents, and the relevant drawings and diagrams

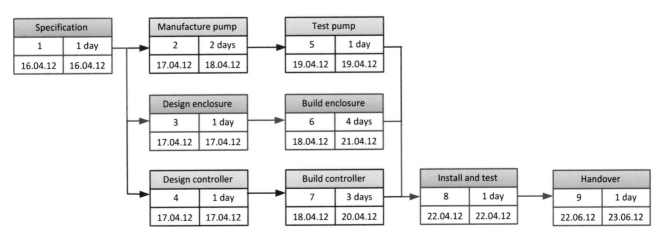

*Legend*

| Task name | |
|---|---|
| Task No. | Length |
| Start date | End date |

**Figure 2.04** A work plan for the design, manufacture and installation of a pumping system

**Hands On**

Write a work plan for removing a flat car battery, charging it on a bench and replacing it. Make sure that your work plan is broken down into a series of tasks. Use a simple flow chart (like the one shown earlier in Figure 2.03) to illustrate your work plan.

The pump will need to be tested before fitting it into the enclosure. This will take one day. Manufacturing the enclosure will take four days and building the control system will take three days. When all three of these tasks have been completed the pump and control system can be installed in the enclosure and tested before handing it over to the client. The whole project requires a total of six days. Notice in Figure 2.04 how the days and dates have been included in the work plan.

# Job cards and work instructions

Job cards and work instructions provide you with detailed information on how to perform a particular engineering task, such as testing a pump, replacing a motor, manufacturing a part, or repairing an electronic circuit. For example, the work instruction in Figure 2.04 for Task 5 (Testing the pump) would provide you with details of each of the tests that need to be carried out on the pump.

Job cards and work instructions usually include some or all of the following:

- the title or job number of the task or activity – each task or activity must have a unique identifier so that it can't be confused with any other task
- a brief description of the task and why it is needed
- where and when the task is being carried out
- the name of the person responsible for carrying out the task
- the tools and equipment required to perform the task – specialised tools, such as jigs and test fixtures may be required in some cases
- the parts and/or materials required to perform the task – these will normally be available from a parts store or may be supplied as a kit of parts for a particular task
- the sequence in which the tasks are performed
- details of any hazards, safety precautions and PPE required – the job card or work instruction will normally assume that you are correctly dressed with suitable clothing and footwear so this will not normally be specified on the job card or work instruction
- diagrams, drawings and sometimes photographs that illustrate the various stages in performing the task.

**Job cards** are usually less detailed than work instructions. They often apply to a single task and include specific information, such as the:

- location the task is to be performed in
- time allocated to performing the task
- names of those responsible for carrying out the task.

Job cards are frequently used to record maintenance tasks because they provide a record showing that a task has been carried out. They can also be kept for tracking and billing purposes. A typical job card is shown in Figure 2.05.

**Work instructions**, which are usually more detailed than job cards, are often used in engineering production and manufacturing. Work instructions often include information such as:

- details of any hazards and safety precautions
- the sequence of operations needed to perform each task
- details of how to check that the work has been carried out safely and correctly.

Typical work instructions are shown in Figure 2.06.

---

**Hands On**

Read the job card shown in Figure 2.05 and use it to answer the following questions.

1. What work is to be carried out?
2. What is the job number and the date of the job?
3. What is the total cost of parts and materials?
4. How many hours of labour are needed to complete the job?
5. Who has 'signed off' the job card?

---

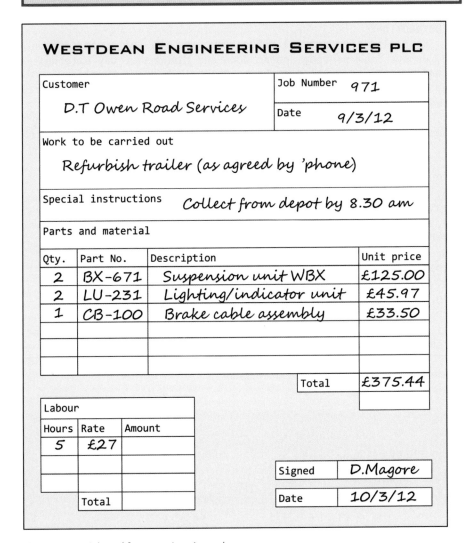

**WESTDEAN ENGINEERING SERVICES PLC**

| Customer | Job Number | 971 |
|---|---|---|
| D.T Owen Road Services | Date | 9/3/12 |

Work to be carried out

Refurbish trailer (as agreed by 'phone)

Special instructions    Collect from depot by 8.30 am

Parts and material

| Qty. | Part No. | Description | Unit price |
|---|---|---|---|
| 2 | BX-671 | Suspension unit WBX | £125.00 |
| 2 | LU-231 | Lighting/indicator unit | £45.97 |
| 1 | CB-100 | Brake cable assembly | £33.50 |
| | | | |
| | | | |
| | | Total | £375.44 |

| Labour | | |
|---|---|---|
| Hours | Rate | Amount |
| 5 | £27 | |
| | | |
| | | |
| | Total | |

| Signed | D.Magore |
|---|---|
| Date | 10/3/12 |

**Figure 2.05** A job card for an engineering task

---

### BLACKWATER AVIATION SERVICES – WORK INSTRUCTION QS-1753/12

**PURPOSE**
This work instruction relates to the routine inspection and maintenance of static inverters type TRS-153 and TRS-253.

**SCOPE**
Models TRS-153A (50 Hz), TRS-153B (60 Hz), TRS-253 (400 Hz)

**ASSOCIATED DOCUMENTS**
Service and maintenance manuals SMM-153, SMM-253

**RESPONSIBLE DEPARTMENT/ENGINEER**
Client Services Department/Tony Groves 01443 397585

**TOOLS AND EQUIPMENT**
Battery service unit BSU-15, load tester LT-55, multimeter

**SAFETY REQUIREMENTS**
Care when lifting battery and battery service unit. Load tester runs hot. Electrolyte spills must be treated with caution.

**INSTRUCTIONS**
1. Seek client's approval before removing the unit from service.
2. Remove from service, power down and disconnect any external load (client approval must be sought before doing this).
3. Remove (6) battery cover retaining screws. Detach cover and gain access to the battery compartment.
4. First disconnect the negative (black) cable from the battery and then disconnect the positive (red) cable from the battery.
5. Connect battery service unit BSU-15 and load tester between the battery and static inverter, taking care to observe the correct polarity.
6. Power up the unit and select 'Maintenance' on the function selector switch.
7. Perform maintenance checks as indicated on the battery service unit LCD panel. Replace the battery unit if indicated.
8. When complete, disconnect the battery service unit and load tester and reconnect the battery to the static inverter.
9. Replace the battery cover and (6) retaining screws.
10. Power up the static inverter and allow it to complete the initial diagnostic checks.
11. When checks are complete (Status Code 99) inform client that the unit is ready to re-enter service.

**Figure 2.06** A work instruction for an engineering task

## QUICK CHECK

**1** What is a work instruction and why would you need one?
**2** How does a job card differ from a work instruction?

# Preparation

Preparation is important because it can save you a lot of time and help you to avoid problems later on. It can also help you to keep your work area safe by making sure you use only the right tools, equipment and PPE.

When you prepare for a work activity there are a number of things you need to think about.

You will need to:

- check that you have **authorisation** to carry out the work – some tasks, such as grinding, can only be performed by people who are properly qualified and therefore authorised to do the work
- make sure that your work area is free from hazards and is ready for the work that you are doing
- check that the required safety procedures are carried out, referring to relevant safety documentation whenever necessary
- obtain the PPE you need to carry out the tasks and activities and ensure that it is in good condition
- check that you have the right tools, work instructions and all of the necessary documents, specifications and drawings
- check that you have the right materials, components and parts required to carry out the job (as with PPE, these will usually be specified in the work instruction).

A summary of the steps discussed above is shown in Figure 2.07.

**Key term**

**Authorisation** – the process of giving someone permission to do or have something. In engineering, authorisation to perform a hazardous task (such as operating a grinding machine) is only given to people who have demonstrated that they are competent to perform the task

**QUICK CHECK**

Why might you need authorisation to carry out a hazardous task? Think of at least three reasons.

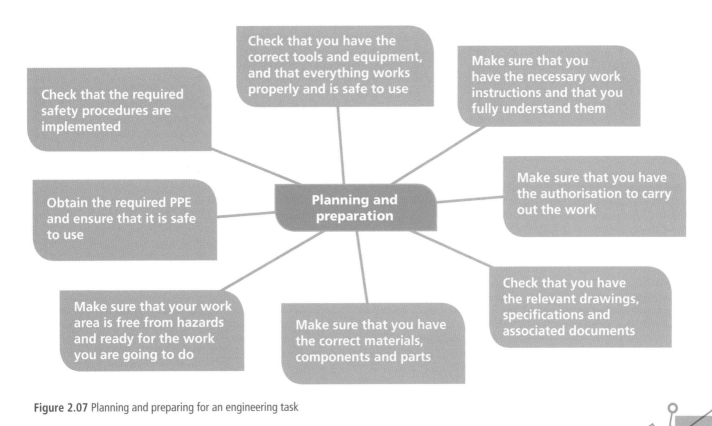

**Figure 2.07** Planning and preparing for an engineering task

**Figure 2.08** Example of a properly lit work area with plenty of space

**Hands On**

Take a careful look at your own work area. Now copy the table below and add your comments in the boxes:

| | |
|---|---|
| Are any hazardous materials present in the work area? Can you identify them? | |
| Are any of the engineering processes hazardous, and if so what makes them hazardous? | |
| Is the correct PPE available and is it all in a usable condition? | |
| Is there enough space to work in? | |
| Is the work area clean and tidy? | |
| Is there enough light to see what you are doing? | |
| Is the work area well ventilated? | |
| Are all of the correct tools and materials available and in usable condition? | |
| Is all of the right information and documentation available (e.g. job cards and work instructions)? | |

(a)                                                    (b)

**Figure 2.09** Examples of (a) a tidy and (b) an untidy work area

In order to manufacture a part you will need a drawing that is accurate and to scale. You will also need the right equipment for marking out, such as a scriber, steel rule, dividers and a square. Think carefully about all the things you need to do *before* starting a particular engineering activity, such as marking out and cutting a sheet of metal, or soldering a connector onto a cable. Make a checklist of everything you will need to do before starting the task.

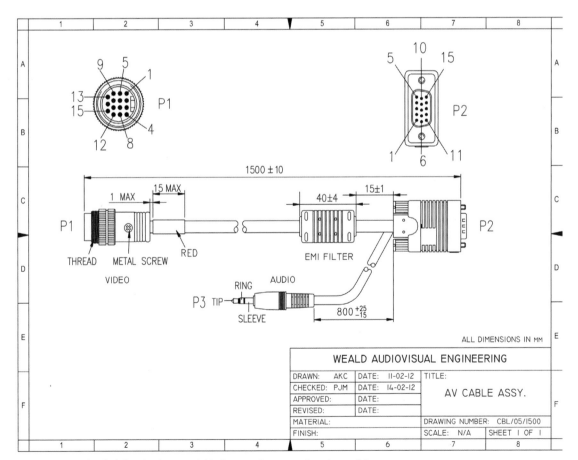

**Figure 2.10** A detailed drawing is essential before starting an engineering activity

# Tools and equipment

It is of course important to have the right tools and equipment that you will need to do a job. In most cases the work instruction or job card will help you select them. In some cases you will need to use your own skills to select the right tool or equipment for a particular task.

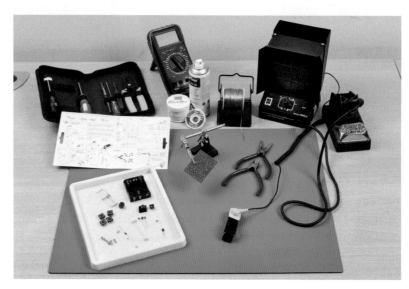

**Figure 2.11** Tools laid out for inspection before carrying out an engineering task

Take a look at the tools shown in Figure 2.11. These have been arranged before assembling a small electronic circuit. Notice how the tools have been arranged in the order in which they will be used and each tool has been checked to make sure that it is safe, functional and in a usable condition.

Any faulty tools, problems or shortages (such as a broken connector or damaged cable) should have been reported. Any tool found to be defective should be clearly marked and not left for someone else to use (see Figure 2.12). Only the minimum number of tools for a given job should be laid out at any one time.

Finally, it is very important *not* to begin a task or activity unless you have the correct tools and equipment. Avoid the temptation to use an incorrect or improper tool (such as using a screwdriver as a chisel!) as this may cause damage not only to the materials that you are working on but also to the tool itself. Work instructions and job cards nearly always include a checklist of the tools and equipment that you need for a task so do make sure that you use it.

**Figure 2.12** Tools that are defective need to be clearly labelled so that they are not used by someone else

## Quick Tip

Common tools such as screwdrivers and spanners come in a wide variety of different types and sizes. It is important to get to know what these are and why you need to use the correct size and type every time you perform an engineering task. Take a look at your tool store and check this out!

## QUICK CHECK

1 What action should you take if you are issued with a drill bit that is broken?
2 List at least four checks that you would make before using a soldering iron to solder a connector onto a cable.

# Dealing with problems

Problem solving is part of the day-to-day work of an engineer. Some of these problems will be minor and you will be able to solve them yourself. Others may be impossible to solve without the help and support of other people. As you gain experience, you will soon get to know which problems you can solve on your own and which you need to refer to other people.

You need to replace the headlamp bulb on a car or motorcycle. What problems could you face when dealing with this problem?

***Shortage of materials, tools or equipment***
The replacement headlamp bulb would need to be the correct type and rating, and you will need to have screwdrivers and/or spanners of the correct size.

***Missing or incomplete drawings and documentation***
You will need the owner's or workshop manual. This will provide you with the information that you need to remove and replace the headlamp unit. It will also tell you what type of bulb is fitted. You will need to know how to check the alignment of the headlamp unit following its replacement.

***Lack of sufficiently detailed work plans or job instructions***
The owner's or workshop manual will tell you in what order you need to perform the various tasks.

***Damaged or defective parts, components and tools***
If you find that any tool or part is damaged or defective (for example, a cracked headlamp unit) you will need to replace them before you start work.

***Disagreements or lack of co-operation from other people***
You may need to have permission in order to use workshop or garage facilities, or have access to a tool or parts store. Normally only 'authorised persons' will have access to these facilities.

***Not enough time to complete the task***
You should allow enough time to replace the bulb and also to check that it has been properly fitted and adjusted.

***Inadequate personal protective equipment***
You will need overalls and safety shoes in order to perform the task.

***Unexpected safety hazards***
Unexpected safety hazards could arise from having to work in a confined space or having to work with inadequate lighting. The low-voltage electrical system of a car or motorcycle is usually safe to work with provided the engine is turned off. You will also need to check that the vehicle is on a flat surface and the brakes are on! For a motorcycle make sure the stand is down and the engine is in gear.

Sometimes it can be difficult to decide just how serious a problem is. In such a case you should always refer the matter to your supervisor and then follow their guidance. Table 2.01 shows three examples of the kinds of problems you can solve by yourself and also of those which will need to be referred to other people.

| Typical problems that you can probably resolve on your own and the action you should take | Typical problems that you should refer to other people and who they should be referred to |
|---|---|
| A ladder has been left across an access way. *Inform your supervisor and move the ladder to a safe place* | You notice that a safety warning sign has been removed from a machine. *Report this to your supervisor and/or safety officer* |
| You have been issued with an electric drill that runs slow and gets very hot. *Mark the drill as unserviceable and return it to the tool store* | A fire exit has been obstructed. *Report this to your supervisor and/or safety officer* |
| A visitor approaches you and tells you that he is lost. *Direct him to reception and phone the receptionist to say that he is on his way* | An electric cable has been damaged and one of the conductors has become exposed. *Switch off, disconnect the supply and report this to your supervisor* |

**Table 2.01** Typical problems encountered by an engineer and who can help

**Hands On**

Make your own list of problems you might have while working. Share your ideas of what to do to solve these problems with each other.

**Quick Tip**

Most companies will provide you with an induction that will give you information about the company as well as who to contact if you have a problem. Make the most of your induction as it could save you a lot of time later on!

## People who can help

Many people will be able to help you with your work. You should not be afraid to ask them for help whenever you need it. Your main sources of help at work are listed below.

### Supervisor or line manager

Your supervisor or line manager is normally the first person to approach because they will have direct responsibility for you and for the work you do. You will often get to know them quite well. They will usually be on hand to help you with any problems you may have, ensure you understand what it is you need to do, and to check you are doing it correctly. They will often inspect your work and provide you with feedback. This will help you improve not only the way you work but also the quality of your work. You can learn a great deal from this feedback and are encouraged never to be afraid of asking them to comment on your work.

### Colleague or co-worker

Your colleagues and co-workers are the people you will have daily contact with. They will often have more experience than you and may have a wide range of knowledge and skills that you can call on. Be careful not to make too many demands on colleagues as they are busy too. In some cases it might be better to refer problems to your supervisor.

## Other people at work

| Job role | Description |
|---|---|
| Counsellor | A person who is trained to give advice and support for any personal or emotional problems you might have |
| First-aider | A person who has received training in first aid. You will often find that one of your colleagues is a first-aider. They are usually the first person to contact whenever there is an accident involving personal injury |
| Payroll officer | A person who is responsible for ensuring that people are paid correctly and on time |
| Personnel or human resources (HR) officer | A person who is responsible for all aspects of recruitment and employment within the company |
| Safety officer | A person who is responsible for all aspects of health and safety within the company |
| Training officer | A person who is responsible for ensuring that people are correctly trained and prepared for the work they do. In a small company the roles of personnel or HR officer, and training officer may be combined. In a large company they are usually separate roles |
| Union official | Within any large organisation there may be one or more trade unions that represent the interests of employees. Union officials are usually elected members of the union who can provide advice and support on issues relating to employment that cannot otherwise be solved by your supervisor or line manager |

**Table 2.02** People you will encounter at work

### QUICK CHECK

1 Who should you contact if you need to report a gas leak at work?
2 Who should you approach when you need to book some time off for a holiday?
3 Who would be the first person to contact if you receive a minor cut or bruise at work?
4 Who should you inform if you need written confirmation of your salary in order to obtain a bank loan?

### Hands On

Work with one other student or in a group to answer the following questions.

1. Think of a problem that occurred at work or college that you were able to solve on your own. How did the problem arise and how were you able to solve it without involving anyone else?

2. Think of a problem that occurred at work or college that you were able to solve with the assistance of at least one other person. How did the problem arise and how were you able to solve it with the involvement of other people?

Discuss your answers and see if you agree.

# Maintaining effective working relationships

Relationships are very important at work. Building and maintaining effective relationships is an important aspect of your work as an engineer. These case studies will help you to understand how this works.

## Case Study A

Paul is a new apprentice working in a large engineering company. He has been working in a small team for about four months and during this time he has witnessed another apprentice making jokes and comments which he thinks are racist. Although Paul feels that this behaviour is unacceptable and offensive, several other apprentices just laugh and join in the banter. When Paul mentions this to his supervisor, he is told to ignore this behaviour and just get on with the job.

What should Paul do and why should he do it? Discuss this with another student and see if you can both agree on your answer.

## Case Study B

Sonali is a junior test engineer working in a research and development environment. She finds it difficult to get on with her supervisor who is frequently critical of her work. Her supervisor told her that girls rarely make good engineers and that she should be applying for other jobs. Sonali feels that she is capable and she has always done whatever has been asked of her.

What should Sonali do and why should she do it? Discuss this with another student and see if you can both agree on your answer.

## Case Study C

Amjad is a very busy technician working on the design and manufacture of printed circuit boards. Amjad's company has asked him to look after two new apprentices. One of these apprentices needs very little supervision and easily gets on with his work. The other apprentice does not seem able to tackle even the most basic job and frequently asks for help. At the end of the first month Amjad is asked to comment on the performance of the two apprentices but feels that he is partly to blame because he has not had enough time to provide the support that the apprentices need.

What should Amjad do and why should he do it? Discuss this with another student and see if you can both agree on your answer.

**Case Study D**

John is a 'loner' and finds it difficult to work with other people. He often takes short cuts and doesn't finish work properly. John's supervisor, Martin, has recently begun to notice that John is regularly late for work. When questioned about this, John seems reluctant to discuss the problem and instead blames his lateness on the bus timetable. Martin feels that he needs to refer this problem to someone else but feels that he should do something first.

What should Martin do and why should he do it? Discuss this with another student and see if you can both agree on your answer.

As you begin your career in engineering you are sure to become a member of a team where other people will depend on you and respect you just as you depend on them and respect them. It is always good to listen to other people's needs and be prepared to give advice and support whenever necessary. If you can't help or don't know the answer, just say so.

Try to understand exactly what it is that you've been asked to do. When you've provided help or given an answer, see if people understand what you have said or done. Some other important things to do when working in a team are shown in Figure 2.13.

**Figure 2.13** How to work effectively in a team

Think of all the teams you belong to. They might be sport teams, social teams, family teams. Do you think that the teamwork diagram applies to all of these? Are any of these elements of teamwork more important than others? What happens when teams break down and how might that affect the work of the team?

## What the law says

Some laws and regulations affect how people should be treated at work. You need to know how these govern what you can and cannot do at work. The **Equality Act 2010** aims to end the discrimination that you might face if you belong to a group of people who may be less favourably treated than others. For example, if you are gay or have a religious faith it is against the law to treat you in a way that will put you at a disadvantage. A list of equal opportunities **legislation** is shown in Table 2.03.

| Equal opportunities legislation | Description |
| --- | --- |
| The Equal Pay Act | A person has a right to the same pay and benefits as a person of the opposite sex in the same employment as long as a man and woman are doing exactly the same work |
| The Race Relations Act | It is against the law to discriminate against anyone on grounds of race, colour, nationality (including citizenship), or ethnic or national origin. It applies to jobs, training, housing, education and the provision of goods, facilities and services |
| The Sex Discrimination Act | Prohibits sex discrimination in employment and education |
| Disability Discrimination Act | Aims to end the discrimination that many disabled people face. It gives disabled people new rights in terms of employment and access to goods, facilities and services, education and public transport |
| Equality Act | Strengthens and extends everyone's rights not to be discriminated against in all areas of life, including work. The Equality Act strengthens, consolidates and extends the laws mentioned above |

**Table 2.03** Different equal opportunities legislation

In addition to the equal opportunities legislation, the **Working Time Directive** limits the hours of work that an employee can be asked to do. It gives the right for workers in the European Union to have a minimum number of holidays each year and at least 11 hours' rest in any 24-hour work period. It also forbids excessive work at night and limits working hours to no more than 48 per week.

**Hands On**

Engineering projects require effective teamwork but each person in a team needs to understand their own role before starting work. Working with two or three other students, allocate individual roles and responsibilities that will allow you to carry out the following team activity.

Using only 2 m bamboo canes and rubber bands, design and construct a stable structure that will support a 2.5 kg load at a height of 2 m above the ground. The task is to be completed in no more than 40 minutes, including a 10 minute planning session.

Then discuss whether or not your teamwork was effective in helping you to carry out the activity.

# Personal training and development

As an engineer you can expect to receive training for the tasks you need to perform and the activities you undertake. You will also receive training that will allow you to gain the knowledge linked to the practical work you do. You are responsible for getting as much as you can from the work you do. This usually involves:

- understanding the levels of skill and knowledge needed to do your job
- paying attention to your own training and development, knowing your personal goals and objectives, and taking part in the process that helped to identify them
- keeping track of the progress you make
- improving your performance at work using the feedback and advice given to you by your supervisor, college tutor and training officer.

You will probably have a regular progress review or **appraisal** with your supervisor or training manager. This will help you to set goals and objectives about your development and training. You will look at what you know now and where you need to get to. Any gaps in your knowledge and skills can be identified and plans can be made for further training and development in order to meet those needs.

**Hands On**

Take a careful look at your training record or portfolio. Check that it is up to date and make sure that everything you've done has been recorded in it.

**Did You Know**

Continuous personal development is your own responsibility. Other people, such as your supervisor or training officer, all have a role to play. In the end it is you who should take charge of your own development.

**Key term**

**Appraisal** – a meeting, usually involving just you and your supervisor, in which your work is reviewed. Many companies have an appraisal scheme that involves every employee in a regular review of their work. In some cases how you perform at work is linked to pay or bonuses

**Quick Tip**

Always make sure that you keep your training record and portfolio up to date whenever you finish an activity or complete an aspect of your training. Not only will this save you a lot of time but it will also ensure that everything you do is accurately recorded and available for later inspection.

# Completing the job

The need to ensure that your work area is clean and tidy when you complete an activity has already been discussed. In addition to this you will also need to:

- return tools and equipment to the proper place – usually a tool or equipment store
- return unused materials and components to the proper place – usually a material or part store
- return drawings, job cards and work instructions (and check that they are complete, clean and unmarked)
- dispose of waste materials properly, following company procedures and environmental requirements
- complete all necessary documentation accurately and neatly
- identify, where appropriate, any damaged or unusable tools or equipment
- report any problems to your supervisor.

## Waste materials

Many engineering activities produce waste materials. Sometimes these materials can be recycled after suitable processing. In other cases the materials need to be disposed of safely and in a way that is not harmful to the environment. Typical waste materials include:

- lubricants, such as oil and grease
- solvents and other chemicals
- metal and plastic swarf.

Whenever you have to dispose of waste material it is essential that you follow the correct procedures as set out by your company. If you are in any way unsure about these, ask your supervisor.

## Storage of tools and equipment

Tools and equipment should be stored in the right place – usually in a separate tool or equipment store where the space for each tool is clearly marked. All tools should be regularly checked and kept in good condition. Many companies use a check system in order to track the use of a particular tool or set of tools. You should make sure that you use this system as it ensures that you always know where a tool is and whether it is being used or not.

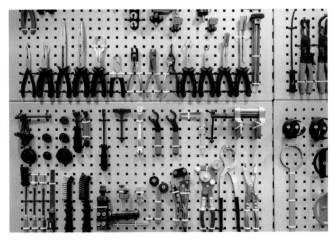

**Figure 2.14** A typical tool store

**Figure 2.15** A typical parts and material store

**Hands On**

Find out where tools, equipment and materials are stored in your workplace. How are they tracked and recorded? Is there a check procedure for tools and equipment and, if so, how does it work?

**Hands On**

Investigate one waste material that is present in your workplace. What procedures are laid down for its disposal and what eventually happens to it? Present your answer in an illustrated A3 poster.

# Improving working procedures

As you gain experience you will find that you become confident in the skills you have gained. You will also find that you are in a position to advise and support others. This is an important part of being a team member. Your company will encourage you to share your skills and knowledge with others. This will help improve working practices and procedures. Don't be afraid to make useful suggestions that will help your company to succeed.

There will usually be several ways in which you can make suggestions. Some companies have a suggestion box in which ideas can be posted. Some companies even offer a reward for the best ideas! Others have regular team meetings in which ideas can be discussed. You might also find that your company arranges a regular appraisal with your supervisor. This will almost certainly provide you with an opportunity to comment on your work and suggest how it can be improved.

Here are just a few of the ways that you can make a positive contribution to working procedures.

- Suggest how working practices and methods can be improved.
- Identify problems that affect quality and suggest how they can be solved.
- Suggest how tools and equipment can be better used.
- Suggest ways of improving internal communication.
- Identify training needs and development opportunities.
- Suggest ways of improving safety and avoiding hazards.
- Suggest modifications/improvements to products and services.

**QUICK CHECK**

List four ways in which you can make a contribution towards improving working practices and procedures.

## CHECK YOUR KNOWLEDGE

**1** The purpose of using personal protective equipment (PPE) is to:

   **a** avoid damage to tools and equipment

   **b** reduce the amount of waste material produced

   **c** protect employees from injury

   **d** improve the quality of engineered products

**2** Which one of the following injuries can be avoided by the use of safety glasses?

   **a** solder splashes

   **b** falling objects

   **c** burns and scalds

   **d** cuts and abrasions

**3** Preparing for a work activity involves:

   **a** using tools and equipment to carry out the task

   **b** making measurements to check quality and accuracy

   **c** checking that you have the right PPE for the job

   **d** tidying up the work you did previously

**4** In order to avoid any unforeseen problems in an engineering activity it is useful to have:

   **a** a full list of PPE

   **b** a work plan

   **c** a risk assessment

   **d** a copy of the relevant equal opportunities legislation

**5** The Working Time Directive:

   **a** helps to ensure equality of opportunity in the workplace

   **b** seeks to prevent discrimination against people with disability

   **c** safeguards health and safety at work

   **d** limits the hours of work that a person can be asked to do

**6** When you encounter a problem at work that you can't solve on your own it is important to:

   **a** carry on working and the problem will go away

   **b** seek guidance and advice from somebody else

   **c** make a note of the problem for future reference

   **d** stop working and go on to another job

**7** After completing a work activity it is necessary to:

   **a** read the job card or work instruction carefully

   **b** retain any unused components and materials for future use

   **c** tidy up and return tools and equipment to their designated locations

   **d** secure the work area by locking all doors, windows and safety exits

**8** Continuous personal development is important because:

   **a** it provides you with a break from work

   **b** it helps you identify problems at work

   **c** it helps you develop new skills and competences

   **d** it gives you an opportunity to forget what you have been doing

**9** Working as a member of a team involves:

   **a** doing other people's work

   **b** solving problems on your own

   **c** working with other people to achieve a goal

   **d** checking that everyone does the same amount of work

**10** Good working relationships are based on:

   **a** an ability to work alone and not to involve other people

   **b** a need for constant supervision and the support of other people

   **c** an ability to amuse and distract people whenever a problem arises

   **d** a positive attitude to work and a willingness to work with other people

# 3 Using and communicating technical information

Being able to use and communicate technical information is an important engineering skill. It is a skill you need to learn at the earliest stage of your engineering career. This chapter will help you to make sense of the information you need to do your job. It will show you how information is presented and how to make the best use of it.

You can communicate in many different ways – drawings, instruction manuals, even how you work with others in meetings. In this chapter you will learn how to make good use of information. This means making sure that you have all of the necessary information, and checking it is accurate and up to date before using it.

In this chapter you will learn about:

- communicating engineering information
- information needed to do the job
- written documentation

- specifications
- drawings and diagrams
- care and control of documents and drawings

In Formula 1 racing every second counts! The success of a Formula 1 racing team not only depends on every team member doing their job to the highest standard but also providing the best possible support for the rest of the team. Everyone needs to work together all of the time, from the mechanics and technical specialists to the race engineer and the driver.

The race engineer's main role is to get the best from the car and the driver at the circuit. However, this is not their only job. They have to communicate with the data analyst and mechanics, decide what changes to make and co-ordinate these changes. Away from the circuits they must analyse the data from previous track times. They also have to get the cars ready for the next circuit and make sure that everyone is updated. Race engineers need very good communication skills – without these skills there's very little chance of winning a race.

**Figure 3.01** A Formula 1 racing team

**Hands On**

1. List three essential skills needed by a race engineer working in the motorsport sector.

2. Use the Internet to find out about the job of a motorsport design engineer. How does this job compare with that of a race engineer?

## Key terms

**Verbal communication** – speaking and listening

**Body language** – gestures, facial expressions and body posture

**Written communication** – memos, notes, letters, reports, email and text messages

**Graphical communications** – charts, sketches, diagrams and drawings

# Communicating engineering information

In your everyday life you communicate with other people in many different ways. The race engineer might talk to someone face to face or on the phone if they are far away. This is **verbal communication**.

They might use **body language**, for example gestures, facial expressions and body posture. In some cases **written communication**, such as text messages, email, notes or letters might be a better way of getting the message across. In other situations, **graphical communications** such as sketches or drawings might be more effective.

You might not work as a race engineer. But whatever role you have, it is important to know how to get hold of the information you need to do your job properly.

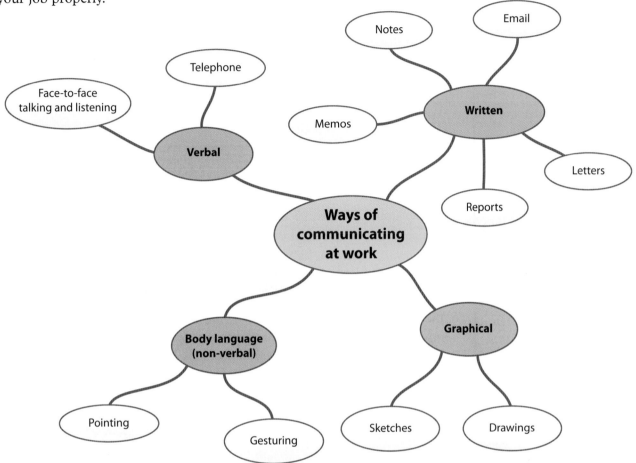

**Figure 3.02** Ways of communicating at work

Working with two or three other students, decide which method of communication you would use in each of the following situations and why.

1. Advertising the sale of your car.
2. Explaining the fire drill to a group of visitors.
3. Giving directions to a stranger who needs to find the nearest railway station.
4. Describing the way in which a sheet of metal can be cut into a number of smaller pieces.

# Information needed to do the job

For many engineering tasks you need information to be written down. This text is usually accompanied by charts, graphs, tables, diagrams and/or drawings. Information needs to be presented in a clear, accurate and up-to-date way. It needs to be set out in a way that makes it is impossible to misunderstand.

Where measurements or **dimensions** are used these need to be clearly written – both the number and the correct unit. Where measurements are critical, for example where **precision** work is being carried out, the required **accuracy** and **tolerance** should also be specified.

For example, if you had to produce a case for a small item of electrical equipment, as an absolute minimum you would need the:

- dimensions of the case
- material the case is to be made from
- **finish** to be applied to the case
- dimensions of any holes, apertures or fixings.

As an example, the information needed to construct an equipment case for a particular application might be as follows:

| | |
|---|---|
| Dimensions: | height 95 mm, width 350 mm, depth 270 mm |
| Material: | mild steel thickness 1.2 mm |
| Finish: | paint, light grey RAL 7035 |
| Fixings: | M4 captive nuts (4), M4 ×12.7 mm screws (4) |

This information is useful but it is still not enough to actually manufacture the enclosure! To be able to make it, you would need a drawing like the one shown in Figure 3.03. This drawing shows the dimensions of the equipment case and a very clear idea of how it will be made.

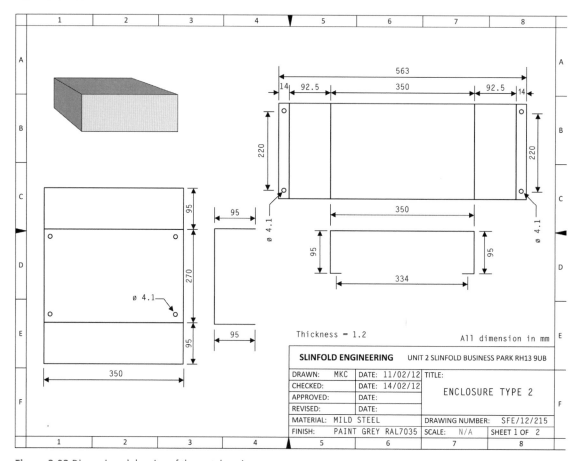

**Figure 3.03** Dimensioned drawing of the metal equipment case

**Hands On**

Take a careful look at the drawing shown in Figure 3.03 and use it to answer the following questions.

1. What is the reference number of the drawing?
2. On what date was the drawing made?
3. What material is used and what is its thickness?
4. What finish is to be applied to the equipment case?
5. What are the overall dimensions (before folding) of the cover and base section of the case?

# Written documentation

Written information is a very important part of communicating in engineering and it can take a variety of different forms.

## Data sheets and data books

Data sheets give essential information on a particular engineering component or device. They usually provide maximum and minimum values, specifications, and information on dimensions, packaging and finish.

Data sheets are usually supplied free of charge on request from manufacturers and suppliers. Collections of data sheets for similar types of engineering components and devices are sometimes also supplied in book form.

**SLINFOLD ENGINEERING** HTA2415 DATASHEET

The HTA series of high performance miniature DC motors are fitted with planetary gears offering outstanding torque to weight ratio and available with six different gear ratios to suit your own particular application.

Applications: Medical electronics, robotics, miniature drives and pumps

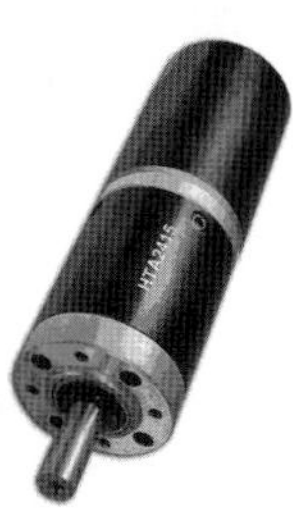

| Voltage (V) | Current (A) | Stalled current (A) | Motor speed (RPM) | Weight (kg) |
|---|---|---|---|---|
| 12 | 0.15 | 0.35 | 3000 | 0.06 |

| Model no. | Gear ratio | No load speed (RPM) | Rated speed (RPM) | Rated torque (Nm) | Peak torque (Nm) |
|---|---|---|---|---|---|
| 2415-1 | 50 | 58 | 48 | 0.09 | 0.82 |
| 2415-2 | 100 | 30 | 24 | 0.18 | 0.86 |
| 2415-3 | 190 | 15 | 12 | 0.32 | 0.90 |
| 2415-4 | 256 | 10 | 9.0 | 0.42 | 0.95 |
| 2415-5 | 520 | 5.8 | 4.5 | 0.50 | 1.10 |
| 2415-6 | 720 | 4.1 | 3.9 | 0.51 | 1.25 |

**Figure 3.04** A data sheet for a small d.c. motor

**Hands On**

Figure 3.04 shows a data sheet for a miniature **d.c.** motor. Read the data sheet carefully and use it to answer the following questions.

1. What is the part number of the motor?
2. What is the name of the company that manufactures the motor?
3. What is (a) the operating voltage and (b) the operating current for the motor?
4. What is the rated speed for a motor with a model number of 2415-4?
5. What is the rated torque for a motor with a model number of 2415-2?
6. Which of the motors delivers the highest value of peak torque?

**Key term**

**d.c.** – direct current (a current that only flows in one direction)

## Application notes

Application notes explain how something is used in a particular application or how it can solve a particular problem. They provide a lot of practical information for designers and others who may be considering using a particular component, process or technology for the first time.

## Technical reports

Technical reports are similar to application notes but they focus more on how engineering components and devices perform. They will usually provide detailed specifications and measurements and also describe how the measurements were obtained. Technical reports are often illustrated with graphs, charts, tables and other data.

## Catalogues

Most manufacturers and suppliers provide catalogues that list the range of products they supply. These usually include part numbers, illustrations, brief specifications and prices.

While catalogues are often very large documents with many hundreds or thousands of pages, short-form catalogues are usually also available. These just list part numbers, brief descriptions and prices but rarely include any illustrations. Catalogues and data sheets are often stored in electronic form to be downloaded from the Internet or distributed on CD-ROM.

## Manuals

Several different types of manual are used in engineering. The two most important types are:

- user or operating manuals – designed to be read by the end user of the product or equipment
- service, repair or maintenance manuals – designed to assist the repair and/or the routine maintenance of a product.

Manuals are usually produced by the company that has manufactured the product but may also be produced by third-party companies that specialise in manual production. Manuals are often supplied as booklets or leaflets but increasingly are being made available as **PDF** files available for download or are supplied on CD-ROM.

> **Key term**
>
> **PDF** – a Portable Document File that can be read on a wide range of electronic devices including desktops and laptops, tablets and book readers

## Job cards and work instructions

Job cards and work instructions are discussed in Chapter 2. Job cards provide information about parts and equipment and what should be done with them. They usually list the work that needs to be done and may also include the time given to each task or sub-task.

Job cards are often used when equipment is sent away for service or repair. They might also relate to a particular stage in the manufacture of a product. See page 33 for an example of a job card.

Work instructions usually contain much more detail than job cards and often describe each of the individual stages of performing a particular task or sub-task. See page 34 for an example of a work instruction.

### QUICK CHECK

1 What would you expect to find in an application note?
2 What is the difference between a data sheet and an application note?
3 What would you use a job card for and what information would you expect to find in it?
4 What would you use a work instruction for and what information would you expect to find in it?

### Hands On

Investigate the operating manual for an item of electronic equipment such as a multimeter, power supply or oscilloscope. List each of the main section headings and describe the information you find in it. Suggest how the manual could be improved to make it more useful. Discuss your findings with the rest of the class.

# Specifications

Specifications are a precise and comprehensive description of an engineered part, product or service. Specifications should relate to the performance of the product in a way that can be measured. They also relate to what the product is going to look like.

In many cases, specifications form the basis of a contract between a manufacturer or supplier and a client or customer. For example, what the purchaser requires and what the manufacturer is going to supply. There are three basic types of specification:

- **General specifications** – a detailed written description of the product including its appearance, construction, and materials used.
- **Performance specification** – a list of features of the product that contribute to its ability to meet the needs of the client or end user. For example, output voltage, power or speed.
- **Standard specification** – a description of the materials and processes (where appropriate) used in the manufacture of the product in terms of relevant **quality** standards (e.g. ISO 9000).

### Key term

**Quality** – when a product or service is 'free from defect' and will operate according to specification. It fully meets the needs and expectations of clients or users

**Figure 3.05** A typical cordless drill

A typical performance specification for a cordless drill might be:

| | |
|---|---|
| Voltage: | 18 V |
| Battery pack: | 1.3 Ah Lithium ion |
| Speed: | 1300 rpm (max) |
| Number of speed settings: | 2 |
| Max. rpm | 1300 |
| Number of clutch settings: | 15 |
| Chuck capacity: | 12 mm |
| Weight: | 2.5 kg |
| Charging time: | 45 minutes |

**Hands On**

Look at the performance specification for the cordless power drill and use it to answer the following questions.

1. What type of battery is fitted to the drill and how long does it take to recharge?
2. What is the maximum size of drill bit that can be used with the drill?
3. What units are used to specify the speed of the drill?

**Hands On**

Obtain detailed specifications for any two of the following engineered products:

1. an electrical test meter
2. a battery charger
3. an angle grinder
4. a mains-operated hammer drill.

For both of your chosen products determine the:

• power supply/energy source
• battery life (where appropriate)
• speed ratings (where appropriate)
• controls and settings
• compliance with relevant standards.

## Drawings and diagrams

Engineers use many different kinds of diagram and drawing as a way of communicating because they can:

• often show what needs to be done more easily than words
• contain extra information including dimensions and materials
• provide different views of a component, sub-assembly or a complete product
• show how component parts fit together to make a complete assembly.

As an engineer you must be able to read and use working drawings as well as producing your own sketches and diagrams. So that everyone can understand them, your drawings must comply with recommended standards, conventions and **projections**.

**Key term**

**Projection** – a way of drawing a 3D object by viewing it from different directions

Drawings can be either formal or informal depending on the way they are presented. Informal drawings are usually sketches or hand-drawn diagrams that provide a quick impression of what something will look like or how something will work (see Figure 3.06). Formal drawings, like the one in Figure 3.07 on page 58, take much longer to produce and usually contain much more detail. They are also much more precise and usually include features such as a scale, dimensions, materials, finishes and a title block.

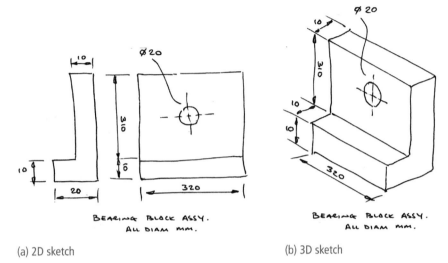

(a) 2D sketch  (b) 3D sketch

**Figure 3.06** A sketch of an engineering component

## Sketches

Sketches are freehand drawings that give a quick impression of what something will look like. A sketch can be either a two-dimensional (2D) representation or a three-dimensional (3D) representation (see Figure 3.06). A sketch can also be used to draw a block diagram or a schematic diagram (see pages 64–65). Additional information, such as labels and dimensions, can be added to sketches. When you draw a sketch you need to ensure that it:

- is clear and easy to read
- is of a suitable size – otherwise it might be difficult for others to read
- uses the correct symbols and drawing conventions
- is in proportion to the real part or component.

If you don't follow this guidance, your sketch will be difficult to read and may even put across the wrong information!

**Quick Tip**

When making a sketch, it is always best to use an HB pencil and an eraser rather than a ballpoint pen. This makes it possible to easily remove any unwanted or incorrect lines. When complete you can always go over your pencil sketch using a permanent ink drawing pen.

**QUICK CHECK**

1  What is a drawing projection and why do you need to show several different projections of the same object?
2  List four things that you need to take into account when sketching a part or component.

Produce simple 3D sketches of any *two* of the following:

- a Vee block
- a pair of dividers
- a torch or inspection lamp
- a standard 13 A three-pin mains plug.

Label your sketch clearly, showing the individual parts and adding approximate dimensions.

## Formal engineering drawings

Formal engineering drawings provide more information than sketches and they are usually produced using a computer-aided design (CAD) package. Most companies use a common template for all of their formal drawings. This has a border so that individual areas of the drawing can be identified. It also has a title block that shows key information like the one below.

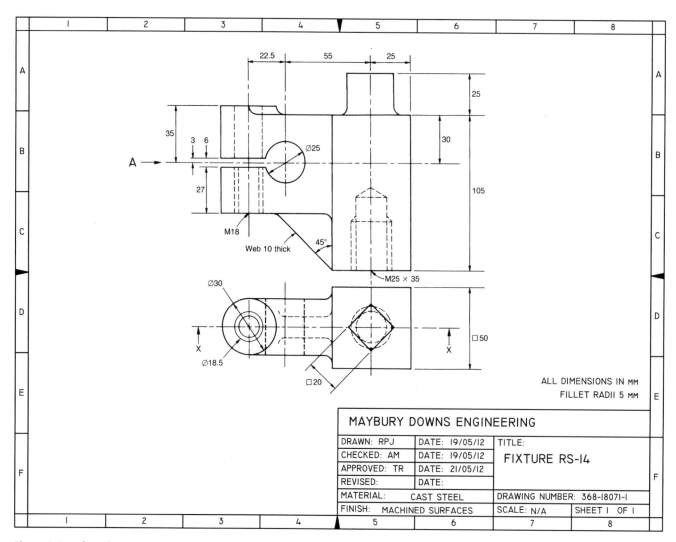

**Figure 3.07** A formal engineering drawing

## Title blocks

The title block (shown in the bottom right-hand corner of Figure 3.07) contains a great deal of important information, such as the name of the company, the title of the drawing, and the names of those responsible for making, checking and approving it. It usually includes the company's contact details and the drawing number (sometimes repeated in the top left-hand corner of the drawing). You may also find the scale or dimensions used for the drawing and the projection used (e.g. first or third angle). Take a look at the examples given in Figures 3.07 to 3.09 to see what other information normally appears in a title block.

## Parts lists

As well as the title block you may find a list of component parts (together with numbered references shown on the drawing) and materials to be used. You might also find information such as:

- the finish to be applied
- the units used for measurement and tolerances
- reference to appropriate standards (e.g. BS 8888)
- guidance notes (such as 'do not scale').

## Drawing scales

Different drawing scales are used depending on the actual size of the part or component shown in the drawing. Scale is normally given as a ratio of the size on the drawing to the size in real life. Hence, 'full size' corresponds to a scale of 1:1. 'Reduced scale' is when the drawing is reduced, for example to 'half size'. This is when one unit on the drawing represents two units in real life and is written as 1:2. Similarly, 'quarter size' is 1:4 (one unit on the drawing is equivalent to four units in real life). Enlarged scales are also used. So, for example, 2:1 is where two units on the drawing represent one unit in real life. A scale of 5:1 is where five drawing units represent one unit in real life.

## General arrangement drawings

General arrangement (GA) drawings show how the various parts used in an assembly are related to one another (see Figure 3.08). The individual parts are often listed in a table together with the quantities required. Each of these parts is drawn with more detail separately in what is referred to as a **detail drawing**.

The numbers of these drawings are usually quoted in the parts list shown in the GA drawing for the particular assembly the parts are used in. Therefore, one GA drawing is usually accompanied by a number of detail drawings. Note that individual parts (such as nuts, screws and washers) may be readily available from other suppliers while other more specialised parts may need to be manufactured especially.

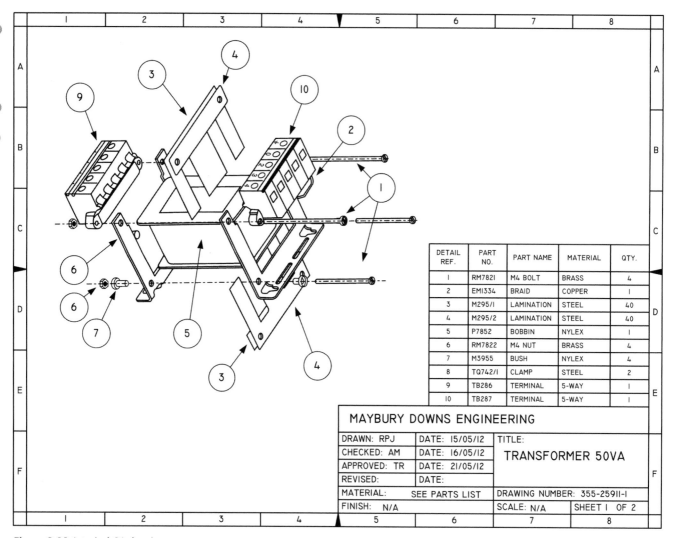

**Figure 3.08** A typical GA drawing

| DETAIL REF. | PART NO. | PART NAME | MATERIAL | QTY. |
|---|---|---|---|---|
| 1 | RM7821 | M4 BOLT | BRASS | 4 |
| 2 | EMI334 | BRAID | COPPER | 1 |
| 3 | M295/1 | LAMINATION | STEEL | 40 |
| 4 | M295/2 | LAMINATION | STEEL | 40 |
| 5 | P7852 | BOBBIN | NYLEX | 1 |
| 6 | RM7822 | M4 NUT | BRASS | 4 |
| 7 | M3955 | BUSH | NYLEX | 4 |
| 8 | TQ742/1 | CLAMP | STEEL | 2 |
| 9 | TB286 | TERMINAL | 5-WAY | 1 |
| 10 | TB287 | TERMINAL | 5-WAY | 1 |

**MAYBURY DOWNS ENGINEERING**

| | | |
|---|---|---|
| DRAWN: RPJ | DATE: 15/05/12 | TITLE: |
| CHECKED: AM | DATE: 16/05/12 | **TRANSFORMER 50VA** |
| APPROVED: TR | DATE: 21/05/12 | |
| REVISED: | DATE: | |
| MATERIAL: SEE PARTS LIST | | DRAWING NUMBER: 355-25911-1 |
| FINISH: N/A | | SCALE: N/A — SHEET 1 OF 2 |

## Detail drawings

Detail drawings, like the one shown in Figure 3.09, need to provide all of the information required to make a particular part or component. Detail drawings usually include dimensions and tolerances as well as details of any finishes that need to be applied. The amount of information given in a detail drawing depends very much on the complexity of the job. For example, drawings for a critical aircraft component need to be much more detailed than those for a garden tool.

## Dimensions

When dimensions are included in a drawing or sketch they should be noted clearly and neatly to avoid confusion or misinterpretation (see Figure 3.10). When adding dimensions, you need to:

- closely follow the conventions associated with dimensioning
- make sure they can't be confused with the original drawing lines and annotation
- use a common fixed reference point.

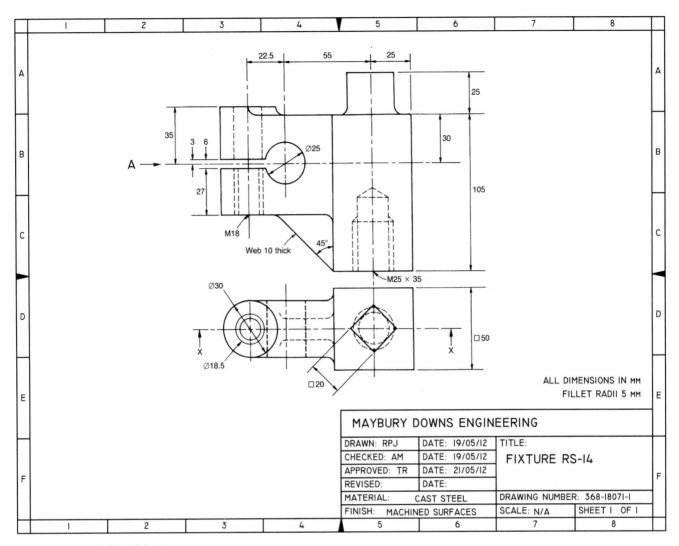

**Figure 3.09** A typical detail drawing

1 What is the difference between (a) a reduced scale and (b) an enlarged scale on an engineering drawing? Give an example of each.
2 What is the difference between a GA drawing and a detail drawing? How are these two types of drawing related?
3 What information would you expect to find in the title block of a formal drawing? Explain why this information is important.

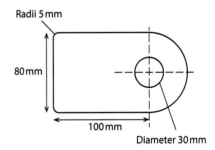

**Figure 3.10** A dimensioned detail drawing of a part

**Hands On**

1. Make a copy of the detail drawing shown in Figure 3.10 using an HB pencil, ruler, square, compasses and an A4 drawing sheet. Don't forget to include a title block.
2. There are two errors in Figure 3.10. Find the two errors and correct them on your drawing.

## Drawing types and projections

As you will have noticed from the sketching you did earlier, it's fairly easy to draw an object in 2D but not quite so easy to produce a 3D view using only a 2D screen or sheet of drawing paper. Modern 3D CAD overcomes this problem and allows engineers to view a part or component from any angle. Despite this, engineers still need to be able to draw a solid object well, using only a pencil and a drawing sheet.

### *Isometric drawings*

Isometric drawings allow you to show 3D objects in a 2D drawing. It does this by drawing vertical lines conventionally and all other lines at an angle of 30° to the horizontal, as shown in Figure 3.11. Lines are normally drawn using their correct (or correctly scaled) length. Modern CAD systems make this easy by helping to snap lines to an isometric grid and also by drawing ellipses to represent circles.

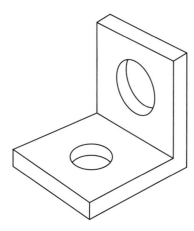

Figure 3.11 An isometric drawing

When you need to show an object in more detail, using a series of views from different directions can be helpful. Two methods are commonly used: first angle (or 'English') projection and third angle (or 'American') projection.

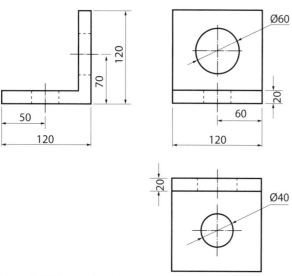

Figure 3.12 First angle projection

### *First angle projection*

To be able to show all of the detail of an object, more than one view is necessary. In most cases three different views (or 'projections') are required. These three views are called front elevation, end elevation and plan view.

In first angle projection, first you draw a front view of the object. Then, by looking from one side of the object, you draw what you would see on the other side. Figure 3.12 shows how this is done.

The two elevations and the plan view are drawn as follows.

- **Front elevation** – to draw this, you look directly at the front of the part and draw what you see. This is the main view from which all the other views are positioned.
- **End elevation** – to draw this, you look directly at the side of the part and draw what you see *at the opposite side*. Note that, for some parts you might need two end views, one at each side of the elevation.
- **Plan view** – to draw this, you look directly down on the part and draw what you see below the elevation.

Figure 3.12 requires only one end view. When there is only one end view, choose the end that is clearer and more easily interpreted.

**Hands On**

Use manual drawing techniques to create a first angle drawing of a simple engineering part such as a flange or bracket. Make sure that you correctly show all three views of the part.

## Third angle projection

In the case of third angle projection the drawing once again starts with a front view of the object. This time, however, you look at one side of the object and draw what you would see on the *same* side. Next you look at the object from above and draw what you would see from above (*not* from underneath as was the case with first angle projection).

Figure 3.13 shows how this appears. It shows a simple part and this only requires one end view.

Here is how the three individual views are produced.

- **Front elevation** – to draw this, you look directly at the front of the part and draw what you see. This is the main view from which all the other views are positioned.
- **End elevation** – to draw this, you look directly at the side of the part and again draw what you see. As before, it is worth noting that, for some parts you may need two end views, one at each end of the elevation.
- **Plan** – to draw this, you look directly down on the part and draw what you see below the elevation.

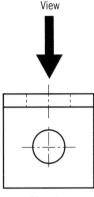

View

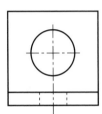

Plan view

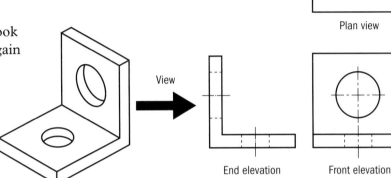

View

End elevation    Front elevation

**Figure 3.13** Third angle projection

## Auxiliary views

In addition to the main views shown on a drawing sheet, it is sometimes necessary to use additional (or 'auxiliary') views in order to clarify the drawing and reduce ambiguity. Auxiliary views are used when you can't show the true outline of the component. They are also used when you wish to illustrate a particular feature of the component.

**QUICK CHECK**

1  What is an isometric drawing and how is it constructed?
2  What is the difference between first angle and third angle projection?

## Other diagrams

As well as sketches, GA and detail drawings, engineers use several other types of diagram including block diagrams, flow diagrams, schematics and exploded views. All of these provide useful information for engineers.

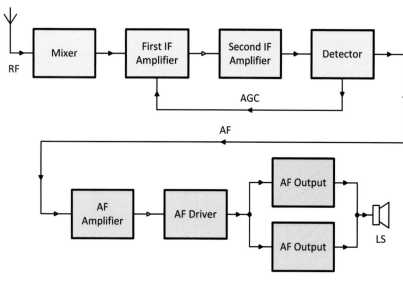

### Block diagrams

Block diagrams are useful for showing how individual parts are connected or linked together. They are not intended to show the physical relationship between the parts but instead they show how the parts are connected together. Block diagrams use shapes – often square or rectangular boxes connected together with arrows to show the flow of signals, power, fluid or information. Figure 3.14 shows the block diagram of a radio receiver. Diagrams like this can be very useful when carrying out fault finding.

**Figure 3.14** A block schematic diagram for a radio receiver

## Flow diagrams

Flow diagrams or flow charts are used to illustrate a sequence of events. They are often used to describe engineering processes such as the stages involved in the manufacture of a product or the maintenance of a piece of equipment (see Figure 3.15).

### Schematic diagrams

Schematic diagrams are used to show how components are connected together in electrical, pneumatic and hydraulic circuits. Schematic diagrams use standard symbols and the links between them are shown with lines. There are several types of schematic diagram including:

- **Circuit diagrams** – used to show how components are connected in an electric or electronic circuit. The components are represented by symbols (see Figure 3.16) and the electrical connections between the components are drawn using straight lines.
- **Wiring diagrams** – used to show the physical connections between electrical and electronic components (i.e. the actual layout of the wires).

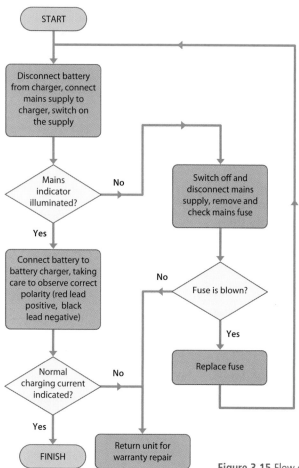

**Figure 3.15** Flow chart for fault finding on a battery charger

- **Pneumatic and hydraulic diagrams** – represent pneumatic circuits and hydraulic circuits using standard symbols.
- **Piping diagrams** – used to show the physical connections between pneumatic and hydraulic components (i.e. the actual layout of the pipes).

More details about the components and symbols used in electronic circuits can be found in Chapter 7. An example of a complete electronic circuit is shown in Figure 3.16. Figure 3.17 shows a hydraulic circuit.

**Key terms**

**Pneumatic** – a system that uses compressed gas (usually air) to produce motion

**Hydraulic** – a system that uses compressed liquid (usually special oil-based hydraulic fluid) to produce motion

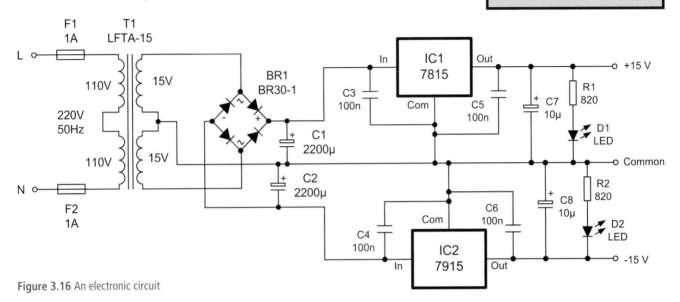

**Figure 3.16** An electronic circuit

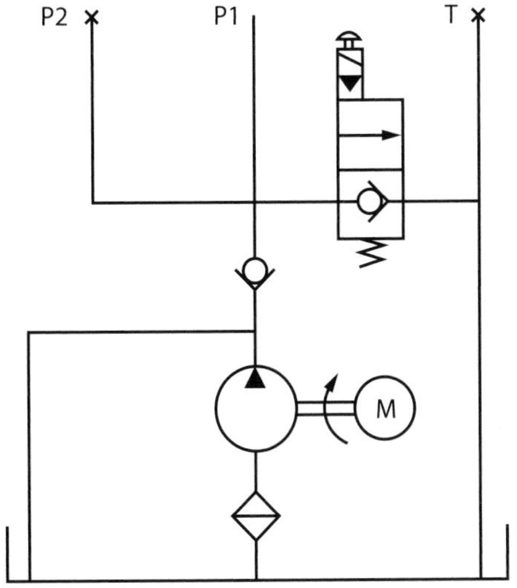

**Figure 3.17** A hydraulic circuit

**Quick Tip**

It is worth remembering that the position of a component in a schematic diagram may not bear any relationship to its actual physical position. This is particularly true for circuit diagrams where a wiring diagram often looks very different from the corresponding circuit diagram.

**Did You Know**

Pneumatic circuits and hydraulic circuits share the same symbols. You can tell which circuit is which because pneumatic circuits should have open arrowheads, whereas hydraulic circuits should have solid arrowheads. Also, pneumatic circuits exhaust to the atmosphere, but hydraulic circuits have to have a return path to a fluid reservoir.

## Exploded views

Exploded views are similar to GA diagrams. The key difference is that GA diagrams show how the parts fit together when a product is manufactured and exploded views show how they can be taken apart and reassembled.

Exploded views can be extremely useful when a product has to be serviced or maintained. A service or maintenance engineer has only to take a look at an exploded diagram to see how the various parts fit together. A typical assembly diagram for an electrical control box is shown in Figure 3.18.

A = Enclosure base with built in contact block clips

B = Contact blocks/lamp holders

C = Locking ring

D = Enclosure lid

E = Legend plate

F = Captive screws (after screw-in) loose in enclosure on delivery

G = Actuators and lens cap

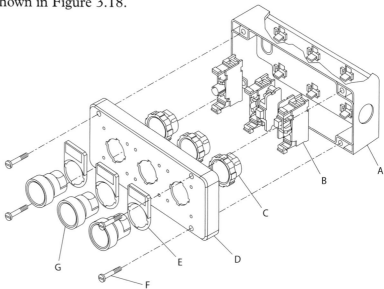

**Figure 3.18** An exploded view of an electrical control box with key

## Charts, graphs and tables

Charts, graphs and tables are used to present data in a way that makes it easy to use and understand. Charts and graphs provide a simple way of showing data as a picture. Tables are ideal for presenting numerical data, such as the different screw threads and clearances.

| Metric size | Nominal diameter (d) | Coarse pitch (p) | Bolt head | | |
|---|---|---|---|---|---|
| | | | Height (H) | Flat size (A/F) | Ext. diam (A/C) |
| M3 | 3.00 mm | 0.50 mm | 2.125 mm | 5.5 mm | 6.4 mm |
| M4 | 4.00 mm | 0.70 mm | 2.925 mm | 7.0 mm | 8.1 mm |
| M5 | 5.00 mm | 0.80 mm | 3.65 mm | 8.0 mm | 9.2 mm |
| M6 | 6.00 mm | 1.00 mm | 4.15 mm | 10.0 mm | 11.5 mm |
| M8 | 8.00 mm | 1.25 mm | 5.65 mm | 13.0 mm | 15.0 mm |
| M10 | 10.00 mm | 1.50 mm | 7.18 mm | 17.0 mm | 19.6 mm |

**Table 3.01** Metric screw threads

## QUICK CHECK

1  What is the difference between a block diagram and a flow chart? Give an example of what you would use each type of diagram for.
2  Sketch four different symbols used in electronic circuits and name each of the components.
3  What is an exploded view used for? What does it help you to do?
4  Give an example of the use of (a) charts and (b) tables to present engineering data.

# Care and control of documents/drawings

Engineering documents and drawings are important so they need to be used and stored correctly. This will ensure that they are not damaged as a result of physical handling or the environment they are used in. Documents must be stored in appropriate cabinets well away from dust, dirt, oil and grease. It is vital to have a system that controls the taking and returning of documents, particularly where a number of people must have access to them. Damaged or lost drawings should always be reported to your supervisor or another responsible person.

Engineering documents/drawings should always be marked with the:

- originator's name
- issue number and/or the date of issue
- date of any subsequent revisions or modifications.

Most companies store drawings and documents electronically. This makes them widely accessible within the company and also makes it easy to update them whenever the need arises.

## Controlled documents

Document control is used in all large engineering companies and the use of computerised systems has made this much easier and more effective. If a controlled document is changed, a record of the change has to be made. Equally importantly, employees should always remember to check they are using the current version of a controlled document.

When a controlled document is changed, everyone who needs it should be made aware and should also make sure they have access to the current version. This means that versions of a document, as well as any revisions made to it, need to be clearly identified.

## Dealing with problems

You will need to deal promptly and effectively with any problems that arise at work and are within your control. Some problems can be solved quite easily by yourself but others may require you to seek help and guidance from other people. Most engineering companies have regular team meetings and these can provide a useful forum for discussing problems and sharing ideas that can lead to a solution. More urgent problems may need to be resolved at the time they crop up. You will normally refer these to your supervisor or team leader.

**Key term**

**Controlled document** – a reference document which, through the course of its lifecycle, may be reviewed, modified and reissued several times

**Hands On**

Find an example of a controlled document used in your company and use it to answer the following questions:

1. What is the title and purpose of the document?
2. What is the name of the person who authorised the document?
3. What is the date of the document?
4. Have any changes been made to the document and how do you know?

**Quick Tip**

Team meetings provide you with an opportunity to ask questions and make a contribution to your work and team. It's always worth keeping a few written notes to act as a reminder of what was discussed and agreed.

**Hands On**

Describe the procedures for (a) reporting discrepancies in data or documents and (b) for reporting lost or damaged documents within your company.

Describe the care and control procedures for documents in your company including (a) reporting errors and changes, and (b) dealing with damaged or lost documents.

## CHECK YOUR KNOWLEDGE

**1** Which one of the following appears in the title block of a drawing?

   **a** a comprehensive parts list

   **b** the dimensions of each component

   **c** the company name and contact information

   **d** isometric or orthographic views, as appropriate

**2** A precision part is manufactured:

   **a** to a high degree of accuracy

   **b** without dimensioned drawings

   **c** using sketches with approximate dimensions

   **d** using only drawings made to a strict 1:1 scale

**3** If a diagram is drawn half size, it means that:

   **a** the scale is 2:1

   **b** only half the drawing area is actually used

   **c** one unit on the drawing represents two units in the real world

   **d** two drawings sheets are needed to represent the part or component

**4** The reference numbers for the individual components used in an assembly are usually found in:

   **a** a parts list

   **b** a specification

   **c** a technical report

   **d** an application note

**5** Formal engineering drawings are normally produced using:

   **a** a CAD package

   **b** a series of sketches

   **c** a single sketch supplemented by a parts list

   **d** word processing software

**6** Which one of the following is a schematic drawing?

   **a** a bar chart

   **b** a circuit diagram

   **c** an isometric view

   **d** a general arrangement (GA) diagram

**7** Changes made to update a drawing are usually found in the:

   **a** parts list

   **b** revision list

   **c** isometric view

   **d** supporting documentation

**8** A flow chart shows:

   **a** how several parts fit together

   **b** an exploded view of a product

   **c** a sequence of events or processes

   **d** the detail of an individual part or component

**9** A summary of the features of a particular part or component can be found in:

   **a** a data sheet

   **b** a technical report

   **c** a service manual

   **d** an operating manual

**10** The plan view of a part is obtained by looking:

   **a** at the front of the component and drawing what you see

   **b** from the side and drawing what you see on the opposite side

   **c** from the rear and drawing what you see on the opposite side

   **d** down at the component from above and drawing what you see

# 4 Wiring electrical equipment and circuits

Almost everything in the modern world runs on electricity. It operates our cookers and washing machines. It lights houses, office blocks, colleges and factories. It powers computers, mobile phones and vehicle engines.

Helpful as it is, electricity is also dangerous. It can cause fire and electric shock. Electrical wiring and equipment must therefore be installed correctly, securely and safely.

This chapter introduces electrical equipment and accessories, and installation methods. It also describes how an installation should be tested, and faults found and repaired.

In this chapter you will learn about:

- cables
- electrical accessories
- safe connections
- circuits

- typical installations
- electrical protection
- inspection and testing
- finding faults

# KITTING UP

## Keeping Safe

Electrical work carries its own risks. An electric shock can be instantly fatal. Faulty wiring and equipment can cause fires. Health and safety are therefore the most important things to think about before starting any job.

It is important to make sure your tools and equipment are of a high standard and are checked before use. Risk assessments must also be written before work starts. If the work is hazardous it must be authorised using the Permit to Work system. Above all, however, the right personal protective equipment (PPE) needs to be selected for the job.

All electrical work must conform to BS 7671 which explains how electrical installations and the people who use them must be protected from fire and shock. It talks about using the correct equipment and wiring methods, how to carry out electrical testing and contains tables which help designers to plan safe, reliable electrical installations.

The *IET On-Site Guide* explains the BS 7671 regulations to the electrician using diagrams and more straightforward language than BS 7671 to cover the same subjects, e.g. protection against electrical shock and fire, and working out what size cable to use. There are also 11 guidance notes which offer lots of support.

**Goggles** – protect the eyes from flying objects when using power tools, such as drills, saws and cutters

**Hi-viz waistcoat** – makes sure you can be seen at all times. Compulsory on most construction sites

**Gloves** – worn to protect hands from sharp edges and rough surfaces when lifting and carrying

**Protective footwear** – protects feet from injury caused by heavy objects. Compulsory on most construction sites

# Toolkit

No job can be carried out without the correct tools. Shown below are the main items of equipment needed for working with electrical equipment

| | |
|---|---|
| **Phillips and flat bladed screwdrivers of various sizes** | Most modern fixing screws now have the x and star-shaped Phillips and Pozidriv slots which require a matching screwdriver. There are two sizes, small and large |
| **Combination pliers** | Made up of gripping jaws and a set of cutting blades, combination pliers enable you to carry out a number of jobs using only one tool |
| **Side cutters** | Designed to cut cables, these can often be used in situations where it is difficult to use combination pliers, e.g. where only the tips of the cutting blades can gain access to the cable or wire |
| **Cable strippers** | Cable strippers are much easier to use for stripping insulation and can be adjusted to fit various cable sizes |
| **Tape measure** | Available in various lengths. Used to measure positions of equipment, saw cuts and drilled holes |
| **Hammer** | Available in various sizes and types, each of which can be used to drive different fixings into materials |
| **Crimping tool** | Specialist tool for securing crimp lugs or terminations onto a cable conductor. Most have a set of various sized slots along the edges of their jaws so they can be used for most standard crimp lug sizes |
| **Electric drill** | Used for drilling holes in masonry, wood or metal, and as electric screwdrivers with appropriate drill bits |
| **Spirit level (small and larger)** | Used to measure the level or plumb of an object |
| **Junior hacksaw** | Smaller version of the hacksaw, used for cutting smaller items of metal and plastic |
| **Sharp knife with retractable blade (Stanley knife)** | Used for a variety of jobs, from stripping cable sheathing to slicing through the tongues in wooden tongued-and-grooved floorboards. When not in use, the blade is hidden inside the handle |
| **Adjustable grips** | There are various types, such as pipe grips and mole grips (shown) – these are adjusted by turning the screw at the bottom of the handle |
| **Adjustable spanner** | Like adjustable grips, can be set to the size of a particular bolt or nut. In this case, the moveable jaw is set using a thumbscrew |
| **Specialist cable termination tools** | Some equipment has non-standard terminals so specialist tools are needed, e.g. for a telephone outlet with a grip-type terminal, a specialist tool to push the conductor into the terminal jaws |
| **Voltage indicator** | Shows whether voltage is present |
| **Continuity tester** | Confirms that a conductor or part of a circuit is unbroken and that current can flow from one end to the other |
| **Insulation resistance tester** | Confirms that the insulation on a cable is intact and that there are no short circuits between line and neutral and earth |

# BS 7671:2008 Requirements for Electrical Installations (17th edition)

The BS 7671:2008 Wiring Regulations are very important. All electrical installation work must comply with its guidelines. BS 7671 covers many things including:

- choosing the right equipment
- cable sizes
- protection against shock and fire.

## Cables

Cables are the nerves of an electrical installation. They carry current from the supply to the sockets, switches, lights and appliances. There are many different types of cable, each one designed to do a certain type of job. For example, a tough environment, such as a factory or agricultural installation, would need a tough cable that can take a lot of punishment.

A cable is made up of a number of components, as shown in Figure 4.01.

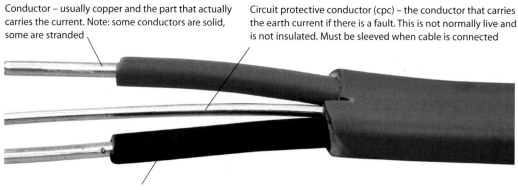

Conductor – usually copper and the part that actually carries the current. Note: some conductors are solid, some are stranded

Circuit protective conductor (cpc) – the conductor that carries the earth current if there is a fault. This is not normally live and is not insulated. Must be sleeved when cable is connected

PVC insulation – colour-coded and prevents short circuit and electric shock

Figure 4.01 A twin-and-earth cable

Choosing the size of a cable for a circuit depends on the amount of current used by the circuit's load. The higher the current, the larger the cable required. Cable size is based on the **cross-sectional area** of its conductor.

BS 7671 contains tables which give the amount of current various cables can carry. The amount of current a cable can carry is also affected by:

- surrounding temperature – the higher the temperature, the less the current it can carry
- length of cable run – the longer the run, the less current it can carry
- **installation method**.

## Twin-and-earth

Twin-and-earth is a cable with an outer PVC **sheath** and three cores; line, neutral and **circuit protective conductor** (cpc). Twin-and-earth is used for wiring:

- houses
- light commercial buildings, such as offices
- public buildings, such as schools.

Three-core and earth is also available. This has a brown, black and grey core as well as the cpc.

## Single cable

Single cable has one layer of insulation and no outer sheath. Because of this, singles must be installed in conduit or trunking. They must never be installed on the surface of a wall or in any situation where they do not have extra **mechanical protection**.

**Keep It Safe**

Always use the correct sized cable. If a cable carries more current than it is designed for it will become hot and possibly cause a fire.

**Key terms**

**Installation method** – how a cable is installed. For example, clipping cable to the surface of a wall, running it in conduit or trunking and running it on cable tray are all wiring methods

**Circuit protective conductor** – a cable's earth conductor

**Sheath** – on a cable, the outer covering that protects the cores. Some cables, such as armoured cable, also have an inner sheath

**Mechanical protection** – protection against physical damage

**Hands On**

Prepare a loom of six, 2.5 mm, two single cables ready to be drawn into conduit. A secure method is as follows.

1. Strip one cable (cable A) back about 200 mm.
2. Strip the other cables back to 10 mm.
3. Wrap the bared conductor of the first of these other cables neatly round the bared conductor of cable A.
4. Wrap the bared conductor of the next conductor tightly round the bared conductor of cable A. Start this at the point where the previous conductor winding finished.
5. Repeat with the remaining three cables.
6. Attach the remaining length of bared conductor from cable A to the draw wire and wind it tightly back on itself.
7. The advantages of this method are as follows.
- The joint is very secure and will not give way while being pulled into a conduit.
- The cables are layered rather than bunched into a cumbersome clump on the end of the draw wire.

It is important to pull all the cables through a conduit run at the same time. If you try to install more cables into a pipe that already contains other circuits, it can damage the cables.

Conduit runs will include a number of inspection boxes. Cables should be pulled out at these boxes then fed into the next section. The cables should be laid carefully into the box and not twisted around each other.

**Figure 4.02** Jointing cables ready to be drawn into a conduit

**Figure 4.03** Single cables on drums being drawn into conduit

## Flexible cable

Flexible cable is also called a flex or a lead. As the name suggests, flex is designed to bend easily. It is used to connect electrical appliances and equipment to the mains supply. There are a number of different types of flex, as shown in Table 4.01.

| Type of flex | Purpose | Example of use |
|---|---|---|
| Standard PVC sheathed and insulated two- and three-core | Connecting appliances and equipment to the supply | Kettle lead |
| Heat resistant | Connecting equipment that gives off heat | Water heater |
| Armoured | Industrial equipment or trailing leads in rough work areas, such as quarries and construction sites | Digging machine in a quarry |
| Multicore | Used where a number of conductors are needed, often as part of a **three-phase** or a control circuit | Three-phase electric motor |
| Ribbon cable | Not strictly a flex but a flat cable used for connecting parts of a control circuit | Part of a control panel which is designed to be pulled out and inspected then re-inserted |

**Table 4.01** Types of flexible cable

### Extension leads

Extension leads (see Figure 4.04) are plugged in when an appliance lead is not long enough to allow the appliance to be used properly. There are a number of rules concerning extension leads.

- Extension leads can be a trip hazard, so if they are trailed across a path or walkway, they should be clearly marked.
- Extension leads should not be plugged into each other (piggybacking).
- An extension lead should be fully unwound before use as the lead can become hot if left coiled round its drum.
- Always use a three-core (line, neutral and earth) extension lead. Never use a two-core.

**Figure 4.04** An extension lead

## Armoured cable

Designed for harsh working environments, such as factories and underground supply routes, armoured cable is protected by strands of steel wire wound round its inner sheath. The sheath not only protects the cable, it can also be used as the cpc.

Cores

Outer sheath – toughened plastic, smoke retardant

Inner sheath    Steel wire armour

**Figure 4.05** Steel-wire armoured cable

## Terminating steel wire armoured cable

| Checklist | | | |
|---|---|---|---|
| PPE | Tools and equipment | Consumables | Source information |
| • Protective footwear<br>• Hi-viz jacket | • Tape measure<br>• Knife – retractable blade type<br>• Junior hacksaw<br>• Adjustable spanner and grips | • Steel wire armoured cable<br>• Cable termination gland kit<br>• Cable shroud | • BS 7671:2008 |

**1**

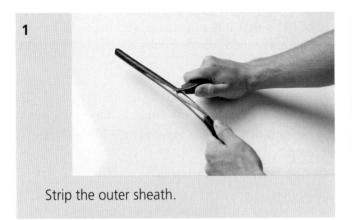

Strip the outer sheath.

**2**

Saw halfway through the armoured wires.

**3**

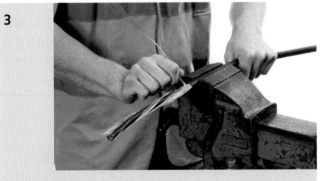

Bend the wires back and forth until they snap off.

**4**

Strip outer sheath another few millimetres, then push the shroud and female gland onto the cable.

**5**

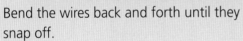

Push the male gland onto the cable. The dome section is seated under the armour wires.

**6**

Secure the female gland onto male thread, clamping the armour wire securely.

## Fireproof cable

Alarms and emergency lighting must continue to work in the event of fire, even after the rest of the electrical installation has failed. To make sure this happens alarm circuits are wired using fireproof cables. There are two main types, as explained below.

### FP cable

FP is widely used in modern installations. It is also known as LSZH (Low Smoke Zero Halogen) cable. It is simple to install and terminate. The main disadvantage of FP is that it is not strong and needs to be handled carefully when being installed. Cable bends should not be tight as this can damage the inner sheath.

FP is made up of:

* an outer plastic sheath that does not give off smoke or fumes if it burns
* an aluminium inner sheath, which adds extra protection and can also be used as a screen
* conductors insulated by fire-resistant plastic.

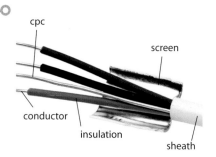

Figure 4.06 FP Gold 200 cable

### Mineral insulated cable

Fire alarm systems in many buildings are still wired in mineral insulated cable, which was the first successful fireproof cable. Mineral insulated cable is tough and has a copper outer sheath. Its conductors are bare and insulated from each other by a white powder called magnesium oxide. The disadvantage of this powder is that it absorbs moisture easily. Because of this, waterproof glands have to be fitted to the end of the cable.

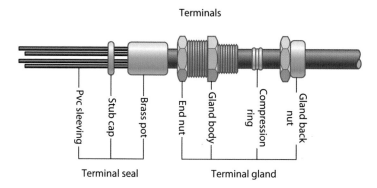

Figure 4.07 Mineral insulated cable and its gland

## Data and signal cables

### Category 5 and telephone cable

Category 5 is used to supply data for computer networks. It is a twisted-pair cable designed with the input and output conductors twisted together. This helps to reduce interference. Category 5 and telephone cables should not be run in the same trunking or conduit as mains electrical cable because the magnetic field around the mains cable will interfere with the data signals. There are other types, such as part 1 type 1 and part 1 type 2.

## Coaxial

Coaxial cable is used for television aerial connections. It has a single copper conductor surrounded by a layer of insulation. The insulation is surrounded by a second conductor. This conductor is usually a copper mesh and is called a screen. The purpose of the screen is to stop the signal from leaking out of the cable.

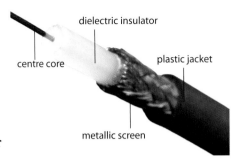

dielectric insulator

centre core

plastic jacket

metallic screen

**Figure 4.08** Coaxial cable

## Fibre-optic

The cores of a fibre-optic cable are made of extremely high-quality clear plastic or glass. The signal travels along this conductor in the form of light pulses. Thousands of data signals can be sent down one fibre-optic conductor in both directions at the same time. Fibre-optic cable must be handled carefully as the conductors are delicate. For example, the cable must not be bent sharply.

### QUICK CHECK

1 What affects the amount of current a cable can carry?
2 How should a single cable run?
3 What are some uses for armoured cables?

# Electrical accessories

Electrical accessories are the fittings which provide a point of connection for appliances and equipment.

| Electrical accessory | Description/use |
|---|---|
| **13 A plug** | Connecting an appliance into the supply. Easily removed and reconnected |
| **13 A socket** | Main type of connection point. The three slots are designed to receive the pins of a 13 A plug. The slots are shuttered for safety and only open when the plug's earth pin is fully pushed in |
| **Double-pole or spur outlet**<br><br>Neutral out to load   Line in from supply<br>Line out to load   Neutral in from supply<br>Earth terminals are linked together so that it doesn't matter which cpc is connected to which earth terminal<br><br>Back of a typical spur outlet and connections   Fused-switched spur with neon indicator lamp | There are many different types of spur outlet. Spurs are a permanent connection to the supply. To disconnect a load from a spur, the power has to be switched off and the cover removed |

**Table 4.02** Some of the main electrical accessories installed by electricians

### Key term

**Double-pole switch** – a switch that opens and closes both the line and the neutral conductors. It is used in isolating switches which completely cut the supply to a load so repairs or other work can be carried out safely

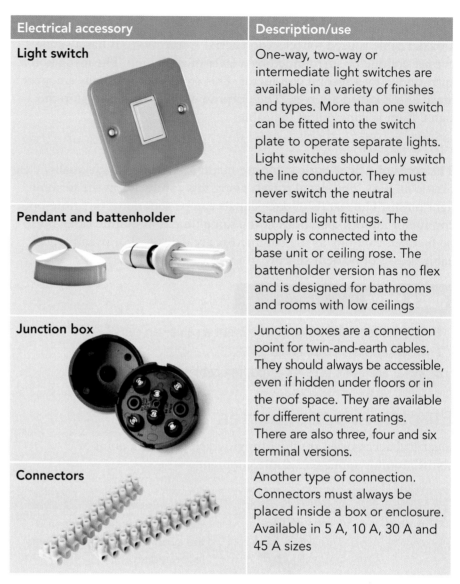

| Electrical accessory | Description/use |
|---|---|
| **Light switch** | One-way, two-way or intermediate light switches are available in a variety of finishes and types. More than one switch can be fitted into the switch plate to operate separate lights. Light switches should only switch the line conductor. They must never switch the neutral |
| **Pendant and battenholder** | Standard light fittings. The supply is connected into the base unit or ceiling rose. The battenholder version has no flex and is designed for bathrooms and rooms with low ceilings |
| **Junction box** | Junction boxes are a connection point for twin-and-earth cables. They should always be accessible, even if hidden under floors or in the roof space. They are available for different current ratings. There are also three, four and six terminal versions. |
| **Connectors** | Another type of connection. Connectors must always be placed inside a box or enclosure. Available in 5 A, 10 A, 30 A and 45 A sizes |

**Table 4.02** Some of the main electrical accessories installed by electricians (continued)

## Fixing accessories and components

Chapter 5 describes fixings in detail. Electrical accessories are fixed using many of the fixings mentioned in that chapter, for example:

- wall plugs
- woodscrews
- cavity wall fixings, such as butterfly bolts.

### Dry liner boxes

Sometimes sockets and switches need to be fixed to plasterboard walls. Dry liner boxes are plastic back boxes that can be secured in plasterboard ready for the socket or switch face to be connected and screwed into place.

A hole should be cut into the plasterboard, just large enough for the box to fit tightly into place. There is a spring-loaded tab at the back and this can be triggered from the inside of the box to fix it securely to the plasterboard.

## Noggins

When fixing a light fitting to a plasterboard ceiling it may not be possible to find a joist to fix it to. In this case, a piece of wood is nailed into place between two of the joists and the light screwed, through the plaster, into this new timber. This short length of wood is called a noggin.

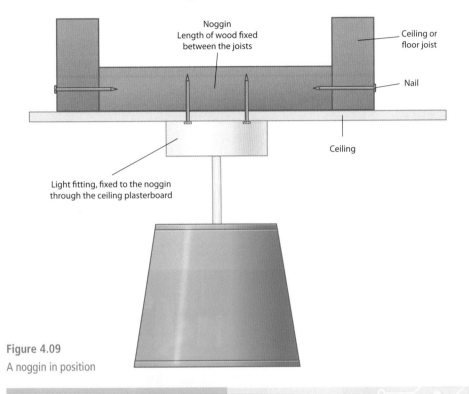

**Figure 4.09**
A noggin in position

### QUICK CHECK

1  How are the safety shutters in a 13 A socket opened?
2  What are the two main parts of a standard light fitting?
3  What is a junction box?

# Safe connections

## Hazards

General health and safety needs to be observed when working on electrical equipment and circuits. Some general hazards might be caused by:

- sharp blades and tools of various types that are used for stripping and connecting cables
- soldering irons for securing connectors to their terminals
- work carried out at height, or in confined spaces, both of which have their own set of regulations (see pages 10–11).

There are hazards that are more specific to electrical work.

As discussed on page 72, the earth (or cpc) in a twin-and-earth is not insulated. This means that the cpc can be used for stripping twin-and-earth without having to use a sharp knife.

### QUICK CHECK

What are the regulations for working at height and in confined spaces? Give two examples of actual regulations from each.

---

**Hands On**

Follow the instructions below to strip a twin-and-earth.

1. Use side cutters to bite into the end of the cable.
2. Peel open the outer sheath so that the cpc can be gripped using pliers.
3. Pull the cpc back using the pliers so that it cuts through the outer sheath.
4. Once the required length is reached, peel away the sheath and cut neatly.
5. Strip the insulation from the conductors using a cable stripping tool. Don't strip away too much insulation. For most terminations 12 mm is about right.

---

## Clipping twin-and-earth cable

| Checklist | | | |
|---|---|---|---|
| **PPE** | **Tools and equipment** | **Consumables** | **Source information** |
| • Safety glasses<br>• Protective footwear<br>• Hi-viz jacket | • Tape measure<br>• Chalk or laser line<br>• Spirit level<br>• Hammer | • Twin-and-earth cable<br>• Cable clips | • BS 7671:2008<br>• *IET On-Site Guide*<br>• Layout drawing |

**1**

Mark a straight line to clip to.

**2**

Straighten the cable.

**3**

Clip at either end of run (in this image one clip is shown in place and the other is being hammered in).

**4**

Fill in with clips at regular intervals.

## Connecting a 13 A socket

When connecting a 13 A socket the following applies:

- L terminal for line conductor
- N terminal for neutral conductor
- E terminal  for cpc.

You must follow these steps.

- The outer sheath must be taken into the socket box.
- Make sure no copper conductor is showing.
- Make sure the terminal screw is not nipping the insulation instead of the conductor.
- If a single conductor is connected into a terminal, bend the conductor double and squeeze tight with a pair of pliers. This makes the conductor bigger and easier to secure into the terminal.
- Pull green-and-yellow sleeving over the cpc.

## Connecting a light fitting

This light is being wired using the loop-in method. The cable sheaths must be taken into the ceiling rose and the conductors also laid neatly inside it.

| | |
|---|---|
| **L terminal** | The blue switch wire that connects the lamp to the switch. Brown sleeving is used to identify that this blue core is *not* being used as a neutral |
| **N terminal** | Neutral |
| **E terminal** | cpc |
| **Loop** | For the supply to the circuit. The feed to the switch is also connected into this terminal |
| **Cord grip** | The flex cores must be passed underneath these anchor points. The flex grip will take the weight of the lamp and the shade |

Table 4.03 The main points to be followed when connecting a lighting circuit

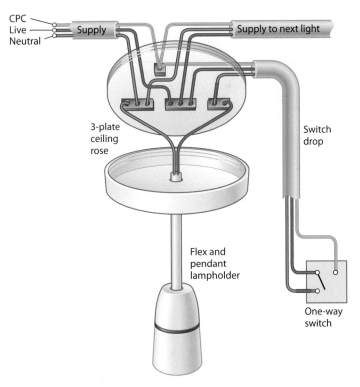

Figure 4.10 A ceiling rose with loop-in connections

**Figure 4.11** A six-terminal junction box, sometimes used for complicated lighting circuits

**Figure 4.12** Crimped lug and crimping tool

## Connecting a junction box

The junction box has no specific line, neutral or earth terminals.

When connecting a junction box make sure:

- the cable sheath is taken into the junction box
- no conductor is showing outside the terminal
- the conductors are laid neatly in the box.

## Crimped termination

Crimped terminations can be fitted onto the end of cable conductors. They can be used to make a more secure connection into a terminal. Some terminals are made up of a threaded post, and a set of washers and nuts. A crimped lug like the one shown in Figure 4.12 is the easiest way to connect a conductor to this type of terminal.

The correct size lug must be fitted to a conductor and be compressed as tightly as possible. Small crimped termination sizes are colour-coded. Larger versions are not insulated and require heavy-duty compression tools.

| Colour code | Conductor size |
|---|---|
| Red | 1.5 mm² |
| Blue | 2.5 mm² |
| Yellow | 6.0 mm² |

**Table 4.04** Crimp lug colour code

### QUICK CHECK

1 What should be done to a single conductor before connecting into a terminal?
2 Which conductor is connected to the loop-in terminal in a ceiling rose?
3 Where and how is a crimped lug fitted?

A church in Suffolk is heated by radiant electrical heaters – electric fires mounted high on the wall. There are five heaters on each side of the church. Sarah is an electrician and was called in because the residual current device (RCD) was operating every time the heaters were switched on. This meant that there was an earth fault. A live part of one of the heaters was touching the heater's metal frame. For example, a cable conductor might have dropped out of its terminal or the insulation between a live conductor and the earth conductor might be damaged, causing a short circuit between them.

The heaters were wired in mineral insulated cable. The insulation in these cables is a powder which absorbs moisture very quickly. If one of the sealed cable terminations was damaged, this could have allowed in moisture and caused a short circuit between live and earth.

Sarah switched off the power using the safe isolation procedure then carried out an insulation resistance test at the supply end of the heater circuit. The reading was higher than 1 M$\Omega$ between all the conductors. This meant that there was no fault on the cable. She switched on the heater isolators and carried out the test again. Everything was still clear. Finally, she switched on the heaters. They glowed red, warmed up and worked for about two minutes. Suddenly, the RCD operated and the power was switched off.

Puzzled, Sarah dismantled one of the heaters. Everything looked fine. She could see no damage at all. Then, just before she reassembled the heater, she noticed that one of the crimped terminals was very close to the metal frame. It was not touching and should not have been a problem. However, she loosened the terminal and moved the crimp lug until it was further from the frame. She went round to each heater and did the same thing. Then she switched the power back on.

The heaters worked. Sarah waited. Two minutes passed. Three, four, five…The fault had been fixed. The cause of the problem was the fact that metal expands when it becomes hot. The heat from the heaters had caused the small crimp lug to expand. This made it bend until it touched the metal frame of the heater.

1. What is an earth fault?

2. What is mineral insulated cable normally used for?

3. What is an insulation resistance test?

4. What is a crimped lug?

# Circuits

All electrical supplies are formed into circuits. In a simple circuit, like the one in Figure 4.13, voltage is produced by a battery or **generator** and flows from positive to negative as current. No matter how complex a circuit might be, it still works on this same simple principle. There must be a power source, a route *to* the load and a route *back*.

Most mains installations are fed by alternating current (a.c.), which is created by an a.c. generator. The main conductors in an a.c. circuit are called line (brown) and neutral (blue). The line brings the supply current to a load, the neutral acts as a return conductor.

**Key term**

**Generator** – a machine that produces electricity. It works by spinning a conductor through a magnetic field

**Did You Know**

In a power station, the energy needed to rotate the conductors, or windings, is provided by steam turbines. The steam is created by heating water using coal, oil, gas or nuclear energy. Wind power is also used to rotate generator windings.

Switch – used to open the circuit and stop current flowing, or close the circuit and allow current through

Conductors – electricity will flow easily along certain types of material such as copper and aluminium. These are made into wires which connect parts of the circuit together

**d.c.** – stands for direct current. This is the type of electricity produced by a battery and d.c. generator

Positive and negative – electrical current flows from the positve to the negative terminal of a circuit

Supply – the power source which generates electricity. Examples of power sources include batteries and generators

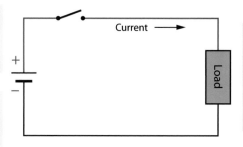

Current →

Load – the reason for creating a circuit. The load is the item that the electricity operates. A load can be a lamp, a heating element, an electronic circuit

Figure 4.13 Diagram of a simple d.c. circuit

1  What three things are needed to make a circuit work?
2  How does a generator work?
3  What are the main conductors in an a.c. circuit?

## Practical circuits

Now the cables have been chosen and the accessories selected, the installation needs to be wired. The BS 7671 Wiring Regulations state that an electrical installation must be divided up into circuits. These circuits all begin at the distribution board (see Figure 4.14).

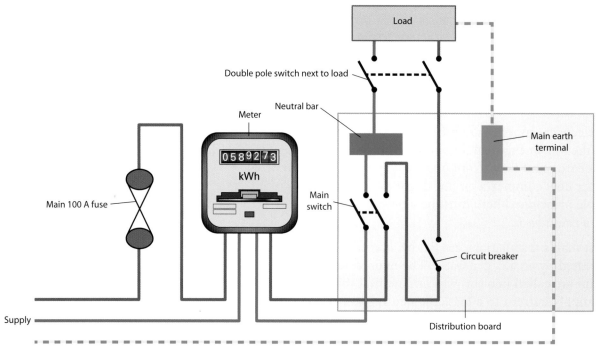

Figure 4.14 Mains position showing meter, distribution board and radial circuit

| Type of circuit | How it is wired | Example of use |
|---|---|---|
| Radial | A line, neutral and earth supply is taken from the distribution board to the load via a double-pole isolator switch. The isolator must be installed close to the load | Cooker<br>Electric shower<br>Water heater<br>13 A sockets |
| Ring final circuit (see Figure 4.15) | A line, neutral and earth are run from the distribution board to a number of 13 A sockets. The supply is connected to each socket, and then returned to the distribution board. This means there will be two line, two neutral and two earth conductors at the supply | 13 A sockets |
| One-way lighting (see Figure 4.16) | A line, neutral and earth is run from the distribution board to a light and switch. If there are other lights on the circuit, a feed is then taken to the next light and the next and so on. The light switch must only switch the line conductor | Rooms or areas where there is only one switch operating a light or set of lights |
| Two-way lighting | Similar to the one-way lighting circuit, except that there are two switches linked by a set of conductors called strappers | Situations where there is at least one light operated by two switches, for example a stairway or a room with an entrance and exit |
| Intermediate switching | A two-way system, but with one or more extra switches added into the circuit | Situations where there is at least one light operated by three or more switches, for example a stairway with two levels, a room with three or more entrances and exits |
| Alarms | Usually supplied from a central control unit, alarm circuits are made up of sensors which detect movement, smoke or heat, alarm sounders, emergency lights etc. They are often wired in fireproof cable | Fire alarms<br>Intruder alarms<br>Gas and flood alarms |
| Control circuits | Sometimes supplied from a central unit, control circuits are made up of remote stop and start buttons as well as automatic switches, such as timers or thermostats. The relay or contactor is at the heart of many control circuits. This is a switch operated by a wire coil that becomes magnetic when **energised** | Electric motors<br>Heating systems<br>Air conditioning |
| Vehicle systems | Although vehicle engines are run on petrol or diesel, the ignition, lighting and combustion systems are electrical. Electricity used in a car is supplied from a battery. The battery's negative terminal is connected to the metal body of the car | Engine ignition<br>Vehicle lights<br>Vehicle heating<br>Vehicle sound system |

Table 4.05 The main types of practical electrical circuit

Ring final circuit

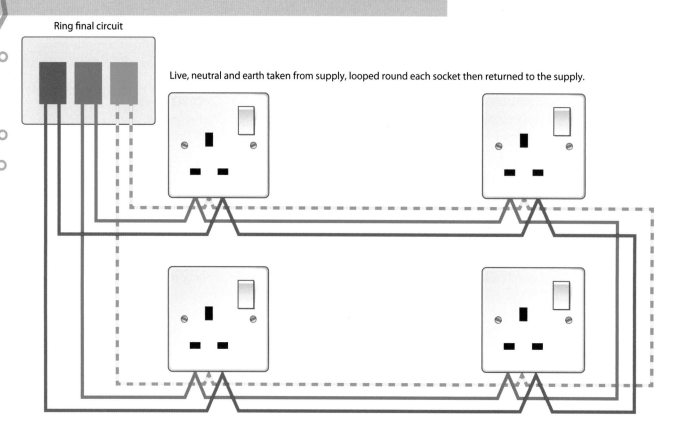

Live, neutral and earth taken from supply, looped round each socket then returned to the supply.

**Figure 4.15** A ring final circuit

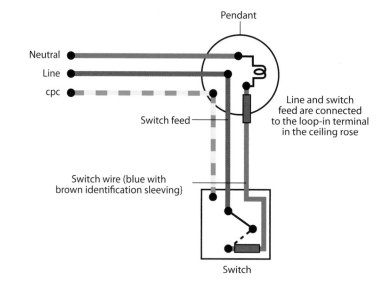

Pendant

Neutral

Line

cpc

Switch feed

Line and switch
feed are connected
to the loop-in terminal
in the ceiling rose

Switch wire (blue with
brown identification sleeving)

Switch

**Figure 4.16** A one-way light loop-in method

### Key term

**Energised** – when a component is connected to the electric supply and has current flowing through it. A lamp is energised when a light switch is operated

### QUICK CHECK

1  What must an electrical installation be divided up into?
2  Describe a radial circuit.
3  What are the conductors joining two two-way switches called?

## Typical installations

The electrician is likely to be called on to undertake a number of
different types of installation. This section looks at some of the main
installation types and their wiring methods.

### Domestic

*Where:* Houses and flats.

*Cable:* Twin-and-earth.

*How are cables run:* Through the roof and floor space. Dropped
down and run up the walls to the sockets and switches etc. in
**chases**.

*Accessories:* Installed flush. A metal back box is set into the wall and
plastered into place. The front plate is connected once the plastering
has been completed. Accessories are usually plastic although some
homeowners prefer a decorative metal, such as brass or brushed steel.

### Commercial

*Where:*  Offices, schools, public buildings.

*Cables:* Twin-and-earth and fireproof alarm.

*How are cables run:* Through the ceiling and floor spaces and chased
into walls. Plastic trunking runs round the walls in areas where large
numbers of 13 A sockets and data points are needed. Alarm cabling
tends to be clipped to the surface using p-clips.

*Accessories:* 'Break glass' alarm buttons, smoke and heat detectors,
and alarms. Switches and sockets are flush, but there may also be
13 A sockets set into the trunking face.

*Other:* Raised floor with removable tiles. Power and data cables can
be run under the floor and fed to desks through sockets and outlets
installed in 'power tiles'.

### Industrial

*Where:* Factories and workshops.

*Cables:* Singles, armoured and fireproof alarm.

*How are cables run:* Singles in steel conduit and trunking (see
Chapter 5), armoured and fireproof on tray (see Chapter 5).

*Accessories:* Metal, surface mounted. Lighting is often by twin
fluorescent fittings fixed to lighting trunking.

**Agricultural**

*Where:* Farms, smallholdings and garden centres.

*Cables:* Singles and armoured.

*How are cables run:* Singles in plastic conduit, which protects the cables from rodent damage. Armoured cable can also be used but this is expensive. Some cables may be run overhead, supported by a catenary-wire designed to take the cable's weight.

*Accessories:* Surface-mounted, damp-proof lights, switches and sockets.

**Construction sites**

*Where:* Large construction sites.

*Cables:* Armoured cables, armoured flexes, extension leads.

*How are cables run:* Supported as securely as possible and out of the way to avoid mechanical damage and becoming a tripping hazard. Some cables may be run overhead, supported by a catenary-wire designed to take the cable's weight.

*Equipment:* 110 V tools, converted from the mains supply using portable **transformers**. Fixed lighting and site office supplies can be 230 V.

> **Key term**
>
> **Transformers** – electrical machines designed to change voltage by either stepping up from a lower voltage to a higher one, or by stepping down from a higher voltage to a lower one

> **Did You Know**
>
> Transformers can be large high-voltage machines seen in power station and local distribution sub-stations. There are also small in-line versions connected between a laptop computer and its 13 A plug.

## QUICK CHECK

1 Where are the conductors run in a domestic installation?
2 In an agricultural installation, what type of conduit are cables run in?
3 How is construction site voltage converted from 230 V to 110 V?

# Electrical protection

Electricity is dangerous. The two main electrical hazards are overcurrent and shock.

## Overcurrent

Overcurrent means that too much current is flowing and this can generate enough heat to cause a fire. Overcurrent results from:

- **Overload** – the cable is too small for the load.
- **Short circuit** – line and neutral come into direct contact. A large fault current (sometimes thousands of amps) will flow resulting in violent explosion and heat.

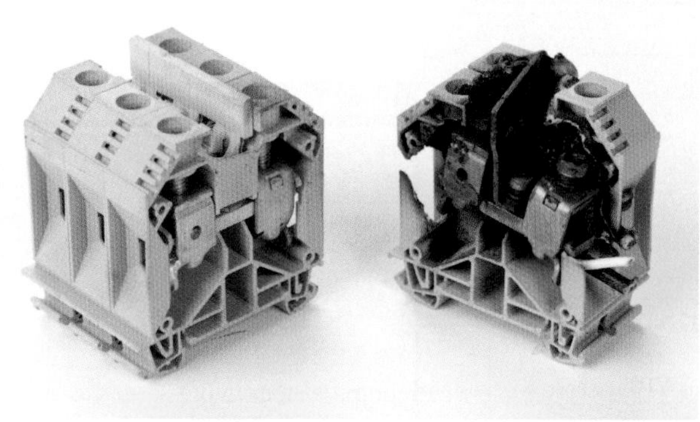

Figure 4.17 Short circuit damage to a component

## Distribution boards

Overcurrent protection is provided by fuses and circuit breakers. These are fitted into a distribution board, which feeds the installation. The installation is divided into a set of circuits. Each of these circuits begins at a circuit breaker or fuse. New installations should be fitted with a residual current device (RCD).

Some large electrical installations have a number of distribution boards, one for each area. All these units are, in turn, fed from a central supply point. This is usually another distribution board.

Each distribution board also contains the main double-pole isolator for the installation, or the part of the installation, it feeds.

## Fuse

A fuse is a short length of conductor. This conductor is designed to carry a certain amount of current. If the current flow increases, the conductor will become hot and break. When it breaks it shuts off the power to the load. A 13 A plug contains a fuse. This should be either 3 A for smaller loads (e.g. a table lamp), or 13 A for larger loads (e.g. a washing machine).

Every complete installation will be protected by a single, large fuse. Houses, for example, are protected by a 100 A main fuse.

## Circuit breaker

A circuit breaker is a switch designed to operate and break the circuit if too much current flows.

## Current ratings

Fuse and circuit breakers are available in different current ratings. Examples of rating and their uses are as follows:

- 6 A – lighting circuits
- 15 A – water heaters
- 32 A – ring final circuit
- 45 A – large cooker.

## Electric shock

Electric shock occurs when a person comes into direct contact with a live electrical supply. Sometimes this can be caused by carelessness, for example when repairs are made to a piece of electrical equipment while it is still switched on. Sometimes it is caused by an electrical fault, for example when a live conductor comes loose and touches the metal case of an item of equipment.

The system used to protect people from electric shock is to connect the metal work of equipment and accessories to the earth itself. The conductor used for this is the cpc. If the metalwork does become live, the current runs along the cpc and operates a protective device, usually an RCD. The RCD must operate in less than 0.04 seconds (40 ms).

**Keep It Safe**

Always use the correctly rated fuse or circuit breaker for a circuit or load. Never use the wrongly rated fuse or device.

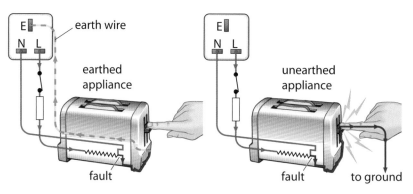

**Figure 4.18** Faulty toaster

To avoid electric shock when working on an electrical circuit, follow the safe isolation procedure below.

1. Identify the circuit to be switched off and isolate it, normally by removing or operating the protective device.

2. If the protective device is a fuse, remove and put in a secure place. If the protective device is a circuit breaker, fit a lock to prevent it from being switched back on before the work is complete. Put up warning notices and barriers.

3. Test the voltage indicator on a known supply or a proving unit.

4. Re-test the isolated circuit.

5. Re-test voltage indicator on known supply or proving unit.

6. If it is dead, work can begin.

## QUICK CHECK

1 What is a short circuit?
2 Where are the protective devices for a circuit located?
3 When does electric shock happen?

**Case Study**

Rock bands have always used high amounts of electrical power. When playing large venues such as football stadiums, this power consumption can be immense. There are cables run all over the stage, all plugged into amplifiers, monitors, microphones and the giant speakers that blast out the sound. Tours are expensive so sometimes shortcuts are taken in an attempt to save money.

The people who build a band's stage set are called roadies, and some of these will be electricians. John is an electrician-roadie. Once when his band was touring he was concerned that the main supply cables to the band's equipment were not big enough. The fuses, which were rated at over 200 A each, were the correct size, but the cable could not carry 200 A. The Road Manager became angry when John told him how concerned he was about this and threatened to sack him. John needed the job and he enjoyed it a great deal. So, knowing that he was making a mistake, he connected the cables and switched the power on.

The band started their sound check. Hundreds of amps flowed. The cable ruptured – it suddenly melted in a flare of heat and flame. John's face and hands were badly burned. Luckily, he survived and his injuries were treated without causing any scars.

It is extremely important that the correctly rated fuses are used to protect a circuit. It is also massively important that the correct sized cables are used. For example, if the fuses are rated at 20 A, then the smallest cable that can be connected to the fuse is 2.5 mm$^2$. If more than 20 A flows, the 2.5 mm$^2$ cable will become hot and cause a fire.

1. What is a fuse?
2. What does 'rating' mean when you are talking about fuses?
3. What does '2.5 mm$^2$' mean when talking about cables?
4. What would you have done in John's situation?

# Inspection and testing

Once an electrical installation is finished, or if it has been in place and working for a number of years, it must be inspected and tested. The schedule for tests is shown in BS 7671. The purpose of this is to make sure the installation is safe and working correctly.

## Visual inspection

Before any actual testing is started, a visual inspection must be carried out. This inspection takes place first with the power on and then with the power off.

'Power on' example checks:

- Are cables clipped and supported safely and correctly (see Figure 4.19)?
- Are lids on?
- Are faceplates secure and not damaged?
- Are fittings, trunking and conduit securely fixed?

'Power off' example checks:

- Are fittings and equipment correctly connected, with no copper showing?
- Are the terminals tight?
- Are the correct cables connected into the correct terminals?
- Are the correct colours used?
- Are there signs of overheating?

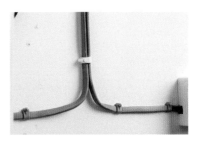

**Figure 4.19** Incorrectly clipped cables

---

**Hands On**

Carry out a visual inspection of a simple lighting circuit.

Wire a simple lighting circuit using a work board, one switch, one light, twin-and-earth cable and cable clips. Design the layout so that there is a right-angle bend in the cable.

Once the circuit has been installed and connected, swap boards with other members of your group and carry out a visual inspection on each other's installations.

1. Are the fittings securely fixed?
2. Are they level and straight?
3. Is the cable correctly clipped?
4. Is the cable damaged?

Take off the front of the switch and the top of the light fitting.

1. Are the connections secure and correct?
2. Is any copper conductor showing at the terminals?
3. Has the earth conductor been sleeved?
4. Are the cores of the flex secured under the anchoring points?

Give feedback.

---

**Quick Tip**

Use your senses for visual inspections:

- Sight – is there any damage or signs of burning? Are terminations under strain?
- Touch – is everything securely fixed, is anything hot?
- Smell – is there a smell of burning?
- Hearing – listen out for any vibrations, crackling sounds. Also listen to any problems the customer may tell you about.
- Speech – ask the customer if there have been any problems with the installation.

**Key term**

**Continuity** – (from 'continuous' and 'continues') describes how complete a cable or circuit is. Lack of continuity or poor continuity means that there is a loose or disconnected conductor in a circuit

## Continuity tests

The first set of tests are to make sure that no cables and conductors are broken or poorly connected. These tests are called **continuity** tests.

Continuity tests are carried out using a low reading ohm meter. This sends a small current into the circuit and then calculates the resistance. If is too high, it indicates that there may be a break or poor connection in the circuit. Continuity tests are carried out on the:

- cpc
- ring final circuit (to make sure that it really is a ring!).

## Polarity tests

Correct polarity means that the line, neutral and earth conductors are connected into the correct terminals. Testing polarity isn't usually carried out as a separate check because the other tests will show up any incorrect polarity.

## Insulation resistance tests

This is similar to the continuity test. This time an insulation resistance tester is used and the test carried out at 500 V. The purpose is to test for short circuits between line, neutral and earth by reading the resistance between them. A resistance reading of less than one million ohms (1 megohm or 1 MΩ) means that there is a problem.

All covers and faceplates must be fitted before carrying out this test. Make sure all sensitive equipment is disconnected, all equipment unplugged, and lamps removed from lighting circuits.

## Live tests

Live tests are tests carried out with the power on. Of course, this can be dangerous so these tests must only be attempted by a qualified electrician. All test instruments must conform to GS38. This is a document which describes the types of instruments, test leads and probes to be used. It also states that test instruments should be calibrated, which means that once a year, the instrument must be sent away to be tested for accuracy.

### Earth fault loop impedance test

This is carried out for each circuit and measures the continuity of the whole earth path, from the end of a circuit to the local supply transformer and back again. The reading must be low. BS 7671 (17th edition) has a set of tables which give the highest readings allowed for this test. These readings depend on the type of fuses or circuit breaker used to protect the circuit. For example, if the circuit is protected by a 20 A Type B circuit breaker, the maximum earth fault loop impedance should be 2.3 Ω.

## *Functionality test*

Once all the tests have been carried out, the installation needs to be checked to make sure everything is working properly. These functionality tests include:

- operating light switches
- plug-in tester in 13 A sockets
- motor start and stop buttons
- isolators on and off.

Part of this test is to make sure that the RCD operates by testing its own test button. An RCD tester is then used to check that the RCD operates:

- within the proper time (usually less than 0.04 s or 40 ms)
- when the minimum fault current flows (usually less than 0.03 A or 30 mA).

# Finding faults

From time to time faults will develop on a circuit. These can be caused by:

- careless use of equipment
- the wrong type of cable or accessories for a particular working environment
- wear and tear
- faulty components provided by the supplier.

Finding and repairing an electrical fault requires a logical, step-by-step approach:

1. Question anyone who uses the equipment or circuit and try to find out as much detail about the fault as possible. It might be that enough information is gathered this way and the cause of the fault becomes obvious.
2. Carry out a visual inspection. Again there might be an obvious sign – a burned-out fitting, some sort of damage that could have caused the problem.
3. If the circuit needs to be tested:
   a. carry out safe isolation
   b. split it up into sections
   c. test each part of the circuit until the fault is located
   d. divide that part of the circuit again and again until the fault is pin-pointed
   e. carry out the repair.

If a repair or replacement cannot be carried out immediately, then the equipment or part of the circuit must be either:

- taken out of service and labelled clearly as faulty or
- left in a safe condition.

Two general rules are:

- if something isn't working at all, carry out continuity testing
- if there has been a short circuit, carry out insulation resistance testing.

**QUICK CHECK**

1 What are the purposes of inspection and testing?
2 What is a continuity test?
3 What is polarity?

**QUICK CHECK**

1 Name two causes of faults.
2 Why carry out a visual inspection?
3 Why split a faulty circuit into sections?

Level 1 Performing Engineering Operations

## CHECK YOUR KNOWLEDGE

**1** The electrical wiring regulations are known as:

a  BS 4536

b  BS 7671

c  BS 1718

d  BS 2139

**2** The practical handbook for the wiring regulations is called the:

a  *Electrician's Guide*

b  *Wiring Guide*

c  *Construction Guide*

d  *On-Site Guide*

**3** What is measured at the supply part of a circuit?

a  current

b  power

c  voltage

d  resistance

**4** Resistance is measured in:

a  ohms

b  amps

c  watts

d  volts

**5** The earth conductor in a circuit is called:

a  an earth protective conductor

b  an overload protective conductor

c  a fault protective conductor

d  a circuit protective conductor

**6** Fire-resistant cable is known as:

a  steel-wire armoured

b  Cat 5

c  FP

d  coaxial

**7** Transformers are used to:

a  change a.c. to d.c.

b  change voltage

c  change polarity

d  change resistance

**8** The standard colours for line, neutral and earth are:

a  brown, black and green/yellow

b  red, blue and green/yellow

c  brown, blue and green

d  brown, blue and green/yellow

**9** The automatic switch used for overcurrent protection is called a:

a  circuit breaker

b  circuit switch

c  circuit protector

d  circuit interrupter

**10** A continuity of protective conductor test is carried out using a:

a  high reading ohm meter

b  low reading ohm meter

c  medium reading ohm meter

d  variable ohm meter

94

# 5 Assembling electrical wiring support systems

Sometimes cables cannot be hidden in roof and ceiling spaces or chased into walls. In some installations, cables need extra mechanical protection. This is when electrical enclosures such as conduit and trunking are needed to provide a secure, practical method for installing cables.

There are many types of electrical enclosure. For example there are basic steel ones which are intended to give maximum mechanical protection in tough environments. Small plastic mini-trunking is used in domestic installations.

In this chapter you will learn about:

- the uses of enclosures and support systems
- hazards
- fixings
- conduit
- trunking
- cable tray
- testing circuits wired in conduit and trunking

# KITTING UP

**Keeping Safe**

Health and safety are always the most important things to think about before starting any job. Electrical enclosure work carries its own risks because it:

- is heavy
- is awkward to handle
- has sharp edges
- requires sawing and drilling operations.

There are times when enclosures and support systems have to be installed at height. This can be dangerous for the electrician and for anyone else working in the vicinity. Risk assessments should be completed before the job starts. They describe the risks and how they should be controlled. Permits to Work must be issued if very hazardous work is to be carried out. The right personal protective equipment (PPE) must also be worn.

*Safety glasses* – protect the eyes from flying objects when using power tools, such as drills, saws and cutters

*Hi-viz waistcoat* – makes sure you can be seen at all times. Compulsory on most construction sites

*Gloves* – worn to protect hands from sharp edges and rough surfaces when lifting and carrying

*Protective footwear* – protects feet from injury caused by heavy objects. Compulsory on most construction sites

## Paperwork

Every job involves some paperwork. Below is a table showing the main documents the electrician will need before starting work on electrical enclosures and support systems.

| Document | What it tells you |
|---|---|
| Layout drawing | Scale drawing showing a 'bird's eye' view of a room or building and the position of electrical accessories and equipment (all represented using the British Standard symbols found in the *IET On-Site Guide*) |
| Specification | Heights of electrical accessories, types of material to be used, fixing methods and any other detailed information needed to carry out the work |
| BS 7671 | The electrical wiring regulations. All electrical work must conform to these regulations |
| *IET On-Site Guide* | A practical handbook which explains the BS 7671 regulations to the electrician |

## Toolkit

Many of the tools you will need for this chapter are shared with Chapter 4. Information on the following tools can be found on page 71.

- Phillips and flat-bladed screwdrivers
- Combination pliers
- Tape measure
- Hammer
- Small and large spirit levels
- Junior hacksaw
- Adjustable grips
- Adjustable spanner
- Continuity tester
- Insulation resistance tester

| **Metal drill bit** | Used for drilling holes in metal | **Specialist conduit tools** | You will need specialist tools when installing enclosures and support systems, for example stocks and dies used for threading metal conduit |
|---|---|---|---|

### BS 7671:2008 Requirements for Electrical Installations (17th edition)

The BS 7671:2008 Wiring Regulations are extremely important to the electrician. Although it is a **non-statutory** document, all electrical installation work must comply with the guidelines it contains. It covers areas such as selection of suitable equipment, cable sizes, and protection against shock and fire.

**Did You Know**

110 V or battery-powered power tools are the only type allowed on most construction sites.

**Key term**

**Non-statutory** – a document that is not law but a code of practice. If it is followed, the electrical installation will be safe and will work properly. Failure to comply with this type of document can be used as evidence of carelessness

## QUICK CHECK

1  What document has to be issued before very hazardous work is carried out?
2  What do electrical enclosures provide?

# The uses of enclosures and support systems

There are three main reasons for using electrical enclosures and support systems:

- mechanical protection
- cable routing
- aesthetics (they look neat and tidy).

## Mechanical protection

Some environments can be harsh on an electrical installation. Some examples are shown in Table 5.01.

| Type of installation | Hazards to electrical installation |
|---|---|
| Factory | Heavy machinery<br>High temperatures<br>Corrosive fumes and chemicals<br>General rough treatment |
| Construction site | Extreme temperatures<br>Dampness<br>Heavy machinery and plant movement around site<br>Trip hazard |
| Agricultural | Dampness<br>Extreme temperatures<br>Threat of electric shock to livestock<br>Threat of cable damage from rodents<br>Old and damaged buildings |

Table 5.01 Installations where extra mechanical protection is needed

## Cable routing

There are times when cables cannot be run on the surface of a wall or ceiling. This might be because:

- the walls have been decorated and the customer does not want the decor disturbed by chasing
- the walls are not plastered, for example finished brick or block walls
- the walls are concrete or another hard surface which is difficult to fix clips to
- there is a gap or open space, such as the roof area of a factory or warehouse, that the cables have to be run through.

In these cases some type of enclosure or support system is needed to provide a route for the cable or cables to run through.

## Aesthetics

Aesthetics is how something looks. In other words, there are certain areas that need to remain neat or attractive even after electrical wiring and equipment has been installed. So, for example:

- a cable clipped down a wall will spoil the look of a room
- industrial and commercial trunking and conduit will always look clumsy and obvious.

One way of running cable without affecting the decor of a room is mini-trunking (see page 112). It is small, and can be painted and tucked away in a corner or run along the top of skirting. It is not ideal but it is not as noticeable as clipped cable would be.

QUICK CHECK

1 What are the hazards affecting the wiring in an agricultural electrical installation?
2 What are 'aesthetics'?
3 Give two reasons why cables cannot be run inside or on the surface of a wall or ceiling.

# Hazards

There are a number of health and safety points specific to installing electrical enclosures and support systems.

## Manual handling

Trunking and conduit are usually sold and delivered in bundles. These bundles are heavy and long. For example, conduit is supplied in 3 m lengths. These bundles should be carried by two people. This is not only because of their weight but because manoeuvring lengths of pipe or trunking around a busy work area could result in injury to other people.

Trunking has sharp edges so it is important to wear gloves when handling. The galvanising used on **galvanised** conduit and trunking rubs off so it is also important to wash hands before eating.

**Key term**

**Galvanised** – having a silver-coloured zinc coating. It is used to prevent corrosion and applied by dipping metal into molten zinc

**Hands On**

Working in pairs, practise carrying bundles of conduit through a crowded workshop. Obstacles and difficulties can be set up so that you have to discuss and plan how to get the conduit from the starting point to the finish.

## Drilling and cutting

Drilling is a common job when installing trunking. Goggles must be worn when drilling. On some sites trunking is cut using a grinder. This also creates showers of sparks so goggles and appropriate gloves and overalls are essential.

**Quick Tip**

When marking trunking and conduit for drilling or cutting, do not use a felt-tip pen. The lines made by these pens can be quite thick and you will not be able to make an accurate cut. Use a scribe or a pencil instead.

**Hands On**

Mark and drill four holes in a piece of metal trunking. Select the correct:

- drill
- drill bit
- PPE.

## Working at height

Enclosures and support systems are often installed at height. Barrier off the work area and make sure the tower or ladders used are erected correctly and are secure. The Working at Height Regulations state that you should:

- only work at height if trained to do so
- use guard rails on towers and scaffolding
- inspect ladders before use
- erect ladders at an angle of 75° with 1.05 m extending above the top resting place.

For more general detail on health and safety in engineering, see Chapter 1.

### QUICK CHECK

1 What PPE must be worn when drilling and handling trunking?
2 Why should you wash your hands after handling galvanised trunking?
3 What must be fixed to the top of scaffolding and towers?

## Fixings

For most electrical enclosure and support system installations, woodscrews, wall plugs and cavity fixings will be all the fixings you need. However, there are a few specialist fixings used for certain types of installation as shown in Table 5.02.

| Fixing type | Use |
|---|---|
| Screws and wall plugs | General fixing to masonry surfaces |
| Girder clamps | Securing conduit and trunking direct to steel girders |
| Studding or threaded rod | Steel rod which has a thread along its whole length. For suspending conduit, trunking or tray when it is routed across an open space. Studding can be screwed into girder clamps |
| Crampets | When metal conduit is chased into a wall, it is secured in place using steel crampets |

Table 5.02 Specialist types of fixings for electrical enclosures and support systems

# Conduit

Conduit is a pipework system designed to carry wiring and protect it from mechanical damage. Conduit is typically used for electrical installations in:

- factories
- workshops
- farms
- the **plant room**.

There are two main types of conduit:

- metal – **black enamelled** and galvanised steel
- PVC.

Single cables are the type of cable usually drawn into conduit. These cables have one conductor and only one layer of insulation.

The *IET On-Site Guide* provides information about a number of conduit sizes – from 16 mm up to 75 mm. However the two sizes normally used are 20 mm and 25 mm.

The conduit sizes are measured using the outside diameter of the pipe.

Conduit does not carry gas or liquid, so it does not have to be watertight. Nonetheless, all conduit joints must be secure so that there is no movement that would damage the cables inside. Metal conduit is exposed metalwork and must be at the same electrical earth **potential** along its entire length.

## Metal conduit

Metal conduit is used as a heavy duty way of enclosing electrical cables. The conduit itself is made of steel and the lengths are joined together by screwed threads. Metal conduit is used in industrial installations and also workshop type areas. It can be cut to length, re-threaded and formed into bends and angles.

### Metal conduit fittings

**Key terms**

**Plant room** – the area of a large building, such as an office block or school, that contains the boilers for the heating system and main equipment for the air-conditioning systems. It may also be the point where the mains electrical supply enters the building. Here it is often connected to a large panel. From there it is distributed throughout the building

**Black enamel** – a black coating designed to resist corrosion in metal

**Potential** – the amount of electrical charge at a certain point in a circuit. To make everything the same potential, they have to be connected together. So, all sections of a steel conduit or trunking system must be securely connected together and then connected to earth

Figure 5.01 A selection of metal conduit fixings

Figure 5.02 Examples of tee, terminal and 90° conduit boxes

| Fitting | Description |
|---|---|
| Conduit boxes | Boxes provide a means of joining different parts of a conduit system together, for example using intersections and tees.<br><br>Through-boxes act as wiring points in long, straight runs of conduit.<br><br>There can only be the equivalent of two right-angle bends between conduit boxes. This prevents strain on the cables when they are drawn around conduit bends.<br><br>Conduit boxes act as connection points for ceiling roses and other fittings.<br><br>Types of box include:<br>• through<br>• 90°<br>• tee<br>• cross<br>• terminal (a single spout)<br><br>Through, tee and 90° boxes are available as:<br>• plain – the threaded spouts are in line with the centre of the box<br>• tangent – the threaded spouts are set along the edge of the box |
| Inspection fittings | No longer widely used, these are a similar diameter to the conduit itself and used when there is no room for a standard conduit box. |
| Loop-in boxes | Loop-in conduit boxes are supplied with holes machine-drilled into the back. The holes are designed to accept conduit.<br><br>Loop-in boxes are used for conduit systems that are buried in 'screeded' concrete floors and ceilings. This method is used in large blocks of flats, public and commercial buildings.<br><br>The conduit and boxes are installed prior to the concrete being poured. The boxes are set so that once the building structure is complete, they are flush with the ceiling surfaces and provide connection and fixing points for lights etc. |
| **General accessories** | |
| Coupler | A short threaded tube used to join lengths of conduit together |
| Male bushes | Brass bushes that screw into couplers and the spouts of conduit boxes. Their main use is to join conduits to the back boxes of accessories, such as 13 A sockets and light switches. Male bushes are available with either short or long threads |
| Female bushes | A brass fitting designed to screw onto the end of a conduit to cover the sharp edge at the end of its thread |
| Lock nuts and rings | Screwed onto bushes and conduit threads to secure them in place |
| Nipple | Male threaded joining piece, designed to be screwed into a coupler or conduit box spout. Used as the main component of a running thread |
| Saddles | Used for fixing conductor. There are two main types of saddle:<br>• spacer bar – the most common version. The spacer bar saddle holds the pipe close to the wall.<br>• deep spacer bar – this has a thicker base and holds the conduit off the wall<br><br>A bigger version of a deep spacer bar is the hospital saddle, so called because it can be used in areas where cleanliness is essential and enables the space behind a conduit to be kept clean |

**Table 5.03** Accessories and fittings for metal conduit

## Specialist tools for metal conduit

Apart from the general tools listed on page 97, conduit work requires a number of specialist tools.

### Combination vice and bender

A combination tool that grips and bends conduit. It has a vice with three sets of gripping teeth for holding the conduit secure while cutting and threading.

The bending part of the tool consists of a bending arm, a block to secure the pipe against while it is bent and a former to bend the pipe around. The former is either 20 mm or 25 mm.

**Figure 5.03** A conduit bender

### Stocks and dies

Lengths of metal conduit are joined together by screwing one to the other. Full lengths are sold with a machined thread on either end of each pipe. Once sawn to length, however, a new thread must be cut onto the pipe. Conduit threads are cut using stocks and dies.

**Stocks** are the handles used to turn the tool and the frame that the dies are secured into. There is also a guide fitted to the back which slides over the conduit and holds the tool straight as the thread is cut.

**Dies** are made up of a steel ring inset with cutting teeth. These cut the thread onto the outside surface of the pipe. Cutting compound should be used to protect the teeth of the dies and to ease the cutting operation.

### Reamer

Once the conduit is cut and threaded, the sharp inner edges of the pipe need to be smoothed away before any cables are installed. These sharp edges are called burrs and will damage cable insulation.

The reamer is a tool designed to be pushed into the end of the pipe and twisted to remove any burrs. A round file can also be used for this job.

## Cutting and threading metal conduit

When cutting and threading conduit, the pipe must always be secured in the conduit vice.

---

**Hands On**

Follow the steps below to thread a length of conduit.

1. Place the length of pipe in the vice, leaving at least 300 mm protruding.
2. Place the stocks and dies over the end of the pipe then turn them clockwise using the handles.
3. Push hard with each turn until the teeth bite – small, sharp turns work best.
4. Once the dies are cutting, make about three or four full turns.
5. Unthread the stocks and dies and remove from the pipe.
6. Smear cutting compound on the end of the pipe.
7. Continue threading until approximately three or four new threads protrude from the end of the dies (the final thread should be about 20 mm long).
8. Unscrew the dies, clean up the thread and ream out any burrs.

---

**Hands On**

Follow the steps below to cut a length of conduit.

1. Measure the conduit to the required length.
2. Mark the pipe clearly, running the mark all the way round the pipe.
3. Cut with a hacksaw.
4. Ream the end of the pipe to remove burrs and jagged internal edges.

## Bending metal conduit

Conduit should always be formed using the bending equipment on the combination conduit vice and bender. The vice stops the pipe from flattening and gives the bend a smooth shape.

There are two measurements in relation to conduit bends:

- back of a bend
- centre of a bend.

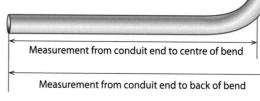

Measurement from conduit end to centre of bend

Measurement from conduit end to back of bend

**Figure 5.04** Difference between back and centre bends

**Hands On**

Follow the steps below to bend conduit into a 90° set.

1. Mark the required measurement on the conduit.
2. Push the conduit into the bending machine.
3. Lift the bending arm and the block.
4. Push the pipe along the slot in the top edge of the former and through the bending arm.
5. Push the pipe under the block.
6. For a centre-of-bend measurement the mark should be three times the pipe diameter from the front edge of the former.
7. Pull the bending arm down to form the bend.
8. If the bend is a right angle, check the bend using a straight edge and set-square or by placing the workpiece in a door frame.

If there is more than one bend, or a double or bridge set to be made in a length of conduit, care should be taken to make sure that the bends are in line with each other.

Once the first set has been formed into the pipe, check that it is sitting at the correct angle before making the second bend.

## Fixing metal conduit

Saddles are normally used to fix conduit to a surface. BS 7671 states that conduit fixings must be no more than 1 m apart. A chalk or laser line should be used to mark a straight line for a long conduit run.

If it is necessary to pass conduit or trunking through an existing wall, the hole must be refilled around the conduit to:

- prevent spread of fire
- maintain the structural strength (integrity) of the wall.

## Wiring metal conduit

Chapter 4 describes how to draw single cables into conduit.

Once all the wiring is complete the lids must be fitted onto the conduit boxes. If the boxes are in a damp environment, damp-proof gaskets should also be fitted under the lids.

If accessories such as ceiling roses are to be fitted to conduit, an earth tail should link the accessory's earth terminal with the conduit box earth terminal. (The conduit box earth terminal is located at the back of the box.) This is to keep the installation earth system and metal conduit at the same potential.

## Case Study

An old house was going to be converted into a conference centre. Before this could be done, the house needed to be rewired. The electrical installation was metal conduit, run under the floors and through the huge loft.

Because the old wiring needed to be removed before the new could be installed, the old installation needed to be switched off. The quickest method for removing the old and then installing the new wiring was to use the old wiring as draw wires. This means that when pulling out old cables, new cables were attached to them and drawn into the conduit at the same time. To do this, the circuits needed to be worked out very carefully because once the new wiring was in there was no possibility of pulling any extra cables into the conduit.

An electrician and an apprentice carried out the rewiring work. The electrician opened up the conduit box at the end of the run and then tugged at each cable in turn. The apprentice shouted when he saw the cable move. These were the ones to be pulled out and discarded. One old cable would be left. The apprentice then jointed the loom of new cable to the end of the remaining old one (using the method described in Chapter 4, page 73). This could take some time but it was important that no cable broke free while the loom was being pulled in.

Once the apprentice was satisfied with the cable joint, he shouted that he was ready and the cables were drawn in as the electrician pulled out the old one. This was done carefully and slowly with constant communication between the two. As the electrician

pulled the draw wire, the apprentice carefully fed the new cables into the pipe. If the cables needed untangling, he shouted to the electrician to stop pulling so he could deal with the problem.

This type of communication is essential when wiring conduit. Cables must not just be dragged into the pipe, they can catch on the edge of the conduit box, and they can tangle and twist. Rewiring in conduit is an advantage because the wiring routes are already in place, however it does take teamwork and a lot careful planning to make sure that all the necessary cables are pulled in each time.

1. What is meant by a 'stranded cable'?
2. What is a loom of cables?
3. What is a conduit box?

## QUICK CHECK

1 Why is some conduit coated with black enamel?
2 What are stocks and dies?
3 What piece of equipment is used for securing conduit while it is being cut and bent?

**Quick Tip**

If the bend has to be formed in the conduit some way from the end:

1. mark the centre of bend on the pipe

2. hold the middle-point of the spring against the measurement

3. knot or tape the spring's draw cord level with the end of the pipe

4. when the spring is pushed into the pipe, the tape or knot will indicate when the spring is in the correct position inside the conduit.

**Figure 5.05** Plastic conduit fittings and bending spring

**Keep It Safe**

Although plastic conduit doesn't have to be secured in a conduit vice when being cut, it still needs to be held safely and securely. Better still, use a specialised plastic conduit cutting tool.

**Quick Tip**

Bend plastic conduit past the required angle because it will try to re-straighten itself once the bending spring is removed.

# Plastic conduit

Plastic conduit is used where a measure of extra mechanical protection is needed. An example of this would be an agricultural installation where it can be damp and where cables can suffer from rodent damage. It is also used in commercial installations, school and colleges as a means of running cables in areas where they cannot be clipped directly onto the surface or hidden in cavity walls.

Plastic conduit is supplied as heavy and light gauge. The gauge is given by the thickness of the conduit wall. The common plastic conduit sizes are 20 mm and 25 mm.

Plastic cable ducting is also available. This is large piping that can be installed underground as a route for supply and data cables.

## Plastic conduit fittings

The fittings used with plastic conduit are similar to those used for metal conduit (see Figure 5.05). They are not normally threaded because they are glued together. The exception is the adaptor.

An adaptor is a coupler that has one glued end and one threaded end. This is used to secure plastic conduit to accessories such as switches and sockets. A plastic bush is used instead of a brass one. Some adaptors have a male thread which means that a plastic lock ring is used to secure the conduit to the accessory.

## Specialist tools for plastic conduit

### Bending spring

Plastic conduit is not formed into bends using a vice and bender but with a bending spring (see Figure 5.05). There are versions for both light (20 mm) and heavy gauge (25 mm) plastic conduit.

A rope or cord should be attached to the back end of the spring so it can be pulled out of the pipe once the bend is complete.

### Cutting tools

There are a number of specialist cutting tools for plastic conduit which give a clean straight cut. A junior hacksaw can also be used.

## Bending plastic conduit

When bending plastic conduit, push the correct sized bending spring into the pipe to the required position. The pipe can be formed around the knee. The bend must not be too tight, otherwise it:

- will be difficult to pull cables around the set
- could put extra strain on the conductors
- may wrinkle or collapse the pipe.

Bending plastic conduit is easier if you warm the pipe before bending. You can do this by rubbing it with a cloth or even running it under hot water.

As with metal conduit, multiple bends should be in line so that the pipe isn't twisted. It is more difficult to achieve this when forming around the knee. This is because the conduit cannot be secured and easily sighted for each bend as it can be in a machine.

### Fixing plastic conduit

Plastic conduit saddles are installed in much the same way as metal conduit. As well as conventional saddles there are clip-fit type fixings similar to those used with copper water pipe.

One problem with plastic conduit is that it will expand when hot. If the pipe is run through an area where there is a high temperature, for example a pig shed, the neat run of plastic conduit left by the electrician at the end of the job will quickly distort and turn into a series of snaking bends.

Expansion couplers are used to get over this problem. These are extra-long couplers which are pushed onto the conduit but not glued. The two ends of the pipes do not meet in the coupler and are allowed to move inside the coupler as the pipe expands and contracts.

**Figure 5.06** Conduit being formed over the knee

## Flexible conduit

Flexible conduit is tubing used to connect electrical equipment to the supply. For example, it is used when the control system for the equipment is complex and requires a large number of cables. It is also used in situations where there is risk of mechanical damage.

Flexible conduit comes in lightweight plastic or metal reinforced versions. The pipe is connected to the isolator and equipment using glands. These provide a secure joint and are important in order to avoid damage to the cable inside.

## Some conduit regulations

BS 7671 contains a number of regulations that apply to conduit installations. This is to make sure that conduit is installed and fixed securely. It also helps to ensure that the cables inside are not damaged when being drawn into the conduit.

- Conduit saddles must be a maximum of 1 m apart for horizontal runs and 2 m apart for vertical runs.
- The radius of a bend must not be so sharp that it causes stress to the cables inside.
- Conduit systems must be completed before cables are installed.
- If conduit is installed with other pipes, such as gas and water, it should be identified as part of the electrical system by painting the conduit orange.

**QUICK CHECK**

1  How would you know if a length of plastic conduit was heavy or light gauge?
2  How are plastic conduit fittings fixed to the pipe?
3  How is plastic conduit formed into bends?

**Figure 5.07** Metal trunking

# Trunking

Trunking is used to hold large amounts of cable. It is also used where it is not possible to clip cables directly onto the surface, or hide them by chasing them into walls or running them through ceiling and floor voids.

## Metal trunking

It is usually made from sheet steel. Metal trunking is available in 2 m lengths which are riveted or bolted together. The joints between lengths of trunking run need to be mechanically secure, both to protect the cables inside from damage and also to provide a good earth connection. Small copper earth bars must be fitted across every joint.

### Fitting metal trunking

There are lots of end caps, angles and tees used to fit metal trunking, and also to join brackets and copper earth bars. You can buy sections of lid pressed out so that accessory face plates – such as 13 A sockets and spur outlets – can be fitted into the trunking.

### Cutting metal trunking

**Hands On**

Follow the steps below to cut a length of metal trunking.

1. Always secure the trunking before cutting. If possible use a vice.
2. Insert wooden blocks into the trunking to prevent damage when tightening in the vice.
3. Measure and mark the trunking all the way round using a scribe marker.
4. Hold the hacksaw with both hands: one on the handle, the other on the end of the frame. This will help keep the saw straight while cutting.
5. Adopt a steady, fluid motion. Use the whole blade and let the blade do the work.
6. Cut on the waste side of the line – i.e. on the side that is not going to be used for the job.
7. Because the trunking is three-sided (the fourth is open), check the cut constantly to make sure it is not wandering off the line.
8. File the cut edge to remove burrs and jagged metal.

### Forming metal trunking

Although tees and angle pieces are available, there may be times when trunking has to be formed by the electrician. For example, when:

- no fittings are available
- an awkward angle has to be formed.

Trunking can be formed by cutting, bending and riveting, or bolting, the bend together.

## Forming trunking by cutting, bending and riveting/bolting the bend together

| Checklist | | | |
|---|---|---|---|
| PPE | Tools and equipment | Consumables | Source information |
| • Protective footwear<br>• Hi-viz jacket<br>• Gloves<br>• Hard hat<br>• Goggles | • Tape measure<br>• Set square<br>• Scribe<br>• Hacksaw/junior hacksaw<br>• Electric drill<br>• File<br>• Twist drill bit for metalwork<br>• Rivet tool | • 50 mm x 50 mm galvanised steel trunking<br>• Rivets | • Layout drawing showing trunking runs<br>• Diagram of bend with measurements |

1   Cut a 300 mm length of 50 mm x 50 mm trunking then divide the trunking into three equal sections and mark the trunking using a scribe and set square.

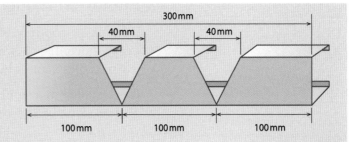

2   Measure 20 mm on either side of 100 mm marks and draw a line using a scribe. Mark angles on the back of the trunking.

3   Cut the triangular-shaped sections out of the trunking. Remember:
   • cut on the waste side of the line, i.e. the side that will be thrown away
   • because you are cutting two sides at the same time, you must constantly check all your saw cuts as you work to make sure that the saw is not wandering from the line
   • once the section has been cut out, file the sawn edges because they will be sharp and slightly ragged. This is to protect you from cutting your hand and to protect the cables that will be installed in the trunking.

4   Cut the small lip in the open side of the trunking with a junior hacksaw then bend the trunking and secure with a plate and either rivets or M5 nuts and bolts.

### *Fixing metal trunking*

Trunking can be fixed to walls and other surfaces using standard fixings, such as woodscrews, rawlplugs and cavity fixings. For long runs use a chalk line or laser level to mark out a level run.

Trunking can also be fitted to girders using the girder clamps described in Table 5.02. It can also be suspended using threaded studding. In this case the trunking is secured to the studding using nuts and washers. Suspension brackets are also available.

Trunking is not designed to be installed outdoors or in damp conditions.

## Plastic trunking

Like plastic conduit, plastic trunking is used in lighter, commercial installations. This is where some mechanical protection is needed, or where cables cannot be clipped to the surface or chased into the walls.

It is installed in a similar way to metal trunking. However, the joints between lengths can be glued together. The lid is usually a snap-on type.

## Multi-compartment trunking

Multi-compartment trunking is typically used in offices and classrooms where it is necessary to run both mains electrical cable and data cabling. It is made up of two or more separate compartments allowing different types of wiring to be run in the same enclosure (see Figure 5.08).

The separation between compartments is enough to protect the data cables from electro-magnetic interference by the mains cabling.

Multi-compartment trunking can be either plastic or metal. The wall-mounted version is sometimes called dado trunking.

**Figure 5.08** Multi-compartment trunking

## Lighting trunking

Lighting trunking is similar to basic metal trunking. The differences are that:

- it has a wide lip
- the lid is usually clip-on plastic.

Lighting trunking is used as a method for supplying and installing large numbers of light fittings. Typically this would be in a factory or large workshop. The trunking is normally suspended from the roof metalwork by means of threaded studding and brackets.

The light fittings are fixed to the trunking by a bush-type fitting which has two metal feet designed to slide under the trunking lip. The bushes are secured using a type of washer-plate and lock ring and are spaced to match up with the fixing holes in the back of the fitting. The fitting is then secured to the bushes using another set of lock rings.

The bushes are hollow so that the lighting supply cables can be run through them and into the light fitting.

Case Study

A large workshop which made prototype parts for a research laboratory was lit by 1,800 mm, triple-tubed fluorescent fittings complete with reflector shades. Unlike newer versions, these fittings were extremely heavy. There was no necessity to replace them as they gave good light and seldom failed. Plus replacement would be expensive.

The section of the fitting containing all the heavy components was in a hinged section that could be unclipped and swung down from the fitting's spine. This was fitted to the lighting trunking with specialist bushes, plates and lock nuts. One day, a fault with the clips caused a small number of these heavy lights to swing open. They broke away from their spines and crashed onto the floor below. Fortunately no one was injured but it was a very dangerous situation.

Electricians were called in to make the fittings safe. They did so by by taking each light down from the lighting trunking and fixing heavy-duty safety wire between the spine and the main body. If the clips failed again and the body swung open, the two safety wires would prevent it from falling. The clips themselves were also repaired as much as possible.

Because the fittings were installed in the workshop roof area, a mobile scaffold tower was needed. The workshop was filled with machines so the tower was constantly in need of dismantling and reassembling, sometimes over and around the machines. There was also a risk of dropping tools, equipment and, of course the heavy lights themselves. So the area around the tower was shut off, using barriers and warning notices.

The job needed careful planning so it didn't interrupt production in the workshop. The project manager and lead electrician met with the heads of the engineering department to work out a programme for the work.

Another issue was light levels. The fittings needed to be isolated from the electrical supply so they could be safely disconnected and re-connected. Temporary emergency lighting was set up so that areas of the workshop were not without full lighting for several hours or days at a time.

The job was completed and the fittings made safe. It took several weeks and was a difficult project. The electrician's job can be very challenging and technically interesting, but it can, like most careers, also be laborious, repetitive and physically hard. In this case, project planning was vital to make sure that the work could be carried out safely both for the electricians and for those working in the area. The Health and Safety at Work Act makes it clear that you are responsible not only for yourself when at work, but also for any others who could be injured by your work.

1. What is lighting trunking?

2. Which regulations apply to working on a scaffold tower?

3. What are bushes and lock rings?

## Busbar trunking

**Busbar** trunking is a method for distributing power supplies around an area and providing flexible take-off points. This means that machines, equipment or work stations can be positioned exactly where they are needed and fed straight from the busbar trunking via some form of take-off connection.

The trunking itself usually consists of a metal or plastic trunking body pre-fitted with busbars. As well as joining the trunking securely the busbars also need to be connected to ensure continuity of supply.

In a factory-type installation, busbar trunking often hangs above the machinery.

In an office area it can be installed under a raised floor. The floors are made up of carpeted tiles above the concrete base. Services are run under the tiles and can be accessed easily.

When power and data is required by a work station or desk, a power tile is fitted. This incorporates a lidded box containing 13 A sockets and telephone outlets. The power tile is then fed, in turn, from the busbar trunking under the raised floor.

> **Key term**
>
> **Busbars** – metal bars, usually copper or aluminium, used as conductors. Because of their size they can carry a high current

> **Did You Know**
>
> Supplies can be taken from the busbar at any point using crimped terminations bolted onto the bars. Mains position switch gear is often fed via a large supply cable that terminates into a busbar. In turn, the other components of the switchgear are then fed from the busbars.

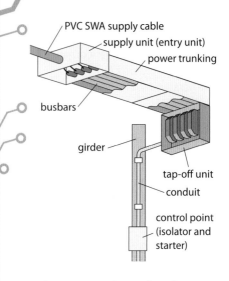

PVC SWA supply cable
supply unit (entry unit)
power trunking
busbars
girder
tap-off unit
conduit
control point (isolator and starter)

**Figure 5.09** Busbar trunking showing tap-off unit

**Figure 5.10** Cable tray

Busbar trunking can also be used as a riser-type power supply in a multi-storey building, such as an office block. In this case power is routed via busbar trunking from the main intake position in a service area at the bottom of the building. The supply for each floor is then taken from the busbar trunking and fed to a local distribution board on each floor.

## Mini-trunking

Mini-trunking sizes range from 16 mm x 8 mm to 60 mm x 60 mm. It provides minimal mechanical protection and is not acceptable as a wiring enclosure for single insulated cables.

Typically mini-trunking is run in domestic installations in situations where the cable cannot be clipped directly onto the surface, or chased into the wall or run in the floor and ceiling voids.

It can be installed using standard fixings such as screws, cavity fixings and rawlplugs. Versions are available that have double-sided tape on the back for quick and easy fitting.

A selection of angles and other fittings are available.

## Some trunking regulations

- Any equipment that is fixed to trunking or into the lid has to be fixed so that it cannot be accidently removed.
- If trunking passes through a fire wall of any sort the interior of the trunking should also be sealed with fire-resistant material.
- Maximum fixing distances for metal trunking are:
  o vertical – 1.0 m
  o horizontal – 0.75 m.
- Maximum fixing distances for plastic trunking are:
  o vertical – 0.5 m
  o horizontal – 0.5 m.

# Cable tray

Cable tray is used to support cables in industrial, public and commercial premises. It is a very workmanlike wiring method and usually kept out of sight.

It consists of lengths of steel tray with its edges formed into lips to prevent cables for falling off.

The tray is stamped with holes and slots which can be used for cable fixings such as p-clips, cleats and cable-ties.

## Types of cable tray

- **Standard** – this is supplied in a range of widths between 50 mm and 900 mm
- **Basket** – rather than being a flat steel tray, this is formed into a vee-shape into which cable can be laid. The sides are generally

made from lengths of wire supported from two parallel rails. Basket tray is not intended to provide fixing facilities for cables and is generally used for data wiring.

- **Ladder** – intended for large cables, this is supplied in sections that resemble a ladder.

## Fixing cable tray

Standard fixings can be used to install cable tray. However, a gap must be left behind the tray to allow cable fastenings to be fitted. For example, if the cable is being secured using cable-ties, the tie must be passed through the back of the tray then out again on the other side of the cable.

Spacers should be used to raise the tray off the surface it is being fixed to. Cable tray can also be suspended using threaded studding, nuts and washers.

## Bending cable tray

Cable tray can be formed into angles in such the same way as conduit. Tray bending machines are available for linear (flat) bends. These consist of a bending arm and two formers into which the lips of the cable tray are fitted. The formers can be adjusted to account of the width of the tray.

For lateral (sideways) bends the tray has to be cut and formed in much the same way as trunking. Bolts can be inserted into the holes of the tray to secure the bends.

**Figure 5.11** A tray bender

# Testing circuits wired in conduit and trunking

Most of the tests carried out on circuits wired in the steel conduit and trunking system are carried out in the same way as those wired using other wiring systems. However, the continuity of the protective conductor test must be completed before the circuits are connected up.

The reason for this is that the metal enclosures provide a **parallel earth path**. The effect of this is to give a low reading, but it does not prove the continuity of the actual protective conductors themselves. This is because the test current is finding its way to earth via the metal enclosures themselves.

**Key term**

**Parallel earth path** – a route back to the installation earth separate from the protective conductor. Metal conduit and trunking systems are designed to provide good continuity and to be at the same potential as the installation earth. This is an advantage when the installation is in use but can give inaccurate readings during a test

## CHECK YOUR KNOWLEDGE

**1** Mini-trunking can be used in a:

  **a** small factory

  **b** farm building

  **c** room that has been decorated

  **d** damp environment

**2** The type of cable normally run through mini-trunking is:

  **a** twin-and-earth

  **b** mineral insulated

  **c** single insulated, non-sheathed

  **d** steel-wire armoured

**3** Continuity tests are carried out on metal trunking and conduit installations:

  **a** before the final connections are made

  **b** after the final connections have been made

  **c** during installation of the conduit and trunking

  **d** during the wiring-up of a conduit or trunking installation

**4** Threads are cut onto metal conduit using:

  **a** arm and reamer

  **b** block and former

  **c** stocks and dies

  **d** vice and hacksaw

**5** A plastic conduit adaptor coupler has:

  **a** a thread in each end

  **b** no threads at all

  **c** two male threads

  **d** a thread at only one end

**6** Common sizes of conduit are:

  **a** 16 mm and 22 mm

  **b** 28 mm and 75 mm

  **c** 32 mm and 10 mm

  **d** 20 mm and 25 mm

**7** The fitting used to prevent plastic conduit from bending when hot is a:

  **a** running coupler

  **b** expansion coupler

  **c** adaptor coupler

  **d** flexible coupler

**8** What should be used to draw cutting lines on trunking?

  **a** felt-tip pen

  **b** ball-point pen

  **c** scribe

  **d** screwdriver blade

**9** What is another name for trunking that is run around the wall of an office or classroom?

  **a** containment trunking

  **b** busbar trunking

  **c** mini-trunking

  **d** dado trunking

**10** The trunking that can be used to supply machines in a factory is:

  **a** lighting trunking

  **b** busbar trunking

  **c** mini-trunking

  **d** dado trunking

# 6 Assembling and wiring electrical panels

There are many types of electrical control panel, from high voltage mains supply to fire alarm panels. These control panels are designed to contain all the necessary components and equipment in one enclosure. This means that switching, protection and monitoring can all be carried out in one central position. Complex processes such as industrial production lines can be controlled from one unit. Alarm systems can be monitored from one central point.

Building and installing electrical control panels is usually carried out by specialist companies. Although much of the wiring and connection work is common to all electrical installation work, there are certain tasks and skills that apply more directly to this branch of the industry.

In this chapter you will learn about:

- types of electrical panels
- electrical panel health and safety
- preparing to work on electrical panels
- components of an electrical panel
- cables and wiring
- inspection and testing

# KITTING UP

## Keeping Safe

Health and safety are always the most important things to think about before starting any job. Electrical control panel work carries its own risks because:

- it is heavy
- it is awkward to handle
- there are often sharp edges
- it requires sawing and drilling operations
- there is the potential for live circuits and equipment in the working environment
- there could be **high voltage** (1000 V and over) in the working environment.

Risk assessments should be completed before the job starts. They describe the risks and how they should be controlled. Permits to Work must be issued if very hazardous work is to be carried out. The right personal protective equipment (PPE) must also be worn.

**Goggles** – *protect the eyes from flying objects when using power tools, such as drills, saws and cutters*

**Hi-viz waistcoat** – *makes sure you can be seen at all times. Compulsory on most construction sites*

**Gloves** – *worn to protect hands from sharp edges and rough surfaces when lifting and carrying*

**Protective footwear** – *protects feet from injury caused by heavy objects. Compulsory on most construction sites*

## Paperwork

Every job involves some paperwork. Below is a table showing the main documents the electrician will need before assembling and wiring electrical panels.

| Document | What it tells you |
|---|---|
| Layout drawing | Scale drawing showing a 'bird's eye' view of a room or building and the position of electrical accessories and equipment (all represented using the British Standard symbols found in the *IET On-Site Guide*). In the case of control panels, these would show actual location of the panel in a room or area |
| Manufacturers' drawings | Diagrams and drawings that show the panel itself. These are normally to scale and there may be a number of views (e.g. front and side). These may also show the position of various components such as switches and instruments |
| Specification | Electrical equipment, types of material to be used, fixing methods and any other detailed information needed to carry out the work |
| BS 7671 | The electrical wiring regulations. All electrical work must conform to these regulations |
| *IET On-Site Guide* | A practical handbook which explains the BS 7671 regulations to the electrician |
| IET Guidance Note 3: Inspection and Testing | Guide to inspection and testing, including test methods, expected results, and correct completion of reports and certificates |
| The Electricity Supply Regulations 1988 | Regulations that include provisions for high-voltage supply and installations |
| HSE Guidance Note GS38 | Guide to test equipment and instrumentation, including calibration and acceptable features of a test instrument |
| IET Code of Practice for In-service Inspection and Testing of Electrical Equipment | Guidelines for testing appliances and electrical equipment |
| BS 60204 | Code of practice for the safety of electrical machinery |

## Toolkit

No job can be carried out without the correct tools. Shown below are the main items of equipment needed for the work in this chapter.

| Tool | Description |
|---|---|
| Phillips and flat-bladed screwdrivers of various sizes | Most modern fixing screws now have the x (Phillips) and star-shaped (Pozidriv) slots which require a matching screwdriver. They come in sizes small and large. Many terminal screw and older fixing screws have a single slot and require a matching screwdriver – there are many different screw and slot sizes requiring large and small screwdrivers |
| Combination pliers | Made up of gripping jaws and a set of cutting blades, combination pliers enable you to carry out a number of jobs using only one tool |
| Tape measure | Available in various lengths. Used to measure positions of equipment, saw cuts and drill holes |
| Hammer | Available in various sizes and types, each of which can be used to drive different fixings into materials |
| Electric drill | Used for drilling holes in masonry, wood or metal, and as electric screwdrivers |

| | | | |
|---|---|---|---|
| **Screwdriver drill bit** | A set of Phillips and flat-bladed screwdriver bits used with electric drills | **Continuity tester** | Confirms that a conductor or part of a circuit is unbroken and that current can flow from one end to the other |
| **Masonry drill bit** | Used for drilling holes in masonry | **Insulation resistance tester** | Confirms that the insulation on a cable is intact and that there are no short circuits between line and neutral and earth |
| **Metal drill bit** | Used for drilling holes in metal. | **Voltalge indicator** | Shows whether voltage is present but does not measure an actual amount |
| **Small spirit level** | Used to measure the level or plumb of a small object | **Voltmeter** | Measures voltage and gives an actual reading |
| **Large spirit level** | Used to measure the level or plumb of a large object | **Clip-on ammeter** | Consists of a meter attached to a pair of jaws. The jaws are closed around a live cable and the current is measured and displayed |
| **Chalk line** | Used to mark horizontal and vertical lines on walls and ceilings, which can be fixed to | **Residual current device (RCD) tester** | Deliberately puts an earth fault into a circuit to make sure that the RCD will operate, cut off the supply and prevent anyone receiving a shock |
| **Junior hacksaw** | Smaller version of the hacksaw, used for cutting smaller items of metal and plastic | **Earth fault loop impedance tester** | Measures the path from the point of an earth fault, along the earth conductor to the start point of the supply transformer, then back along the line conductor to the point of fault. There is a table in BS 7671 which gives the maximum readings for circuits with different types of protective device (e.g. fuses and circuit breakers) |
| **Adjustable grips** | There are various types of adjustable grips, such as pipe grips and mole grips (shown). These are adjusted by turning the screw at the bottom of the handle | | |
| **Adjustable spanner** | Can be set to the size of a particular bolt or nut. In this case, the moveable jaw is set using a thumbscrew | **Flash tester** | Carries out a high-voltage insulation resistance test. For main supply panels this can be carried to at 2 kV (2,000 V). The purpose is to thoroughly check that the insulation is able to withstand this type of voltage |

### BS 7671:2008 Requirements for Electrical Installations (17th edition)

The BS 7671:2008 Wiring Regulations are extremely important to the electrician. All electrical installation work must comply with the guidelines it contains. It covers areas such as selection of suitable equipment, cable sizes, and protection against shock and fire.

### QUICK CHECK

1 Give two examples of electrical control panels.
2 Which regulations include provisions for high voltage supply and installation?
3 What is BS 60204?

# Types of electrical panels

The basic types of electrical panels are:

- main supply intake panels
- control panels for automated systems
- control panels for monitoring and alarm systems
- back-up and emergency supply control panels.

## Main supply intake panels

In the past the electrical supply for a building would be connected to a main switch. This switch would then feed a large **busbar**. A set of switches and distribution boards were fed from the main busbar. This collection of equipment was called switchgear. Switchgear is still used but in many new installations it is collected into an electrical panel. This is called a mains intake panel.

Figure 6.01 A typical electrical panel

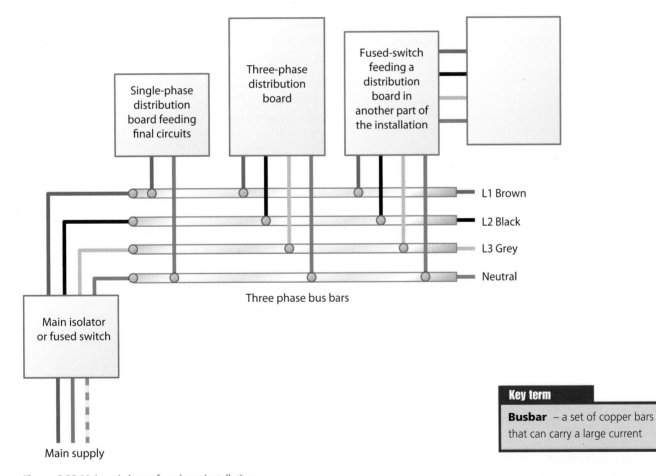

Figure 6.02 Main switchgear for a large installation

L1 Brown
L2 Black
L3 Grey
Neutral

Three phase bus bars

Single-phase distribution board feeding final circuits

Three-phase distribution board

Fused-switch feeding a distribution board in another part of the installation

Main isolator or fused switch

Main supply

---

**Key term**

**Busbar** – a set of copper bars that can carry a large current

A modern electrical panel includes switches and distribution fuses, voltmeters and ammeters, and other recording devices to monitor the supply. The **electricity supply meter** may also be fitted to the control panel.

The main components in a mains intake panel are as follows and are looked at in turn below:

- a main isolator
- a busbar
- a fused switch
- a distribution board
- a voltmeter
- an ammeter
- stop buttons and alarms.

## Main isolators

The main isolator is the switch at the point where the customer's supply begins. This switch connects and disconnects the whole supply, including the neutral. It must *never* switch the earth conductor.

Isolators should only be used when all the individual circuits are switched off. They are designed to make electrical equipment and installations safe to work on and not for regular on/off switching.

The main isolator might be a fused-switch (see page 121).

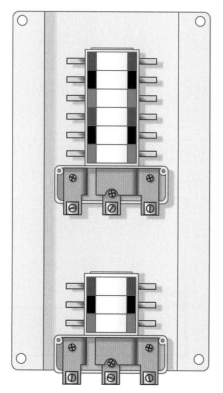

**Figure 6.04** Circuit breaker connection tabs on a distribution board busbar

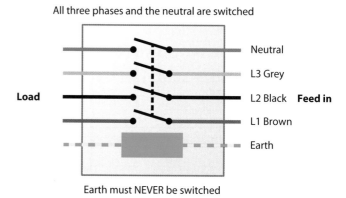

**Figure 6.03** A multi-pole isolator

## Busbars

The supply cables from the main isolator are connected to the busbar. The rest of the switchgear is then connected to the same busbar by short lengths of cable called tails. In a control panel the busbar may have a set of connection points which allow components to be fixed directly to them. For example, a circuit breaker is fitted directly onto a small busbar in the distribution board.

## Fused switches

A fused switch is a switch that opens and closes a supply by physically connecting and disconnecting a set of fuses. These are used for main supplies and so the fuses are generally rated for a high current, for example 100 A.

## Distribution boards

BS 7671 states that all electrical installations must be divided into separate circuits. Each circuit is protected from overcurrent (see Chapter 4) by either a fuse or circuit breaker. These components are enclosed in a distribution board. A distribution board will also contain:

- a **neutral bar** – where the main neutral cables for each circuit are connected
- an **earth bar** – where the circuit protective conductors for each circuit are connected.

There will also be a main switch. This must be a double pole isolator which disconnects both the line and neutral. If the panel is a **poly** or **three-phase** panel, then the main switch will disconnect all the phases and the neutral.

There may be more than one distribution board in an electrical panel, each one feeding a separate area of the installation or different types of equipment.

## Voltmeters

A voltmeter reads the amount of voltage present at any point in a circuit. Voltmeters are connected in **parallel** with the circuit.

In a very large commercial or heavy industrial installation, the supply side may be 11,000 V (11 kV), 33,000 V (33 kV) or higher.

One of the purposes of the voltmeter is to make sure that all three phases are connected and working. A recording version will show if there have been any:

- **surges** – when the voltage is much higher than it should be. This can be caused by a lightning strike. Surge protectors can be fitted into a sensitive installation
- **dips** – when the voltage is much lower than it should be.

**Figure 6.05** A fused switch

---

**Did You Know**

The difference between a fused switch and a switch-fuse is that a **fused switch** physically connects and disconnects a set of fuses each time the handle is operated. A **switch-fuse** makes and breaks a connection to a fixed fuse each time the switch is operated (e.g. a switch-fused spur).

---

**Key terms**

**Poly** or **three-phase** – the main supply from the power station, through the national grid and out into a neighbourhood or large installation is via its local sub-station and consists of three line conductors. The power is generated in such a way that the voltage is fed into each line in turn

---

**Did You Know**

The supply into many large installations, for example hospitals, factories and colleges, will be three-phase. In this case the voltage between each phase is 400 V, the voltage between each phase and neutral is 230 V. Many large electric motors need three-phase to operate.

**Figure 6.06** A voltmeter

**Figure 6.07** An ammeter

## Ammeters

An ammeter shows how much current is being used. For a three-phase supply, the current should be balanced, as far as possible, across all three phases. The ammeter will show if one phase has to work harder than the others.

If there is too much difference, current will flow in the neutral. This reduces the efficiency of the supply and increases the cost.

Ammeters are normally connected in **series**. However, clip-on ammeters can be used instead. These use the magnetic field around a conductor to read the current. In electrical panels, the clip-on jaws are replaced by a permanent coil wound round the conductors.

## Stop buttons and alarms

The mains panel may well be fitted with a set of stop buttons which can be operated in the event of an emergency, for example, if someone is suffering an electric shock. Stop buttons will break a high current supply by means of a contactor. (See page 129 for more detail on how a contactor works.)

Alarms may be installed so that the maintenance staff can be alerted if anything goes wrong. Many electrical panels include alarms in their circuitry. These can make a loud noise, light lamps on the panel itself or send a signal or message to a remote monitoring station to raise the alarm.

## Electrical panel forms

As well as being designed for specific jobs, electrical panels are divided into forms.

- **Form 1 panels** – there is no segregation (physical separation) between the busbars in the panel and the rest of the equipment in the panel.
- **Form 2 panels** – busbars are segregated from the rest of the panel by being run in a separate compartment.

## Control panels for automated systems

An automated system, such as a manufacturing process, may require each part of the production line to stop and start in a set sequence. Or perhaps one section of the line should only start when a product container reaches a certain weight or a fluid tank is filled to a certain level.

The type of control panel used in automated systems often requires a mixture of electrical and electronic circuits. The main part of this type of control panel is the programmable logic controller (PLC).

## Programmable logic controller (PLC)

The PLC is fitted to the main control panel or item of electrical equipment. It allows you to set the equipment or system to work in a certain way. For example, the PLC in a central heating system allows you to set the temperature, and the times and even the days when the heating is turned on and off.

## Electronic components

Chapter 4 describes the main components of electronic circuits and how they work. Basically they have no moving parts, are fed by an extra low voltage d.c. supply and route small amounts of current around the system.

Electronic circuits can be used to create very complex processes and sequences. They control voltage and current, direction of current and timing. Examples of electronic components are shown in Table 6.01.

| Electronic component | Purpose |
| --- | --- |
| **Resistor** | Resistors provide a set amount of resistance which controls the amount of current that can flow |
| **Capacitor** | Capacitors are charged up while current is flowing, much like batteries. However, unlike batteries, they will discharge all their stored electrical charge as soon as the supply is switched off. They are used to 'smooth' circuits and to counteract electro-magnetic interference |
| **Diode** | Diodes only allow current to flow in one direction. They are used to convert a.c. to d.c. |
| **Transistors** | A type of switch that routes different amounts of current through the circuit |

**Table 6.01** Some basic electronic components

## Electrical components

The main electrical component of a control circuit is the relay. This is an automatic switch operated by a coil. The coil is a length of insulated conductor, usually copper, wrapped into a hollow spiral.

When the coil is energised, a strong magnetic field is set up inside the coil. If an iron (ferrous) or iron-based rod is inserted into the coil it will be drawn in by the magnetic field. This can be used as the basis of an automatic switch. The switches can be:

- **normally open (N/O)** – closing when the coil is energised
- **normally closed (N/C)** – opening when the coil is energised
- **normally open/normally closed (NO/NC)** – changing the direction of current flow by opening one set of switches and closing another, like the points on a railway.

The coil can be connected to a timer or sensor, which will energise and de-energise the coil according to their settings.

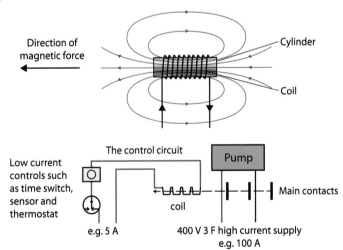

Control circuits often use one supply to switch another e.g. a low current supply to switch a high current load. An example of this is a heavy duty pump operated by a time switch and thermostat.

**Figure 6.08** The principle of a simple control circuit

**Figure 6.09** A relay

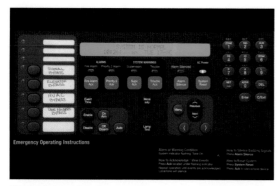

**Figure 6.10** A fire alarm panel

Relays can be used to switch high-current loads. The coil only needs a low current. This means that low current control devices, such as thermostats and timers, can be connected into the coil circuit. A contactor is a larger version of a relay. (See page 129 for information on contactors.)

## Control panels for monitoring and alarm systems

Alarm panels are the central control point in an alarm system. The alarms can be set, tested and monitored from this panel.

A typical alarm is the fire alarm system. This is usually divided up into zones. These can be areas of a building or separate buildings in a large complex, such as a hospital or factory.

Each zone has a set of heat and smoke detectors, fire alarm buttons, and possibly sprinklers or some other method for automatically fighting the fire.

### Heat detectors

Heat detectors send an alarm signal to the control panel when the surrounding temperature reaches a certain level. The detector contains a heat-sensitive element, which, in some types will melt and trigger the sensor.

There are two main types of heat detector:

- **fixed temperature** – operates when the temperature reaches a certain level
- **rate of rise of heat** – operates when the temperature begins to increase rapidly.

### Smoke detectors

Smoke detectors send an alarm signal to the control panel when there is smoke in the atmosphere. There are two main types of smoke detector:

- **photoelectric** – contains an infrared beam that sets off the alarm when it is broken by smoke
- **ionisation** – detects smoke particles in the air.

### Fire alarm buttons

The most familiar type or fire alarm buttons are the 'break glass' type. The glass front holds the button in. When the glass is broken the button pops out and operates the alarm.

### Alarm sounders

These are sirens or bells which operate when alarm signals reach the panel. Anyone who works in a building equipped with fire alarms should become familiar with the sound of the alarm.

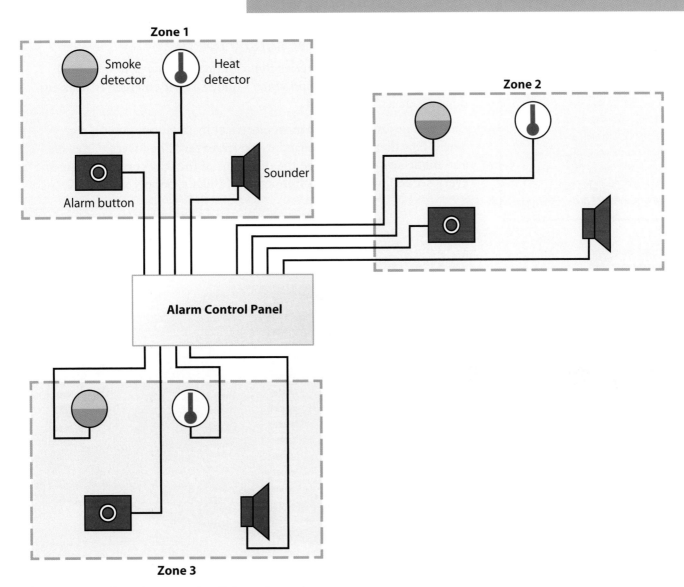

**Figure 6.11** Zones in an alarm system installation on the panel

## Back-up and emergency supply control panels

Emergency back-up power is provided for installations where it is vital that certain power supplies are maintained at all times. Examples of this are:

- emergency lighting for evacuation during a fire
- hospital equipment.

The emergency back-up power process is controlled by an electrical panel. They are equipped with changeover switching that will operate automatically when the mains power fails. While the back-up power is running, the panel will monitor voltage, current and generator fuel levels.

The main source of emergency back-up power is the generator. However, it may take several seconds for a generator to start and reach the speed necessary to provide the power needed. The uninterrupted power supply (UPS) is a means of filling in during the generator start-up time.

## Uninterrupted power supply (UPS)

The UPS is a bank of batteries that can provide power long enough for the generator to start and come online so that emergency back-up power is never interrupted.

Batteries produce d.c. but most electrical installations run on a.c. The d.c. is therefore converted by an **inverter**. The inverter uses an automatic switch to change the direction of the d.c. current 50 times every second, which is the frequency of the a.c. supply in the UK.

### Case Study

A large computer centre was upgraded so that it could provide switching and computing services to the 999 emergency service telephone system. The centre was already equipped with a generator for electricity supply back-up in the event of a power cut. However, it took several seconds for the generator to get up to full speed and power output, and in that time the 999 system would be under serious strain. The solution was to install an uninterrupted power supply (UPS).

A company designed and built the UPS especially for this job. It was important that it would fit into the space available where it would be installed.

Before it was delivered, however, it needed to undergo a 'witness test'. This test takes place at the factory and is attended by representatives from the customer's company.

The representatives for the computer centre watched as the panel was given a series of tests. These included insulation resistance, earth continuity and a flash test – a test carried out at high voltage to check that the insulation will not break down. The batteries were tested and the panel put under full load. It passed with no problems and was successfully installed at the computer centre.

Often the tests have already been carried out once before the customers arrive for a witness test. This doesn't matter because it means that very thorough testing takes place and that expensive items of electrical equipment like this panel are safe and will work properly when installed.

1. What is used to convert d.c. to a.c. in a UPS?

2. What is a flash test?

### QUICK CHECK

1  What is the purpose of an isolator?
2  How should an electrical installation be divided up?
3  What does a programmable controller do?

# Electrical panel health and safety

Although assembling and wiring electrical panels is covered by the general health and safety regulations, there are a number of health and safety issues that are directly related to this type of work. Panel assembly and wiring usually takes place at a factory and the finished unit is then transported to its site. There will, of course, be some work involved in installing the panel then connecting it to the general installation or the systems it feeds and controls.

Hazards relating directly to panel construction and installation are shown in Table 6.02.

| Task | Hazard | Control |
|---|---|---|
| **Manual handling** | Panels and many of their components are heavy | Correct transportation. Lifted using mechanical aids or approved lifting techniques |
| **Sharp edges** | Because they are constructed from metal there will be sharp edges, particularly as a result of cutting and drilling | Wear gloves when handling metal sections and components |
| **Drilling** | Drilling work can result in eye injuries caused by flying debris | Wear safety glasses and gloves when drilling |
| **Cutting** | This may be hand sawing or using electric bench saws and grinding equipment, which create sparks and flying debris | Wear safety glasses and gloves when cutting |
| **Electric shock** | As with all electrical work there is a risk of shock | Always follow the safe isolation procedure (see Chapter 1) when working on an electrical installation |
| **High voltage (HV = 1,000 V+)** | Many panels are fed by high-voltage supplies | Only electricians qualified in high-voltage work can deal with these systems |
| **Confined spaces** | Because electrical panels are usually installed in power rooms and plant rooms, they are often located in confined spaces | Follow the Confined Spaces Regulations, e.g.: <br>• make sure there is a good supply of fresh air <br>• make sure one person is always stationed outside the confined space area to give assistance if necessary <br>• raise a Permit to Work before work starts and carry out a risk assessment to see how hazardous the work is |

**Table 6.02** Hazards that can arise when working on electrical control panels

## Earthing

All metal equipment and enclosures must be connected to earth. This means that if there is a fault and the metalwork becomes live, the fault current will be diverted straight to earth. On its way it will operate a protective device – a circuit breaker or a residual current device (RCD) – and cut off the power before anyone can receive an electric shock.

The earth conductor is connected either directly to the metalwork or to a terminal which is, in turn, connected to the metalwork.

**QUICK CHECK**

1 What is HV?
2 What parts of an electrical panel must be earthed?
3 Where are electrical panels often installed?

## Preparing to work with electrical panels

When constructing electrical panels, a clean, tidy area is needed. Components need to be laid out ready in a place where they will not be damaged or get dirty. If working with electronic components, earthed wrist straps should be worn to protect the components from electrostatic discharge (ESD) hazards (see Chapter 7).

You will need various diagrams and drawings. These are:

- **wiring diagrams** – these show how the panel is wired. The connections correspond to real life. The terminations are often numbered for identification

- **circuit diagrams** – these show how the panel actually works but do not always show the wiring and connections exactly as they are in real life

- **manufacturer's drawings and instructions** – these show the construction of the panel and the positions of the various instruments and components. They may also contain an exploded view of the panel, showing how it fits together

- **layout drawing** – this is used when installing the panel. It shows the exact position of the panel

- **commissioning instructions** – these list the tests and checks to be carried out during the commissioning. They may also list possible common faults and their causes. Once the panel is installed, it needs to be commissioned. This is a thorough test carried out to make sure that the panel actually works

- **user manual** – this is supplied by the manufacturer and shows how the panel should be used. It details:
  - settings
  - what certain instrument readings actually mean
  - how to switch the panel on and off
  - test schedules.

These documents will usually be supplied with the panel and may be collected together into the user manual. Wiring and circuit diagrams are sometimes displayed on the panel itself for quick reference.

**QUICK CHECK**

1 How should your work area be presented when working on electrical panels?
2 When should you wear an ESD wrist strap?
3 List two things the user manual tells you about an electrical panel.

# Components of an electrical panel

As well as the components described in relation to specific types of electrical panel, there are other general components that may need to be installed.

## Types of component

The other components you may need to install are:

- transformers
- contactors
- switches
- ballast chokes
- terminal blocks.

### Transformers

Transformers are electrical machines that change voltage, either from low to high (step-up versions), or high to low (step-down versions). Transformers can be large or small. The national power transmission system uses large transformers to convert extremely high voltage (e.g. 25,000 V to 400,000 V). Smaller versions can be found in the power leads for laptop computers where they are used to transform 230 V a.c. to 24 V d.c.

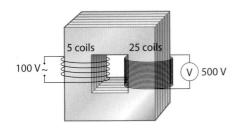

5 coils    25 coils

100 V ~              (V) 500 V

A step-up transformer has more turns in the secondary coil than in the primary coil. The potential difference across the secondary coil is greater than that across the primary coil.

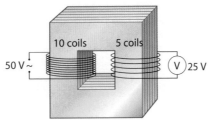

10 coils    5 coils

50 V ~              (V) 25 V

A step-down transformer has fewer turns in the secondary coil than in the primary coil. The potential difference across the secondary coil is less than that across the primary coil.

**Figure 6.12** A transformer showing step-up and step-down versions

### Contactors

A contactor works on the same principle as a relay (see page 123). The difference is that a contactor is designed to work on higher current and to operate larger equipment and circuits. Stop buttons will usually be connected to the coil of a contactor.

The main use for contactors is to start and control electrical motors. These allow for low current start-up and also feature a no-volt safety system. This means that if a motor stops working because of a power failure, it will not automatically restart when the power returns. The start button has to be operated to restart the motor.

**Figure 6.13** A DoL starter

The different types of contactor starters are outlined below.

### Direct on line (DoL)

The DoL is the most basic type of motor starter. It consists simply of a set of contacts operated by a coil. The coil circuit can include control devices such as timers and sensors, and also remote start and stop buttons, for example the control box for an overhead crane or gantry.

### Star-delta

A star-delta is a three-phase starter for large industrial motors. Because electric motors draw a high current when starting to connect, a method is needed for reducing this start current as much as possible.

The star-delta starter changes the connections to the motor between start and run. At start, it connects the motor connections in star. This reduces the amount of current that flows as the motor tries to get up to its running speed.

When the motor is running, the connections change to delta, which allows enough current to flow.

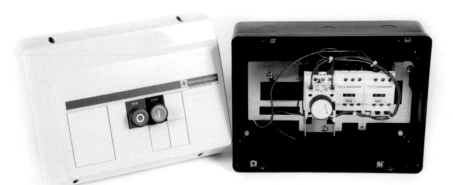

**Figure 6.14** Star-delta starter

### Auto-transformer

Like the star-delta starter, the auto-transformer limits the amount of current that flows during motor start-up. It does this by changing the voltage from a low voltage at start to a higher voltage at run. See page 129 for more information on transformers.

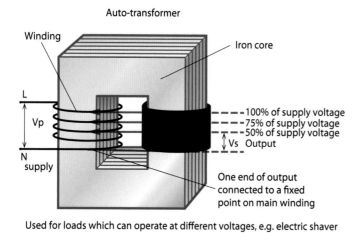

**Figure 6.15** An auto-transformer

## Soft Start

Star-delta and auto-transformer starters are being replaced by soft start motor starters. These use electronic circuits and components to reduce the high currents that flow when a motor starts. Some only allow current through to the motor at certain points in the a.c. sine wave, when the voltage is lower. Others change a.c. to d.c. then convert it back to a.c. at a different frequency to the supply. This means that the speed of the motor can also be controlled.

## *Switches*

As well as isolators there are functional switches that operate as part of the normal function of a circuit. Light switches are an example of functional switches.

### Push button

Usually connected to a contactor or relay, the button makes or breaks the supply to the relay coil. Many push button switches are spring-loaded so that once pressed they return to their original position. Fire alarm break glass and emergency stop buttons are both push button switches.

### Toggle and rocker switches

Light switches are usually rocker or toggle switches. These have an 'off' and 'on' position and stay in position once switched.

### Multi-position switches

Multi-position switches allow you to set a system in a certain way. For example, the switches on an oven often have a number of temperature settings. These are multi-position switches.

### *Ballast chokes*

Ballast chokes are usually found in fluorescent light fittings. They consist of an insulated conductor wound around an iron core. They are designed to provide a second or back-voltage (back EMF) to assist the start-up process.

### *Terminal blocks*

Dim-rail clip-on terminal blocks are the type usually found in electrical panels. These are designed to clip onto a rail, which can be cut to the length needed. The higher the current, the larger and more robust the terminal.

## Installing components

Components must be installed according to either the manufacturer's instructions or to the panel specification. They must be level, the right way up and secure.

If fixing holes are being drilled or punched out in the panel faceplates for buttons and instruments, these need to be carefully measured so that components are in line and neat.

Instruments can be fixed in place in a variety of ways. The back section of some instruments has a plate or bracket on either side in which the fixing holes are located. The panel must be drilled in line with these fixing holes. The drilled holes must be big enough for the fixing screws but small enough to be hidden under the screw or bolt head when the instrument is fitted. Some components have a threaded back section that a nut or locking ring is screwed onto.

### *Correct connection*

Instruments and other components must be connected correctly. Polarity is important. Correct polarity means that the line and neutral (if a.c.) and positive and negative (if d.c.) are connected to the correct terminals. If polarity is reversed, some instruments will read backwards or even be damaged.

---

**QUICK CHECK**

1  What is a typical use for contactor?
2  How must components be installed?
3  What does correct polarity mean?

# Cables and wiring

As with all electrical equipment and systems, the cable is the nervous system which carries electrical current to the various parts of the installation. The amount of current a cable can carry depends on its size. The larger the **cross-sectional area** of a conductor, the more current it can carry.

## Components of a cable

The main components of a cable are:

- **conductor** – the metal core that carries the actual current
- **insulation** – the layer of material around the outside of the conductor that prevents shock and short circuit between the conductors
- **sheaths** – the outer layers of insulation, and sometimes armouring, which package all the cores of a cable together and give mechanical protection. Some outer sheaths are toughened for use in harsh environments while others are treated to prevent them giving off smoke when they burn.

### Multi-core cables

Multi-core cables have more than one core, such as twin-and-earth and three-core flex. The cores are usually colour-coded.

| Supply type | Core names | Colour |
| --- | --- | --- |
| d.c. | Positive (+) | Red |
| | Negative (-) | Black |
| a.c. single-phase | Line (L) | Brown |
| | Neutral (N) | Blue |
| | Earth (E) | Green and yellow |
| a.c. poly or three-phase | Line 1 (L1) | Brown |
| | Line 2 (L2) | Black |
| | Line 3 (L3) | Grey |

Table 6.03 Cable-core identification colours

In addition to those shown in Table 6.03 there are the following:

- **General control circuits and extra low voltage** – these can be brown, black, red, orange, yellow, violet, grey, white, pink or turquoise.
- **Control panel power circuits** – a.c. phase is black, a.c. neutral is light blue, d.c.+ is black and the earth green and yellow.
- **Control panel control circuits a.c. and d.c.** – the a.c. live and a.c. neutral via a transformer is red, the a.c. neutral (mains) is light blue, the d.c.+ blue, the interlocks and circuits supplied from remote panels are orange and the earth is green and yellow.
- **Control panel services** – the cables feeding the lights and fans and other equipment that is part of the control panel itself:

- o **Multi-core cables** – the sheath, a.c. live cores and a.c. neutral cores are orange and the earth cores green and yellow.
- o **Single-core cables** – the a.c. live is orange, the a.c. neutral is light blue and the earth is green and yellow.

Control cables used in complex circuits or electronic circuits may not have the standard colours shown in Table 6.03. Because of this, there may be **looms** of cables which are all the same colour. The individual cables in such a loom will need to be identified. There are a number of ways to do this. Push-on tags that display a number or letter are often used. The number or letter will be the same at each end of the cable. They usually correspond to those used in the wiring diagrams.

Make sure both ends are identified before installing a cable. If this has not been done, a continuity test can be used to identify the ends of a cable.

### Key terms

**Loom** – a collection of cables run together

**Resistance** – a property of all matter. It limits the amount of electrical current that can flow through it

### Did You Know

A material with a very low resistance is called a **conductor**. A material with a very high resistance is called an **insulator**. The symbol for resistance is R and it is measured in ohms ($\Omega$).

### Hands On

Follow the steps of the continuity test below to identify a cable in a loom.

1. Strip both ends of the cables in the loom.
2. Obtain a low reading ohmmeter and set to the ohm ($\Omega$) scale. This will read the **resistance** of the conductor.
3. Connect one lead of the ohmmeter to one end of the cable to be identified.
4. Connect the ohmmeter lead to one of the cables at the other end of the loom.
5. If the ohmmeter gives a low reading, for example 0.01 $\Omega$, then you have identified both ends of the same cable.
6. If the ohmmeter gives a high reading or shows an off-the-scale symbol, then you have not found the other end of the cable. Try again until you obtain a very low reading.
7. Once you have identified both ends of the cable, mark them using a push-on tag (or insulation tape as a temporary measure).

## Single-core cables

Single-core cables have one **conductor**, insulation and an outer sheath. They are often used as tails at the supply end of an installation.

## Single-insulated cables

Single-insulated cables have a conductor and one layer of insulation, but no outer sheath. They must not be used on the surface but must always be contained in an enclosure. Single-insulated earth cables can be installed on the surface because they do not normally carry current.

## Ribbon cables

This is a single-insulated multi-core cable which is flat and colour-coded for identification of each core. They often have a specially coloured outer core, or reference core. This means the outer core can be identified by counting in from the reference core. They are used mainly for control circuits. Ribbon cables are usually very small and used for low current, extra-low-voltage circuits and electronic circuits. Because of problems with air flow in electronic equipment, caused by the shape of ribbon cables, new versions are contained and folded in a circular sheath.

**Figure 6.16** A ribbon cable

## Data/communication cables

Signals and data in a panel will be carried by data or Category 5 **twisted pair** cables. Data cables must not be run next to mains electrical cables. This is because the magnetic field caused by the current flowing in main cables interferes with the data being carried by the Category 5 cables. There are several other different types.

### Screened cables

Screened cable carries signals and data. It is protected from electro-magnetic interference by a layer of metal screen around the main core. Coaxial cable used as television aerial cable is a type of screened cable.

### Tri-rated cables

Tri-rated cables are used in main supply panels and can be used to carry high voltage, i.e. 1,000 V and over. They are available in sizes from 0.5 mm$^2$ to 120 mm$^2$. They are stranded and flexible, which is necessary when running cables around the confines of a panel.

This type of cable is heat resistant and can be either single or multi-core.

## Cable routing

Care must be taken when installing cables in an electrical control panel to keep the cable run neat and accessible. Loose cables can interfere with the function of the panel equipment and also become damaged, for example by getting caught in a door or removable section.

### Cable-ties

Cable-ties are plastic or nylon cable retainers that wrap around the cable loom. The tail of the cable-tie is drawn through the slotted head. The tail is pulled tight and held in place by a ratchet action between the slot and the teeth in the tail.

When securing cables using cable-ties, try to keep the loom of cables untangled. Work out which cables will branch off the loom first and run the cables so that as each cable branches off it does not cross or twist around the others.

### Slotted trunking

Another routing method for cables is plastic trunking with a clip-on lid. The sides of the trunking are slotted so that cables can be branched off the main run wherever necessary. Again, try to run the cables in the trunking without twisting them around each other or tangling them together.

### Slot and holes

When running cables through holes or slots in metal plate, use either a **grommet** or **beading** to protect the cable from the sharp sides of the hole.

## Stripping cable

When stripping the outer sheath, the insulation must not be penetrated or damaged. See Chapter 4, page 80 for instructions on stripping cable.

When stripping insulation, use a specialised cable-stripping tool. Do not cut out any conductor strands from a stranded cable because this reduces its cross-sectional area and reduces the amount of current it can carry. The result will be a hot area which could cause a fire.

Do not nick or damage the solid core. It could become loose and hot or snap off completely.

## Terminating cables

There are various types of cable terminals. These are outlined in Table 6.04 and described in more detail in Chapter 4.

| Termination type | Description | Use |
|---|---|---|
| **Standard clamped terminal** | Usually a brass cylinder in which the conductor is secured using a grub screw | If a single conductor is to be terminated, strip the insulation away to twice the required length then bend the conductor double. This creates a larger conductor for the retaining screw to grip onto. BS 7671 states all stranded conductors must have their ends treated to make sure all strands go into their terminals. Another method is to crimp a pin-type lug to the end of the cable. |
| **Post** | A threaded post onto which the conductor is secured using a set of nuts and washers | Wrap the conductor tightly round the post in the same direction as the locknut is turned for tightening (usually clockwise) |
| **Crimped termination** | A fitting that can be pushed onto the conductor then crimped tight with a specialised crimping tool. The smaller versions are usually colour-coded. The larger ones, bare metal. These have a variety of terminal types such as a ring, spade and fork. The ring type is a good method for securing cables to post terminations | The crimping tool crushes the body of the crimp lug onto the conductor. Make sure the crimped lug is securely fitted to the cable before connecting |
| **Soldered** | The conductor is secured to the terminal using solder which is melted onto the terminal using the tip of a soldering iron | Often used for very small conductors in electronic circuits. Precautions must be taken because solder can give off toxic fumes (see Chapter 7) |
| **Push** | Designed to allow the conductor to be pushed home. A spring-loaded clamp secures the conductor. Check that the termination is tight because a loose termination can create a hot spot | An example of this are certain telephone outlets. A specialist tool might be needed for this type of termination |

**Table 6.04** Cable termination types

# Inspection and testing

As with all electrical systems, electrical control panels must be properly tested and checked to make sure they are safe and work correctly.

## Visual inspection

> **Key term**
>
> **Visual inspection** – a check of an installation or piece of equipment that you carry out with your eyes. There is usually a checklist you need to follow

Before any instruments are used it is important to carry out a **visual inspection** to make sure the installation itself is wired and constructed correctly. The inspection includes checks for damaged cables and fittings, and incorrect wiring methods.

Visual inspections involve carrying out the following checks.

- Check all instruments on the panel are in the correct place and are the correct way round.
- Check that the correct instruments are connected to the correct circuits.
- Check that all components are securely fixed in place.
- Check terminations are secure and correct (the instrument test will also confirm this).
- Check for general damage to cable and components.
- Check that all jobs have been carried out.
- Check that no cables are badly terminated.
- Check that no components are missing.

## Test instruments

> **Key term**
>
> **Calibration** – the resetting of a test instrument to make sure it is reading accurately. This must be carried out by a registered calibration company and the date recorded

Test instruments must conform to HSE Guidance Note GS38. The main points of this Guidance Note are as follows:

- Test probes must be insulated and have finger barriers to guard against accidental contact with live terminals. Their metal tips must be less than 4 mm long. Spring-loaded tips that retract into the probe holder are recommended.
- Leads must be insulated and sheathed. They should be coloured-coded to make identification easier, and permanently and securely connected to the probe with no conductor showing.
- Test leads must be fused and fitted with a current limiting resistor.

All test instruments must be regularly calibrated. This has to be carried out by a registered **calibration** company.

The main items of electrical test equipment are described in Table 6.05.

| Instrument | Description |
|---|---|
| Voltage indicator | The voltage indicator is not intended to measure actual voltage but to show if a voltage is present. It is typically a lamp and two probes which are connected to line and neutral or line and earth<br><br>*Do not* use a neon screwdriver for this task because they are unreliable and dangerous<br><br>*Do not* use a cheap indicator. An electrician's life may depend on this piece of equipment! |
| Low reading ohmmeter | Intended to test for continuity, the low reading ohmmeter gives a resistance reading in ohms ($\Omega$). The scale can be set to $\Omega$ and m$\Omega$. End-to-end continuity tests are carried out to make sure that all the metalwork is connected to earth, and that all conductors and connections are secure and not broken |
| Insulation resistance tester | The scale on an insulation resistance tester is usually set to megohms (M$\Omega$). (1 M$\Omega$ = 1 million $\Omega$.) This is because the insulation resistance test is used to check that there are no short circuits or faults to earth caused by failed or damaged insulation. The lowest acceptable reading is 1 M$\Omega$. Readings are taken between:<br><br>• line and earth<br>• neutral and earth<br>• line and neutral<br><br>Insulation resistance testing is carried out at 500 V d.c. so take care to ensure all sensitive equipment is unplugged or isolated before doing the test. All covers and faceplates must be in place |
| Earth fault loop impedance tester | This measures the path from the point of an earth fault, along the earth conductor to the star point of the supply transformer, then back along the line conductor to the point of fault. Only a low reading that complies with the maximum earth loop impedance stated in BS 7671:2008 is acceptable |
| Prospective fault current tester | Usually incorporated into the earth loop fault impedance tester, this measures the maximum fault current that will flow in the event of a short circuit or earth fault. The reading will be high, typically thousands of amps (kA) |

Table 6.05 The main instruments used for tests on electrical panels

| Instrument | Description |
|---|---|
| Residual current device (RCD) tester | Any circuit protected by an RCD has to be tested. This is carried out using an RCD tester. This instrument creates an earth fault in the circuit then measures how long it takes for the RCD to operate and cut off the supply. The sequence of tests that have to be carried out are:<br>• 50% of the RCD operating current – RCD should not operate. This proves that the RCD will not 'nuisance-trip', in other words, it will not trip when there is no fault<br>• 100% of the RCD operating current – RCD should trip within stated operating time<br>• 150% of tripping current – RCD should trip more quickly than operating time |
| Clip-on ammeter | Current normally has to be read by an instrument connected in series with the circuit. This means that the circuit has to be switched off so that the ammeter can be connected safely. The clip-on ammeter avoids the need for this. The instrument is basically a current transformer and consists of a pair of sprung jaws which are closed around a cable where current is to be measured. The result is shown on the indicator screen |
| Voltmeter | Unlike the voltage indicator, the voltmeter is designed to give an actual, recordable voltage measurement. It should be connected in parallel with a circuit. Because of this, a reading can be taken by touching the instrument's probes to the live terminals of a load or supply |
| Plug-in socket tester | This displays the correct operation of a 13 A socket. Combinations of green, red or similar indicator lamps (and sometimes a buzzer) give a quick confirmation of correct operation or presence of certain faults. Plug-in testers should be used only as indicators and not as a recordable test or fault-finding tool |
| Plug-in test leads | Plug-in test leads can be as simple as a 13 A plug with its flex terminated into a connector block. They are intended as a method for taking readings at a 13 A socket without having to remove the socket's faceplate. This must only be used for dead tests. |
| Recording instrument – voltage, current or power | Recording instruments are sometimes connected to a supply or circuit for a number of hours or days. These are intended to show if there are any dips or surges in the voltage, current or power consumption |

**Table 6.05** The main instruments used for tests on electrical panels (continued)

## Other tests

### *Touch current*

If the 500 V d.c. insulation resistance test cannot be carried out, a touch current test can be used to test equipment insulation. Care has to be taken as this test is done while the equipment is switched on and operating. The test is carried out between the internal live parts of the equipment and its metalwork and insulation.

An acceptable reading should be 3.5 mA. For appliances with heating elements it should be 0.75 mA.

### *Flash test*

A flash test is a high-voltage insulation resistance test. For main supply panels this can be carried to at 2 kV (2,000 V). The purpose is to thoroughly check that the insulation is able to withstand this type of voltage.

### *Phase rotation*

This is a test carried out on three-phase supplies to make sure that L1, L2 and L3 are connected to the correct phases. The brown (L1) sine wave should reach its peak first, followed by black (L2) and then grey (L3). A specialised test instrument is used for this.

## Commissioning

Commissioning is the process of checking that all functions of the panel are tested. This means that all buttons are pressed, and isolators and fuse switches operated. This is done without the full load, then with the load connected.

Elements included in this functionality test are:

- switchgear
- controls
- interlocks (e.g. panel doors cannot be opened until the power is switched off)
- no-volt cut-out (built into motor controls so that if there is a power failure the motor will not restart until the start button is pressed)
- sequences (making sure the panel operates a system in the correct sequence)
- programming
- all warning lights, on/off lamps etc.
- stop buttons

**Quick Tip**

For quickness when carrying out an insulation resistance test, connect line and neutral together so both can be tested to earth at the same time. A few seconds saved at each test will soon add up.

**QUICK CHECK**

1   What is an insulation resistance tester used for?
2   What is the difference between a voltage indicator and a voltmeter?
3   List three tests carried out while commissioning an electrical panel.

## CHECK YOUR KNOWLEDGE

1 A main switch that works by physically connecting and disconnecting a set of fuses is called a:

   a switch-fuse

   b switch-isolator

   c fuse-switch

   d fuse-circuit breaker

2 An electrical panel in which the busbar is run in a separate compartment from the rest of the components is a:

   a Form 1

   b Form 2

   c Form 3

   d Form 4

3 The set of tests which include all the buttons, instruments and functions of an electrical panel is called:

   a commissioning

   b continuity

   c confirmation

   d completeness

4 A supply made up of three line conductors is called:

   a poly-phase

   b multi-phase

   c tri-phase

   d line-phase

5 Fire alarm equipment is controlled by a panel and divided into:

   a areas

   b sectors

   c zones

   d quadrants

6 The battery cabinet used to provide emergency back-up power while a generator is starting up is called an:

   a uniform power supply

   b uninterrupted power supply

   c uncontrolled power supply

   d unauthorised power supply

7 The component that converts d.c. supplies to a.c. is:

   a a rectifier

   b an auto-transformer

   c a capacitor

   d an inverter

8 Cable looms can be held together neatly using:

   a plastic beading

   b rubber grommets

   c cable-ties

   d crimp lugs

9 One type of starter used for large industrial electric motors is the:

   a star-delta

   b star-star

   c delta-star

   d delta-delta

10 A flash test is carried out at:

   a 500 V

   b 3,300 V

   c 12 V

   d 2,000 V

# 7 Assembling electronic circuits

Electronics is just about everywhere, from the mobile phones in our pockets to the satellites in space. The modern world just wouldn't be the same place without it! Our houses contain hundreds of circuit boards and every day there are new products becoming available that use the latest advances in the field.

In this chapter you'll find out what makes these electronic products tick, how they're made and assembled. You will gain some of the essential skills of an electronics engineer. This chapter is an introduction to the fascinating, exciting and cutting-edge world of electronics.

In this chapter you will learn about:

- electronic components
- electronic drawings and diagrams
- printed circuit boards (PCBs)
- different types of circuit

- component and tool storage and preparation
- hand soldering
- quality control

# KITTING UP

## Keeping safe

Health and safety are always the most important things to think about before starting any job. Working with electronic circuitry carries its own risks.

### Electricity
Even relatively low voltages are able to deliver a potentially serious electric shock. Therefore, great care should always be taken when working on any circuit. All portable electronic equipment should be routinely **PAT** tested and carefully inspected before every use.

### Heat
The tip of a soldering iron is between 200 °C and 400 °C. This is hot enough to give you a nasty burn as soon as you touch it. It is also more than hot enough to burn paper and or melt plastic. Therefore, you should take great care not to touch the metal barrel and tip of the soldering iron at any time. Should you or someone you are working with suffer a burn, make sure to receive the appropriate first aid immediately.

When not in use, the soldering iron should always be returned to the stand and never simply laid to rest on a workbench. Always keep your workspace clear of any potentially flammable materials. You should also allow the soldering iron to cool down completely before packing it away.

### Fumes
Solder contains a corrosive additive called **flux** that helps the soldering process. However, the flux 'boils off' when soldering and creates irritant fumes. Therefore, a **fume extractor** should always be placed near to the soldering work to draw away fumes effectively.

### Eye protection
Stray wire clippings, molten solder and chemicals used during circuit construction can all be very damaging if they get into your eyes. Therefore, it is important to wear safety glasses at all times.

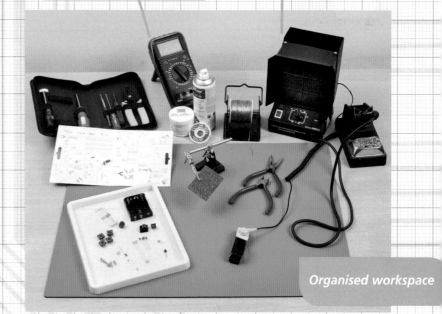

Electrical equipment PAT tested and safety inspected before each use

Extractor fan

Organised workspace

Safety glasses to protect eyes from sparks

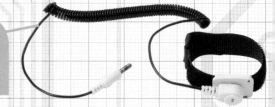

Anti-static wrist band to avoid damage to static sensitive components

### Key terms

**Portable Appliance Testing (PAT)** – used to check the electrical safety of a portable mains appliance

**Flux** – often contained within solder wire to help the soldering process

**Fume extractor** – a device used to draw away the irritant fumes from soldering

## Toolkit

No job can be carried out without the correct tool. Shown below are the main items of equipment needed for the work in this chapter.

| | |
|---|---|
| **Soldering iron and extractor** | The soldering iron is used to make soldered joints. The extractor removes irritant fumes from solder flux  |
| **Side cutters** | Used to cut wires to size and trim component legs 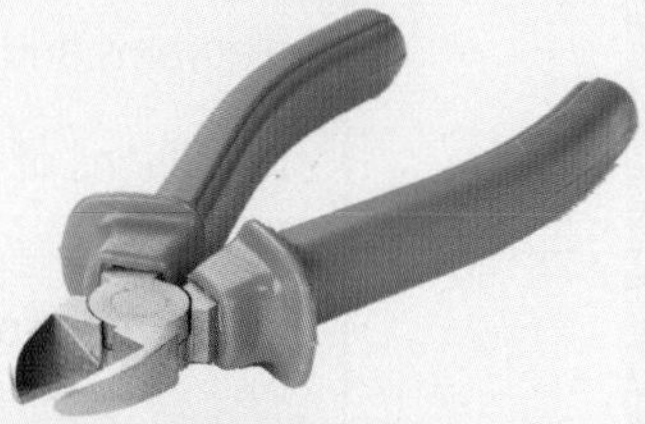 |
| **Long/snipe nosed pliers** | Used to form components to the required shape as well as holding/positioning items 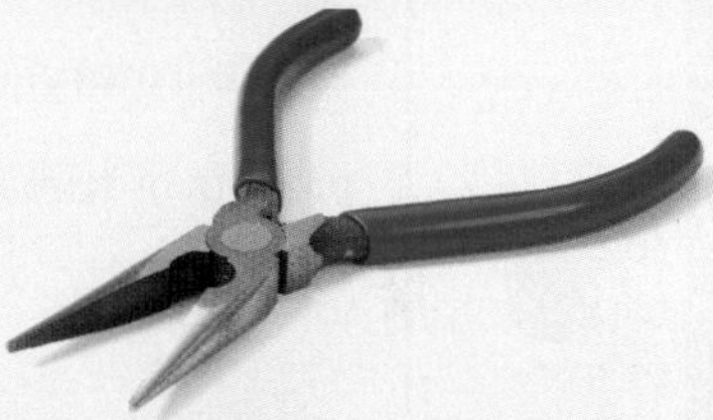 |
| **Wire strippers** | Used to strip insulation from wires and cables  |
| **Screwdrivers/spanners** | Used to open/close cases and enclosures as well as mechanical fixings of components and circuit boards 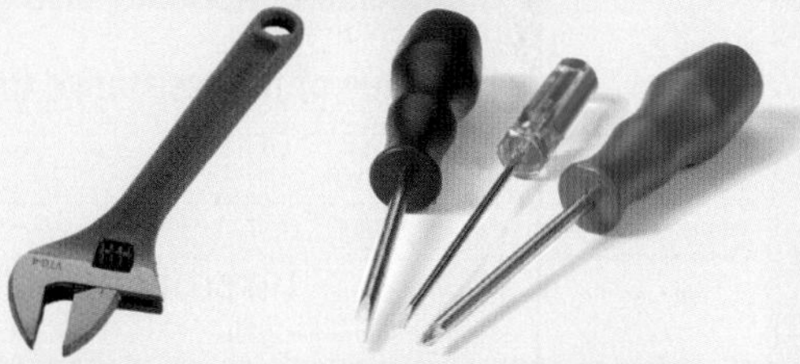 |
| **Trimmer tool** | Used to make adjustments to electronic circuits 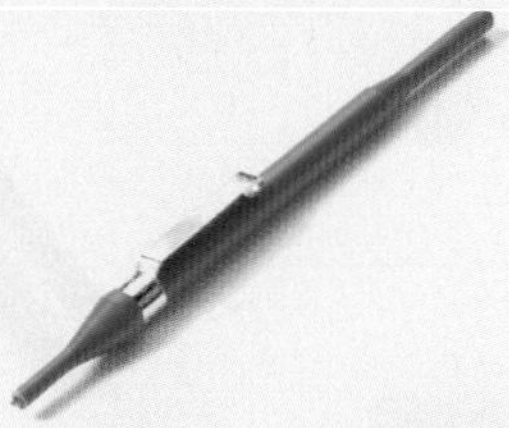 |
| **De-soldering pump** | Used to remove solder when de-soldering 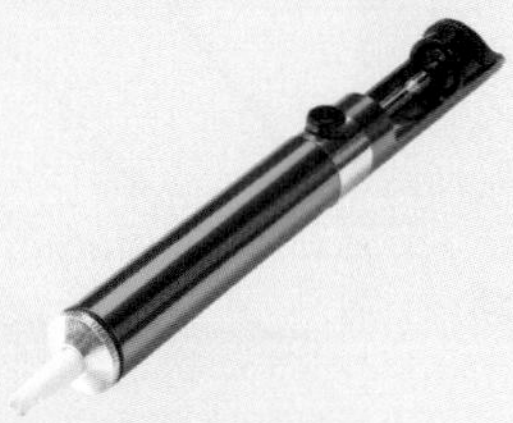 |

# Resistors

## What are they?

**Resistors** are very common electronic components and you'll find them in almost every electronic device. They are labelled with an R in circuit diagrams and are available in huge range of values from just a few Ohms to millions of Ohms! Resistors come in various types, shapes and sizes.

**Fixed resistors** have a specific value that can't be changed and **variable resistors** have a resistance that can be changed, for example by turning a knob (**rotary**) or moving a slider (**linear**). Small variable resistors called **presets** or **trimmers** are used to set up or calibrate a circuit before it goes into use.

### *What else do I need to know?*

The **resistor colour code** is used to tell the value of a resistor from the coloured bands around the component.

The value of a resistor in not always exactly what it should be. The manufacturer normally also gives a **tolerance** – this is the percentage of the value of the resistance that it could be 'out' by.

Fixed resistors

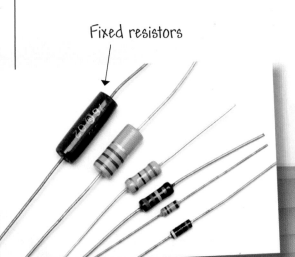

Rotary variable resistor or potentiometer

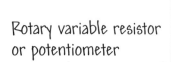

| Type | Circuit symbol |
|---|---|
| **Fixed resistor** | 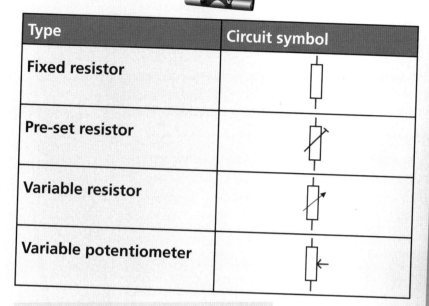 |
| **Pre-set resistor** | |
| **Variable resistor** | |
| **Variable potentiometer** | |

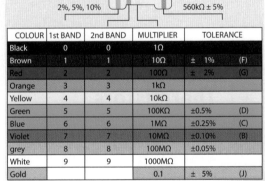

4-Band-Code

2%, 5%, 10%      560kΩ ± 5%

| COLOUR | 1st BAND | 2nd BAND | MULTIPLIER | TOLERANCE | |
|---|---|---|---|---|---|
| Black | 0 | 0 | 1Ω | | |
| Brown | 1 | 1 | 10Ω | ± 1% | (F) |
| Red | 2 | 2 | 100Ω | ± 2% | (G) |
| Orange | 3 | 3 | 1kΩ | | |
| Yellow | 4 | 4 | 10kΩ | | |
| Green | 5 | 5 | 100KΩ | ±0.5% | (D) |
| Blue | 6 | 6 | 1MΩ | ±0.25% | (C) |
| Violet | 7 | 7 | 10MΩ | ±0.10% | (B) |
| grey | 8 | 8 | 100MΩ | ±0.05% | |
| White | 9 | 9 | 1000MΩ | | |
| Gold | | | 0.1 | ± 5% | (J) |

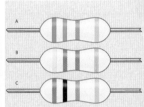

Resistors are used in mixing boards.

## Hands On

Make your own 'colour-code poster' – this can then be put up on the wall to help you identify resistors when you are constructing circuits.

### Quick Check

Use the resistor colour-code table to help you give the values of the three resistors a, b and c.
State the colour code for the following resistors; 10K ±5%, 470Ω ±10% and 6K 8 ±5%.

# Light dependent resistors (LDRs)

## What are they?

LDRs are special resistors whose value changes depending on how much light falls on them. They are used in circuits that need to know the light level such as automatic lights.

### What else do I need to know?

They work by using a special chemical which has a resistance that changes when light falls on it.

LDRs need to be mounted where they are exposed to the light.

| Type | Circuit symbol |
|------|----------------|
| Light dependent resistor | |

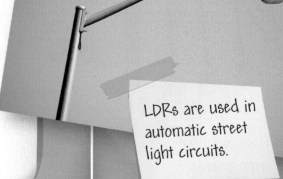

LDRs are used in automatic street light circuits.

# Thermistors

## What are they?

A thermistor is a temperature-sensitive resistor; its resistance changes depending on what the temperature is.

| Type | Circuit symbol |
|------|----------------|
| Thermistor | −t°C |

Thermistors are used in cars to control the heating.

### Hands On

For each type of resistor give an example of what type of circuit they might be used in and why.

### Hands On

Use a multimeter (set to resistance) to measure the resistance of an LDR and thermistor as you vary the light level and temperature. What happenes to the resistance?

# Capacitors

## What are they?

Capacitors store electrical charge like a bucket. They are very common components used in all sorts of circuits.

They come in lots of different varieties, shapes and sizes.

They often have their value (in Farads) written on them. They are labelled 'C' on circuit diagrams.

### What else do I need to know?

They can give a nasty shock – take care!

Some must be put in the right way round.

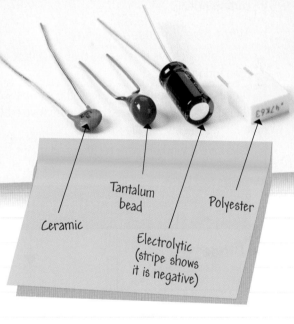

Ceramic

Tantalum bead

Electrolytic (stripe shows it is negative)

Polyester

| Type | Circuit symbol |
|------|----------------|
| Fixed | 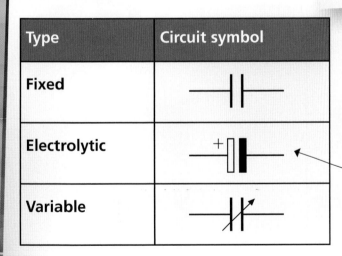 |
| Electrolytic | |
| Variable | |

must be the right way round '+' shows the positive connection

*Keep it safe*

Capacitors can give you a nasty shock – always take care and allow them to discharge before working on a circuit.

# Diodes

## What are they?

Diodes are like one-way valves – only letting current run through them in one direction.

**Zener diodes** are special types of diode that will let current pass through them in the 'wrong' direction, but only after a certain voltage is reached across them. This voltage is often written on the side of the diode's case.

Diodes are also used in **bridge rectifiers** that change alternating current (a.c.) to direct current (d.c.). You'll find these in power supplies.

**Thyristors** are special devices that act like diodes but a third leg called the 'gate' is used to control whether they block current or not.

## What else do I need to know?

Some diodes have glass cases that can crack easily when preparing the leads.

Diodes must be put into a circuit the correct way round – the stripe/band on the case is the negative (cathode) and matches the line on the symbol.

Take care if working with rectifiers on mains power supplies!

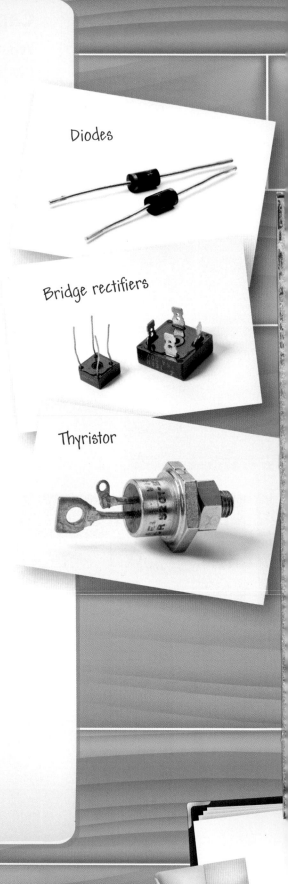

Diodes

Bridge rectifiers

Thyristor

| Type | Circuit symbol |
|------|----------------|
| **Diode** | |
| **Bridge rectifier** | |
| **Zener diode** | |
| **Thyristor** | |

Shorter leg shows the negative leg

Flat shows the negative leg

# Light emitting diodes

## What are they?

Light emitting diodes (LEDs) are special types of diode that give off light. They come in a range of of different shapes, sizes and colours.

### *What else do I need to know?*

Like other diodes they must be inserted the right way round – the flat on the neck of an LED and the shorter leg show the negative leg (cathode).

| Type | Circuit symbol |
|------|----------------|
| Light emitting diode | |

The line shows the negative cathode

Many thousands of tiny LEDs are used in an LED TV.

# Transistors

## What are they?

Transistors can act like tiny electrical switches or amplifiers. Millions of them are also found inside a computer chip. They come in various shapes and sizes depending on the job they have to do.

### What else do I need to know?

They have three connections and normally their model number is printed on the case. It is important that you use the correct model.

Try not to let them get too hot when you solder them as this can damage them.

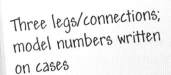

*Three legs/connections; model numbers written on cases*

| Type | Circuit symbol |
|------|----------------|
| BJT | |
| FET | |

# Voltage regulators

## What are they?

Voltage regulators are a special semiconductor device that are designed to give a really accurate output voltage even if the input voltage is not steady.

| Type | Circuit symbol |
|------|----------------|
| Voltage regulator | IN OUT REF |

# Integrated circuits

## What are they?

Integrated circuits (ICs or 'chips' for short) are amazing – inside are tiny circuits all of their own! They are designed to have a specific purpose and there are thousands of different ICs on the market. Many modern circuits use microprocessors – large and often expensive ICs that are able to run programmes and make decisions.

## *What else do I need to know?*

ICs often have lots of legs connected closely together. Take care not to bridge them when soldering and always be careful not to bend the pins when they are being inserted.

Many ICs are sensitive to static – special anti-static packaging/storage should be used as well as a wrist/leg straps being worn when soldering.

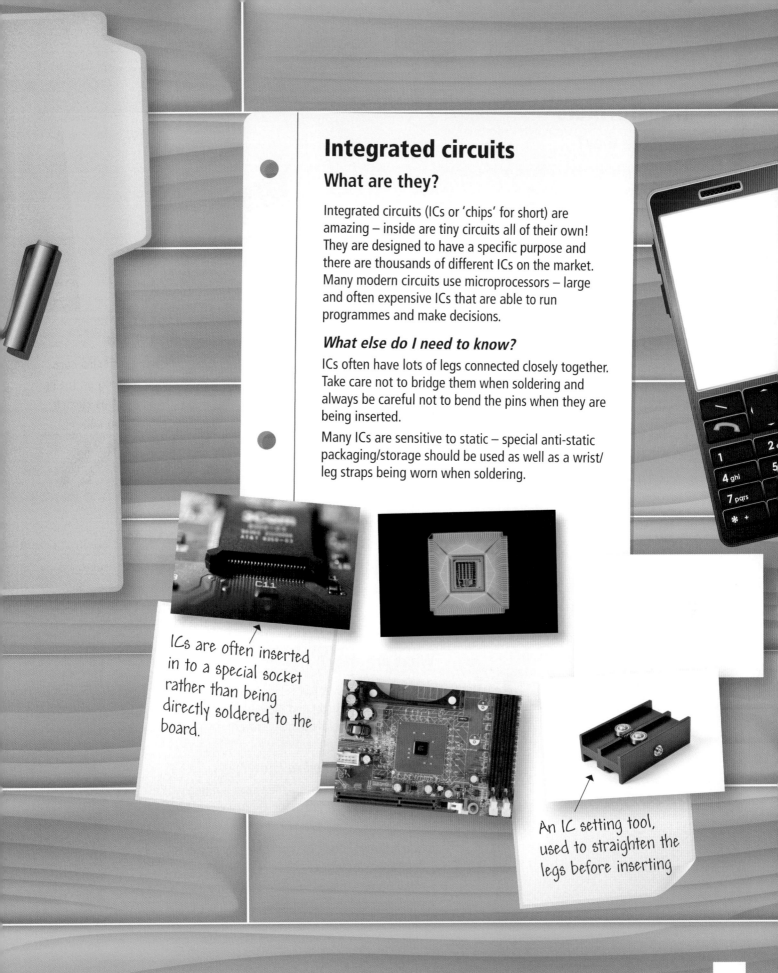

ICs are often inserted in to a special socket rather than being directly soldered to the board.

An IC setting tool, used to straighten the legs before inserting

# Transformers

## What are they?

Transformers are used to step-up or step-down voltages. For example they are often used in power supplies to step-down the high mains voltage to lower voltages used to power all of our gadgets.

### What else do I need to know?

Transformers are often quite large and heavy and need to be mounted securely.

| Type | Circuit symbol |
|------|----------------|
| Transformer | |

**Keep it safe**
Always take extra care when working on mains equipment as electric shocks can kill.

# Fuses

## What are they?

Fuses act like a weak link in a circuit. If something goes wrong in a circuit and there is too much current flowing, they will blow to help prevent damage to the rest of the components.

### What else do I need to know?

Always use the right fuse – they have a rating which is the amount of current at which they will blow.

Fuses can be:

- **quick blow** – don't tolerate much extra current before they blow
- **slow blow** – tolerate a little extra current for a short time before they blow.

# Heatsinks

## What are they?

Heatsinks are a bit like mini radiators attached to components to keep them cool.

### What else do I need to know?

All components get warm when they run but some can get very hot and need to be kept cool or they could be damaged or start operating unreliably.

Thermal compound can be put between the component and the heatsink to help the heat transfer away.

Heat sink and fan on a computer processor

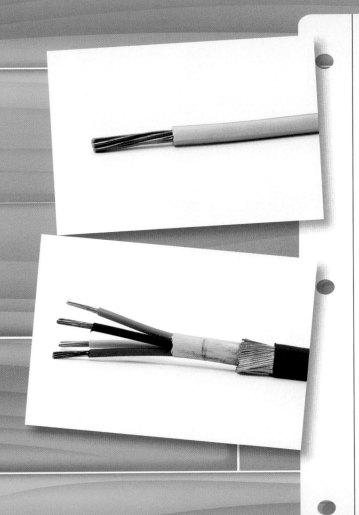

# Cables/wires

## What are they?

Cables are used to connect off-board components to the circuit boards or to connect circuit boards to each other. There are many different types of wires and to select them you must take in to account a number of factors such as how much current will be running through them and the environment which they are being used in. Cables may be single core with a single metal centre or multi-core with several more flexible strands inside.

### What else do I need to know?

The BS 7671 regulations detail how to select the correct wire/cable.

Colour coding, labels, markers and tabs are often used to help identify cables.

Crimping is a solder-less way of attaching wires to connectors where a metal sheath is squeezed (crimped) on to the wire.

**Hands On**

Use the Internet and/or other resources to investigate circuit diagram standards. What are the differences/similarities between them?

Make a poster or reference sheet of the most common components and their symbols. You'll be able to use this as a reference for the rest of the chapter.

# Electronic drawings and diagrams

Electronic engineers use many different types of diagrams to help them construct electronic circuits.

## Circuit diagrams

A schematic or circuit diagram shows how all of the components are connected together. The components are shown as symbols linked together by lines representing the wires.

There are certain standards for how circuit diagrams should look. The two main standards are the British Standard BS 3939 (also known as IEC 60617) and the American ANSI standard Y32.

Each component is labelled with a letter and number combination. The letter tells you what kind of component it is and the number counts up the amount of that type of component in the circuit. Circuit diagrams can be a little confusing, especially when they are complicated. Also, where the components are positioned on the diagram may be different from where they are actually located on the circuit board.

**QUICK CHECK**

What are the names and values of R2, C5, IC1, L1 and B1 in Figure 7.01?

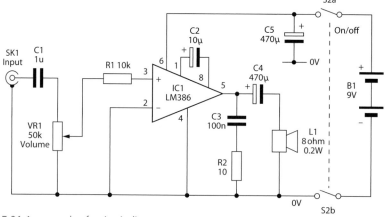

**Figure 7.01** An example of a circuit diagram

Many other types of diagrams might be used when constructing a circuit. These might include assembly diagrams, exploded views, step-by-step guides, and flow charts.

**Hands On**

Use the Internet to find one example of each of the following:

• assembly diagram
• exploded view
• flow chart.

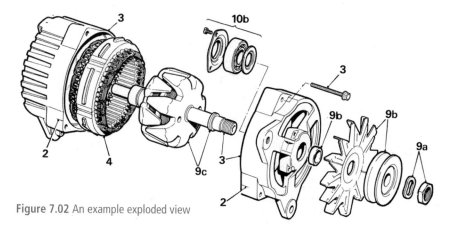

**Figure 7.02** An example exploded view

# Printed circuit boards (PCBs)

Printed circuit boards (PCBs) often have a **silk screen** printed on them. This tells you where the components need to be located on the board. It might also indicate the correct way round that a component needs to be mounted (see the surface mount image below).

## Types of PCB

There are many different types, shapes and sizes of PCB. They hold the components in position and connect them together using tracks. Some of the common PCB types are explained in Table 7.01.

| Type | Description |
| --- | --- |
| **Single sided** | The most common type of PCB that you will assemble. The legs of the components go through holes in the board and are soldered to pads on the track side. This is known as '**through-hole**'. |
| **Multi-layer** | Used for more complicated circuits with several layers of tracks and board sandwiched together to make all of the connections. |
| **Surface mount** | Components are soldered on to the surface of the PCB. Surface-mount components are much smaller and can be hard to solder by hand. Instead they are soldered using a solder paste that is put on the pads and then heated in an oven to melt it and make the connections. |
| **Flexible** | Used when connections need to be made that bend around a product or need to flex/bend when the product is in use. |
| **Film** | A very specialist type of PCB that have a very thin layer (or film) of tracks on a backing board of glass, ceramic or plastic. They are used where circuits must be extremely small and/or complex. |

Table 7.01 Common types of PCB

# Different types of circuit

There are different types of circuits performing lots of different tasks. During this unit you are required to produce a minimum of two assessed electronic circuits from a range of different circuit types. Below are some examples of different types of circuits along with a few pointers to help you construct them.

| Type | Description | Examples | Things to look out for |
|---|---|---|---|
| **Audio circuits** | Circuits that take an audio input and change it in some way. | Amplifier<br>Voice changer<br>Filter<br>Signal processor | Can be sensitive so construct well and use accurate components. Powerful amplifiers can get hot and may require heatsinks |
| **Microprocessor circuits** | These use complex integrated circuits that are programmed to perform a task. | Many more complex circuits now utilise microprocessors<br>PIC (Programmable Integrated Circuit) based circuits | The expensive ICs can be static sensitive and easily damaged<br>Often an IC socket is used rather than soldering the microprocessor directly to the PCB |
| **Sensing circuits** | This type of circuit monitors or senses the environment and then reacts accordingly. | Automatic lights<br>Automatic fan<br>Climate control<br>Rain alarm<br>Moisture detector<br>Process control systems | Often need to be calibrated before being used<br>Sensing components may need to be mounted off-board to monitor the appropriate area |
| **Power supplies** | All circuits need the right power to operate. Power supplies are used to take mains voltage and convert it to what is required for the circuit. | Power supply | Take care with mains voltages and test carefully before applying to the circuit. Always have electrical appliances PAT tested before use |
| **Timer/oscillator** | This type of circuit tends to repeat over-and-over (oscillate) at a set time. Engineers can use this signal to control things over time or count up/down. It can also be used to produce signals and sounds. | Signal generator<br>Siren sound generator<br>Clock<br>Timer<br>Countdown | Careful calibration might be required to get the timing just right |

**Table 7.02** Common types of circuit

# Component and tool storage and preparation

Electronic circuits can contain hundreds or even thousands of different components so it is important that you can easily get hold of the right components when you need them. Similarly, the components need to be in good shape so that they can be soldered easily and effectively. You will often need to use precision tools and equipment, sometimes of a specialist nature. It is also important that these are kept in good condition so that you can work to a high standard.

## Storage

Components are often fragile, small and look similar to each other. It is therefore important to have well-devised storage systems in place. Trays or drawers are often used to safely store components and allow them to be found easily when needed. Some components are sensitive to static electricity so specially designed packaging or storage systems are needed. Over time the metal leads of components can tarnish or oxidise so they need to be kept clean and dry.

**Hands On**

What is the component storage like where you work or study? Could it be improved? If so, how?

**QUICK CHECK**

What would be the consequences if components were not stored properly?

As with all engineering activities it is vital that tools are stored safely and maintained properly. You should check equipment before and after use, and report any problems. Some tasks may require specialist tools – never attempt to 'make do' with an incorrect tool or you could risk damaging the tool, component or worse, yourself!

## Preparation

When assembling an electronic circuit, there are lots of bits and pieces that you will need to hand. For example, tools, solder, wires, PCB and documentation, not to mention all of the components. Therefore, it is essential that you prepare well before you begin.

Completing a preparation sheet (see Figure 7.03) will help you to identify everything you need, as well as giving you a list of the steps you need to take to complete the job.

**Keep It Safe**

Never 'make do' with the wrong tool – this could reduce the quality of your work.

## Work Plan

| Engineer's Name: | | Assembly/Product Name: |
|---|---|---|
| C. G. Tooley | | Battery charger |

| Date: | | Drawing Reference: |
|---|---|---|
| 11th September 2012 | | BC001 |

| Step No. | Description of Operation | Required Tools, Equipment & Resources |
|---|---|---|
| 1 | Prepare work area | All tools and components, BC001 PCB<br><br>Assembly instructions and reference materials |
| 2 | Insert and solder diode D1<br><br>Take care with polarity – negative cathode is shown by stripe on component and PCB | D1 – 1N4007 diode<br><br>Soldering iron/extractor, solder, side cutters, long nosed pliers, PCB holder, work plan |
| 3 | Insert and solder resistors R1-R2 | R1 – 120 Ω 1/4W, R2 – 47 kΩ 1/2 W<br><br>Soldering iron/extractor, solder, side cutters, long nosed pliers, PCB holder, work plan |
| 4 | Insert and solder light emitting diode LED1<br>Take care with polarity – negative cathode shown by short leg and flat on LED neck | LED1 – 3 mm red LED<br><br>Soldering iron/extractor, solder, side cutters, long nosed pliers, PCB holder, work plan |
| 5 | Insert and solder capacitor C1<br>Take care with polarity – negative leg is marked by '-' on component body | C1 – 220 μF radial electrolytic capacitor<br><br>Soldering iron/extractor, solder, side cutters, long nosed pliers, PCB holder, work plan |
| 6 | Mount transistor TR1 on to heatsink; apply thermal compound and secure both to PCB with M3 nut, bolt and lock washer (as exploded diagram). | M3 10 mm bolt, M3 nut, M3 lock washer<br><br>Phillips screwdriver, 3mm spanner<br><br>Exploded diagram |
| 7 | Solder transistor TR1 | TR1 BD135 NPN transistor<br><br>Soldering iron/extractor, solder, side cutters, long nosed pliers, PCB holder, work plan |
| 8 | Insert and solder off-board connectors CN1/2 | CN1/2 two-pin screw connectors<br><br>Soldering iron/extractor, solder, side cutters, long nosed pliers, PCB holder, work plan |
| 9 | Mount PCB in enclosure and connect power socket and battery compartment leads to CN1/2 respectively<br><br>Ensure polarity is correct – red wire is positive, black is negative | Completed PCB assembly<br><br>Phillips screwdriver, Electronic screwdriver (small flat head)<br><br>Work plan, exploded diagram |
| 10 | Assemble, inspect and test | Test and inspection plan<br><br>Power supply, multimeter<br><br>Inspection checklist/report paperwork, faultfinding flow charts etc |

**Figure 7.03** A preparation sheet

# Hand soldering – a step-by-step guide

An essential skill for an electronics engineer is being able to make good-quality soldered joints. It can take a little time to master the skill, but practice really does make perfect. By the time you have completed this chapter, you should be soldering like a pro!

# Hand soldering

| Checklist | | | |
|---|---|---|---|
| **PPE** | **Tools and equipment** | **Consumables** | **Source information** |
| • Eye protection<br>• Extractor<br>• Anti-static strap (if applicable) | • Soldering iron<br>• Side cutters<br>• Long nosed pliers<br>• PCB holder | • Solder | • Circuit reference material |

**1** Put on your PPE, check all of your equipment and prepare your workspace.

**2** Prepare the component legs and insert the component into the PCB, making sure that it is in the right place, the right way round (if applicable) and seated neatly.

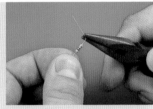

**3** Clean the tip of the iron then tin the tip by melting a small amount of solder onto it. Do this every time you remove it from the holder before making joints.

**4** Place the tip so that it touches both the leg of the component and the pad, then carefully feed in solder to the opposite side of the pad. Remove the solder first and then the soldering iron. A 'perfect' joint will have a shiny volcano shape and should take only a few seconds to make. Always return the iron safely back to the stand after use.

**5** Once the joint has cooled, use side cutters to trim the leg down to just above the top of the soldered joint. When you get more experience you might like to consider trimming the legs down to size before soldering (see Step 2)

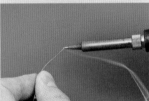

**6** You should now have a good-quality final joint! Once you've made your soldered joints, check out page 161 on good and bad soldered joints – how do yours compare?

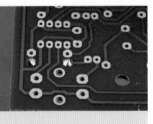

**Hands On**

Use a camera or mobile phone to record a short video of making a soldered joint.

**Hands On**

Make several soldered joints then evaluate your work. Refer to pages 160–61 to help you assess the quality of your work.

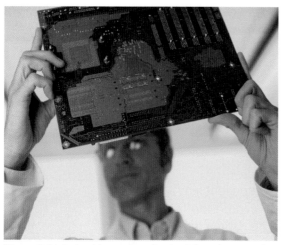

**Figure 7.04** A visual inspection of a circuit board as part of quality control

# Quality control

Once an electronic product has been assembled it is important to check that everything has been done properly. This is known as quality control.

## Visual inspection

The most basic form of quality control is simply looking carefully at the finished board and seeing if you can identify any problems. This is known as visual inspection and many basic assembly errors can be found with these simple checks. If a problem is found at this point it can easily be fixed before it goes any further in the manufacturing process. Here is what to look out for when you carry out a visual inspection.

### Component placement

It is important to check that all the components are placed correctly.

* Have the correct components been put into the right places and are they the correct value?
* Are all of the components seated properly?
* Have they been inserted the correct way round (if they are polarity sensitive)?

### Signs of damage

As part of your quality control checks, look for any signs of overheating, physical damage, cracking, warping, etc.

**Hands On**

Write a visual inspection checklist of all the things to look out for. Now use your checklist to assess one of your completed circuit boards or one of your classmate's.

**Figure 7.05** Poorly seated component

**Figure 7.06** Damaged component

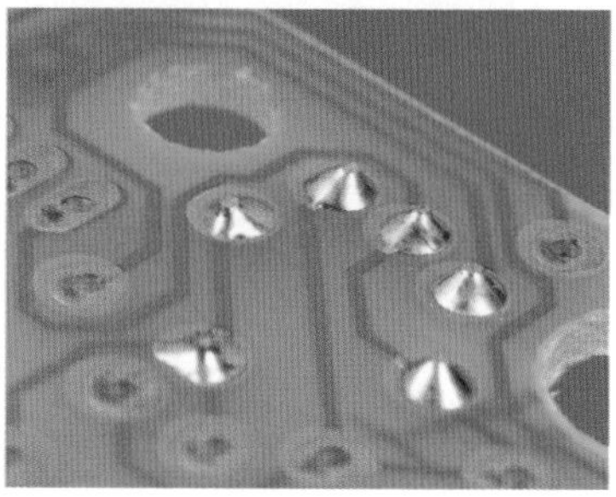

### Quality of soldering

An important part of the visual inspection is to assess the quality of the soldered joints. An ideal soldered joint has a smooth shiny appearance and a 'volcano' shape (see Figure 7.07). Table 7.03 shows some common soldered joint problems.

**Figure 7.07** A perfectly soldered joint

| Type of error | Cause of error | Example |
|---|---|---|
| **Excessive solder** | Too much solder applied | |
| **Missed and incomplete joints** | Too little solder or entirely missing a joint | |
| **Bridged joint** | A pad and/or track are accidentally connected to each other | |
| **Dry joint** | Solder has not properly stuck to either the track or pad properly | |
| **Disturbed joint** | Often caused when components are moved before the soldered joint has cooled completely. They appear dull grey and rough in appearance | |
| **Lifted pad or track** | Too much heat or force can make a pad/track come away from the board | |

**Table 7.03** Some common soldering errors

## De-soldering

If you find a problem during the visual inspection you might need to remove and replace a component by de-soldering it.

To de-solder a component:

1. clean and tin the soldering iron tip
2. apply heat to one side of the existing soldered joint to melt the solder
3. push the plunger of the de-soldering tool down
4. place the nozzle of the de-soldering tool up to the other side of the joint
5. press the button on the de-soldering tool to release the cylinder and extract the molten solder.

You may need to repeat the above steps a few times to remove all of the solder but never force the component out.

**Figure 7.08** De-soldering a component

## CHECK YOUR KNOWLEDGE

1 Which of the following statements is **not** true about resistors?

   a They oppose the flow of current.

   b They are very common.

   c They store electrical charge.

   d Their value is shown by colour bands.

2 LDR stands for:

   a low diameter resistor

   b light dependent resistor

   c large diode rating

   d light deciding resistor

3 Which of the following is not a type of capacitor?

   a electrolytic

   b ceramic

   c polyester

   d potentiometer

4 When a fuse allows peaks of high current without immediately blowing it is known as:

   a quick blow

   b high current limit

   c slow blow

   d tolerant

5 A bridge rectifier is likely to be found in:

   a a filter circuit

   b a microprocessor circuit

   c a power supply circuit

   d an audio circuit

6 Which of the following must be considered when selecting a wire?

   a the working current of the circuit

   b the environment the wire is to be used in

   c BS 7671/IET regulations

   d all of the above

7 The temperature of a soldering iron is:

   a 200°C – 400°C

   b 1,500°C – 1,600°C

   c Less than 150°C

   d About 600°C

8 When components are soldered to the top of the PCB it is known as:

   a top soldered

   b surface mount

   c external soldering

   d miniature assembly

9 The correct steps to making a soldered joint are:

   a tin the tip, make the joint, clean the tip

   b clean the tip, tin the tip, make the joint

   c make the joint, tin the tip, clean the tip

   d tin the tip, clean the tip, make the joint

10 When solder fails to stick completely to the leg of a component and/or pad it is known as:

   a a bridged joint

   b a disturbed joint

   c a dry joint

   d a solder spike

# 8 Making components using hand tools and fitting techniques

This chapter introduces you to a wide range of tools and skills that you will need to work safely on a variety of products. Hand fitting is skilled work that involves attention to detail and careful consideration with every task you do. Learning about hand fitting techniques will give you the expertise to work in many different areas of employment, not just engineering.

In this chapter you will learn about:

- hand fitting tools and equipment
- marking out
- sawing, cutting and shaping materials

- checking your work
- dealing with problems
- making the work area safe and tidy

# KITTING UP

## Keeping Safe

Health and safety is very important when you are using hand tools and fitting techniques. It is important to think carefully about what you are about to do and what might go wrong. You also need to think about the people around you and how they might be affected by your activities. Before starting work, make sure you know where all the safety equipment is that you may need as you work.

To work safely in the workshop make sure you understand:

- all the safety signs and other safety information in the workshop. If you are not sure, ask your trainer or supervisor to explain them to you
- what to do in an emergency, such as using fire doors and turning off machinery power supplies
- all the relevant health and safety rules (see Chapter 1, pages 2–6) and are able to follow them
- how to keep your work area safe and tidy before you start work, when working and how to tidy up after you have finished, putting tools back in the correct place for the next day. Make sure:
  o power leads and air hoses are not a trip hazard
  o work surfaces are clean and free of swarf, grease, oils and tools
  o measuring tools are calibrated and put in a safe place in your work area where they are less likely to be damaged.

Hand tool and fitting activities can be varied, so your PPE needs to be right for each job. You may need:

- **gloves** – protect your hands when lifting and carrying
- **ear defenders** – protect your ears when using noisy power tools
- **safety goggles** – must be worn while using grinders
- **dust mask** – protects your lungs when carrying out jobs that create dust.

*Safety glasses* – protect your eyes from flying objects when using power tools, they also protect your eyes when using maintenance sprays, oils and sealants. Must be worn when using grinders

*Overalls* – protect your skin and clothes from contamination by oils, metal particles and sealants, they can also keep loose or baggy clothing from getting caught in equipment or machinery

*Barrier cream* – protects your hands from dirt and oil and makes them easier to wash

*Safety boots or shoes* – protect your feet from falling objects or tools

### Keep It Safe

Compressed air travels very fast. Any dirt or metal particles blown by it can do a lot of damage, so always wear safety glasses and never point it at anyone.

# Hand fitting tools and equipment

Before starting your fitting activity, get all the tools, materials, equipment and safety equipment you need to complete the job.

Materials and tools are often kept in stores. Your workplace or college will have a system that keeps a check on stock. If a material has run out, you may need to fill in a form before you order anything from the store. Remember to order materials and tools in good time if you need them to complete a job.

**Figure 8.01** Tools, materials and equipment you need to get the job done

## Checking tools before starting work

All the tools and equipment you use must be checked before you use them to make sure they are safe, suitable and in good condition. This is your responsibility, not just your employer's or trainer's.

Poor fitting handle – could fall off and cause you to slip

Missing handle – the tang may stick in your hand as you file

**Checks for files**

Cracked or split handle – may pinch you or give you a splinter

**Figure 8.02** Checks when using files

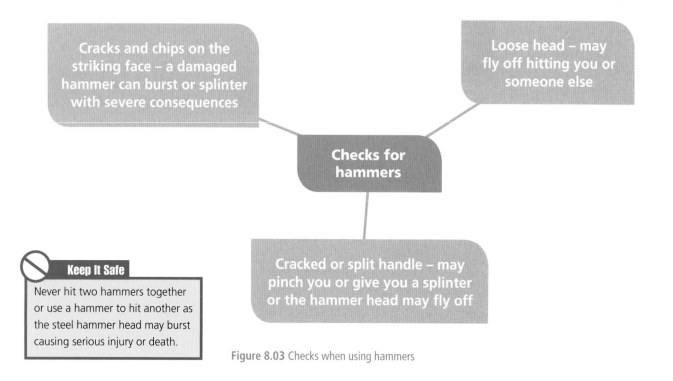

Cracks and chips on the striking face – a damaged hammer can burst or splinter with severe consequences

Loose head – may fly off hitting you or someone else

**Checks for hammers**

Cracked or split handle – may pinch you or give you a splinter or the hammer head may fly off

**Keep It Safe**

Never hit two hammers together or use a hammer to hit another as the steel hammer head may burst causing serious injury or death.

**Figure 8.03** Checks when using hammers

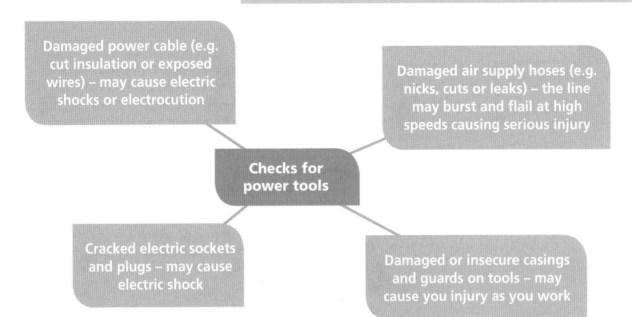

Damaged power cable (e.g. cut insulation or exposed wires) – may cause electric shocks or electrocution

Damaged air supply hoses (e.g. nicks, cuts or leaks) – the line may burst and flail at high speeds causing serious injury

Checks for power tools

Cracked electric sockets and plugs – may cause electric shock

Damaged or insecure casings and guards on tools – may cause you injury as you work

**Figure 8.04** Checks when using power tools

Any tools that are damaged, blunt or unsafe should be dealt with straight away. If you are not sure what to do, always ask your trainer or supervisor.

Sometimes materials are supplied with faults such as cracks or defects that will affect the finished workpiece, so visually inspect them carefully. You also need to make sure you have the correct specification of material for the work you are doing. Checking its colour code or code number will make sure you have got it right.

A visual inspection involves looking for:

- **Cracks** – these can seriously weaken materials so any with cracks should not be used. Cracks can be formed as the metal is cold rolled in the factory.
- **Cavities** – these are also called blowholes and pinholes, caused by poor metal casting. They are not as serious as cracks but can often be bigger below the surface so take care.
- **Oxidisation and corrosion** – this can weaken materials and cause a poor surface finish. It is often found on poorly stored or old stock.
- **Distortion** – material could be warped, twisted or bent as it is transported and handled making it very hard to produce a component to the correct specification.

> **Key terms**
>
> **Oxidisation** – metal is affected by the oxygen in the air (moisture also plays a part) causing steel to rust and copper, aluminium and brass to tarnish
>
> **Corrosion** – the damage caused to a material when chemically attacked by a substance
>
> **Distortion** – as metals are worked they can lose their shape and bend and warp out of shape

> **Hands On**
>
> Make a list of all the tools, materials and equipment you need to produce a finished component you have recently worked.

## QUICK CHECK

1 What should you check files and hammers for before use?
2 Where do you find the tools and materials that you need to start working?
3 How do you check the tools you are about to use to make sure they are safe?
4 Find out what personal protective equipment you have where you work extra to the safety boots, safety glasses and overalls that you already wear.

# Marking out

Marking out is very important as it sets out where everything should be on the **workpiece**, so it is essential not to make mistakes. Always double-check what you have done before you start to cut and shape the work. Table 8.01 shows some of the marking out tools you will need.

| | | |
|---|---|---|
| **Steel rule** |  | Normally 150 mm or 300 mm long but can be 75 mm or 1 m. Often marked every 0.5 mm. A useful tool for checking and laying out work. Can also be used to check for straightness |
| **Tape measure** |  | Can measure longer distances than the steel rule for larger workpieces but may not be as accurate |
| **Scriber** |  | Scribers are used to scratch fine lines on the workpiece when marking out. |
| **Plate protractor** | 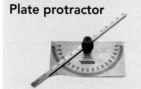 | Used to measure an angle on the workpiece. Always measure and set from **datum** edge. Angles should be marked on workpieces with a scriber |
| **Centre punch** |  | Used to make a neat, small dint that helps to position a drill or mark a point |
| **Engineer's tri-square** |  | Helps mark out lines at 90° to another face or datum. Made of a stock and blade. The stock should always be positioned on the datum and the measurement made using the blade |
| **Scribing block** |  | A scriber mounted on an adjustable stand. The scriber can be set to a fixed height to ensure accuracy when marking out. Used on a surface table. Sometimes called a surface gauge |
| **Dividers** | 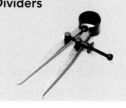 | Used for scribing circles and curves accurately, or for stepping of distances along a datum line |

Table 8.01 Marking out tools you may need

| | |
|---|---|
| **Trammels**  | Used for drawing large diameter circles that are too big to be drawn by dividers. One head may be fitted with a fine adjuster to make setting easier |
| **Vernier height gauge**  | Used when greater accuracy is needed than is possible with a steel rule and scribing block. When well maintained they are accurate to 0.02 mm |
| **Combination set**  | A set of four instruments in one: a steel rule, centre finder, tri-square and protractor. Not always as accurate as single tools especially if not looked after |
| **Radius gauges**  | Often come in sets like a bunch of keys. They can be used as a template to scribe internal or external radiuses. Can also be held against a radius for checking purposes. Handy for marking radiuses that are too small for dividers |

Table 8.01 Marking out tools you may need (continued)

Workholding or support devices you may need to mark out are listed in Table 8.02.

| | |
|---|---|
| **Surface table**  | A surface table is an accurate flat surface that measuring and marking out equipment is used on. The flatness of the plate allows scribing blocks or height gauges to scribe lines a precise distance from the table surface |
| **Angle plate** | Angle plates are 'L' shaped blocks that can be used to clamp or position work 90° to the surface table. Slots are machined in the block so that the workpiece can be bolted to it or it can be bolted to a machine table |
| **Vee block** | Normally come as a pair. Used to hold and position round bars for marking or drilling. Round bars can be clamped in a horizontal or vertical position using the block's matching clamp |

Table 8.02 Workholding or support devices

| Parallels | Used to raise the workpiece accurately to help either with marking out or clamping while drilling. They always come as matched pairs and are ground with square corners and faces parallel |
|---|---|
| Screw jacks | Useful in supporting uneven shapes (e.g. casting) while marking out |
| Toolmaker's clamp | Toolmaker's clamps are used for setting and holding work in place while marking out. The screw farthest from the jaws can be tightened to give a very firm grip without marking the workpiece |

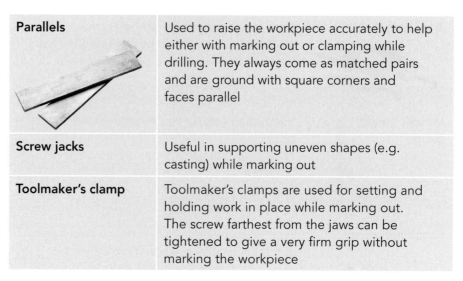

Table 8.02 Workholding or support devices (continued)

## Deburring

Before working you need to clean and **deburr** your workpiece.

### Cleaning and deburring

Remove all traces of protective oils and greases, and swarf or metal particles from the workpiece. Use a rag or industrial tissue to wipe and clean the material. If it is very dirty or oily, you might have to use a degreasant. Remember to wear the appropriate PPE when cleaning, as degreasants can irritate your skin and have other harmful effects.

Once the workpiece has been cleaned, then you can deburr it. A variety of tools can be used depending on the type of burr and the shape of the workpiece.

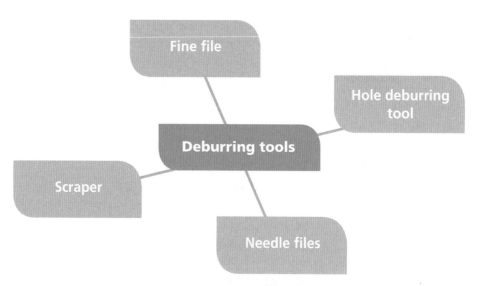

Figure 8.05 Tools you may need when deburring

## Types of datum

Once the workpiece is cleaned and deburred you can establish your datums. Datums are your workpiece reference points so they must be right as the accuracy of your work depends on them. Datums are often written on the drawings, so check here first.

If no datums are specified then think carefully how you are going to mark out the component ensuring all necessary features are covered. If you're working on a complex component, you may need a planning sheet so you don't miss any important features.

There are three types of datum or workpiece reference points. You can use:

- **Edge or face datum** – this is taken from a true (accurate) edge or flat face that is filed true. For a complex component three faces may be needed, 90° apart. This type of datum is very useful as it allows accurate marking out using a surface table. This could be the side and face of a rectangular bar. The other datum could be the sawn end that may need to be filed true, checking with a square.
- **Linear datum** – this is often a line marked on the component. It could be a line through the centre of the workpiece or a line marked in a convenient position for a range of features such as a row of holes.
- **Point datum** – this is the simplest datum, referenced from a single point, i.e. a hole or mark (e.g. a scribed cross or punch mark). It is often used on castings where the cored hole position is the most important feature so must be central.

To make the marking out clearer on the workpiece **marking blue** can be used to put a thin layer of blue colouring on the workpiece surface.

## Templates

You can use a template to mark out complex components or profiles that would be hard to mark out individually. They can also be used where the same workpiece is needed several times to ensure each workpiece looks the same.

Templates can be made of paper or card. Steel templates, however, are more accurate and last longer.

Card and paper templates can be produced using CAD and are stuck on the material to be marked out. Use a dot punch to lightly mark the workpiece through the template. Check that every detail has been transferred onto the workpiece, as it is easy to miss features out when using this method.

Metal templates are easier to use as they can be scribed round without damaging their edges. However they are harder to position on the workpiece and so will need to be pinned, screwed or clamped in place using a toolmaker's clamp. Always check the workpiece carefully to make sure all the features are marked and the template has not slipped.

**Key term**

**Marking blue** – a strong dye dissolved in a methanol base, which dries very quickly at room temperature

 **Keep It Safe**

Marking blue contains methanol, which is highly flammable and toxic. It must be used in a well-ventilated area where nothing can cause it to catch fire.

**Quick Tip**

Things to remember while you mark out.

- Always measure from datums to make sure your work is accurate.
- Always try to use a surface table and Vernier height gauge.
- Use an angle plate or Vee block to ensure the workpiece is upright on the surface table.
- Use a steel rule to check measurements before cutting.

**Did You Know**

Hardened round templates with a hole in the centre are called toolmaker's buttons. They can be used to mark and file radiuses on the corners of the workpiece and are clamped or screwed in place. Their hardened surface is not damaged when filed.

**Hands On**

Practise marking out lines and point positions using a height gauge. Afterwards, check your work using a steel rule to make sure you have used the height gauge correctly.

**QUICK CHECK**

1 What are the three types of datum used for marking out a workpiece?
2 Why is it important to always measure from a datum?
3 How should a workpiece be prepared before marking out?

**Figure 8.06** Hacksaw

# Sawing, cutting and shaping materials

Once the workpiece has been marked out, it then needs to be shaped to meet the correct specification. It is roughly cut to shape using a saw then filed until it is correct.

## Hacksaws

Hacksaws are designed to cut metal. They can often be fitted with a range of blade sizes. The blade can be rotated through 90° so that long cuts can be made without the hacksaw frame hitting the workpiece.

If you need to cut internal shapes you can remove the blade from the frame, put it into a drilled hole in the work and then reattach it to the frame to begin sawing.

### Hacksaw blades

Hacksaw blades are normally made from three different types of material. Make sure you have chosen the correct blade for the material you are working with.

- **High carbon steel** – these are cheap blades that are used to cut softer materials but don't last long when sawing steel. They are tough and hard to break.
- **High speed steel** – these are very hard and brittle, and easily shatter if twisted when cutting. They are not very easy to use if you are a beginner but they last a long time and cut well.
- **Bi-metal blades** – these have high speed steel teeth welded onto a carbon steel backing. They are more expensive than the other types of blade but have long-lasting teeth and are tough and hard to break.

Some experienced fitters prefer the solid high speed steel blades, as they allow more control in skilled hands, enabling cuts to be made closer to the line.

Hacksaw blades also come in four tooth sizes or 'pitches'. The most common pitches are 14, 18, 24 and 32 teeth per inch (TPI) or per 25 mm.

When using a hacksaw at least three teeth should be in contact with the work at all times. So if you were sawing a 3 mm plate, the coarsest blade selected should be 24 TPI. If the material you are cutting is too thin to get 3 teeth in contact, even with a 32 TPI blade, you can angle the handle of the saw down and cut in an upward direction. This prevents teeth snagging on thin metal.

| Imperial pitch | Metric pitch | Use |
| --- | --- | --- |
| 14 TPI | 1.8 mm | Soft metals and polymers (plastics) that are quite thick in section |
| 18 TPI | 1.4 mm | Tough metals that have a thick section and soft materials with a medium section |
| 24 TPI | 1.0 mm | Tough medium section metals and thin soft materials. Also good for brittle polymers such as acrylic. A good general purpose blade |
| 32 TPI | 0.8 mm | For very hard materials and thin section tough metals such as steel. Good for accurate cutting |

**Table 8.03** Different pitches for hacksaw blades

## Using the hacksaw

First of all select the correct blade for the material you are cutting. If you are cutting lots of different materials, or are new to hacksawing, then a good all-round blade is a bi-metal, 24 TPI (1 mm) pitch blade.

Before cutting, check the blade is:

- tight in the frame
- the correct type for the material being cut
- the right way round.

Then follow these five simple steps.

1. Fit the blade to the frame. The teeth should point away from the handle.
2. Tighten the blade by hand until the blade is taut. You should not be able to flex the blade or twist it. Old saw frames can bend, which means the blade is not tight enough to keep the cut straight.
3. If you are right-handed, stand facing the vice and hold the saw in your right hand. This hand provides the power for the cutting. (Do it the opposite way round if you're left-handed.)
4. Use your left hand to hold the front of the saw, helping to steer it and hold it straight.
5. Concentrate on moving the saw forward and back, slowly and with control. Use the full length of the blade and try not to push down too hard. As you gain in skill and confidence, apply more pressure to speed up your cutting.

**Did You Know**

Hard metals (e.g medium carbon steel and stainless steels) need fine blades. Aluminium and brass are easier to cut with coarse blades as they do not clog up so easily.

**Did You Know**

There is often an arrow on the blade showing which way the blade should point.

Tips for cutting:

- Make a trial saw cut (or kerf) when starting the cut. This will mark your position and stop the blade from sliding over your work.
- If possible always cut straight down and not at an angle. Move the work in the vice to make this possible.
- If you have to change blades before finishing the cut, do not put the new blade in the old cut. The new blade will be thicker as it is not worn yet. Instead start a new cut by the side of it.
- Cut as close to the line as possible. This will save on filing.
- Remember that there is another side to the metal so make sure you are cutting down the line on the back face too.
- You can add a second blade to a hacksaw to make a wider cut or slot.

## Files

Files are used for a range of tasks, from roughing down to finishing flat and curved surfaces. You therefore need the right type of file for the job. Files are named by their length, grade of cut and shape.

The length of a file refers to the cutting surface and does not include the handle. Make sure the handle is fitted before use.

| Type of file | Use |
|---|---|
| **Flat file** | Used for large flat surfaces. It tapers in thickness and width at the front |
| **Hand file** | Has a safe edge with no teeth so that you can use it up to a shoulder without marking the workpiece |
| **Half round file** | Used to file the inside of curved surfaces |
| **Round file** | Used for opening up holes or filing internal radiuses. Sometimes called a rat-tail file |
| **Square file** | Used for widening square holes |
| **Three square file** | Used for filing square corners. Sometimes called a triangular file |
| **Knife file** | Used for tapered narrow slots |

Table 8.04 Types of file and their uses

| Grade | Pitch of teeth | Use |
|---|---|---|
| Rough | 1.8 – 1.3 mm | Used on soft metals and polymers (plastics) where material needs to be removed quickly |
| Bastard | 1.6 – 0.65 mm | Used for general roughing out work |
| Second cut | 1.4 – 0.60 mm | Used for roughing out tough materials and finishing soft materials |
| Smooth | 0.8 – 0.45 mm | Used for finishing and draw filing where a good surface finish is needed |
| Dead smooth | 0.5 – 0.25 mm | Not often used except on tough steels where a good finish and high accuracy is needed |

Table 8.05 Common grades of file and their uses

Files can also have double or single cut teeth. Double cut teeth are the most common and are more efficient at removing metal. However they can be damaged by harder tough materials, so it is better to use single cut files for these materials.

## Three steps for good filing

### Step 1 – Hold tight

When filing, most work has to be held firmly in place. This is often done using a bench vice. To file flat, the vice must be at the correct height. This makes the file easier to control. The top of the vice should be at elbow height when you are standing in front of the bench. Don't have too much metal sticking out of the vice as it can vibrate, making **chatter** marks.

### Step 2 – Stand right

Stand almost sideways to the bench with your feet shoulder-width apart. If you are right-handed, your left foot should be nearest the bench. As you use the file, the line the file moves in should be roughly in line with your right toes.

### Step 3 – Grip right

If you are right-handed, grip the file handle in your right hand and support the front of the file with your left. As with the hacksaw, the right hand is for power, the left hand to steer and control. As you file your weight should gradually move from the front of the file to the back. This stops the file rocking and making a curved surface. Check as you file to ensure sure you do not take too much metal off.

## Looking after your files

Tips for looking after your files.

- Keep the file clean with a special wire brush called a file card.
- Keep your files in a rack so the teeth are not damaged.
- Never file quickly as it just wears you and the files out. Use slow even strokes, using the full length of the file.

**Did You Know**

Needle files are very small files for precise work.

Single-cut file

Double-cut file

Figure 8.07 Single and double cut teeth

**Key term**

**Chatter** – the name given to a poor surface finish when a tool vibrates on the surface rather than cutting

Figure 8.08 A worker standing in the correct position at a vice ready to file

**Quick Tip**

Use soft jaws with the vice to protect your work from getting damaged.

- Push the file a little more lightly on the backward stroke as the file only cuts on the forward stroke.
- Try to break in new files on soft materials to prevent damage to teeth.

## Using a file correctly

### Straight filing

This is where you file straight across the workpiece.

- The file should be held flat and not rocked.
- One hand should hold the file by the handle.
- The other hand should be supporting the other end of the file to help guide it and keep it level.

### Flat filing

Flat filing uses a process called cross filing to achieve a flat surface.

- Use a flat file because the tapering of the cutting edges means you only remove metal from where you want to.
- Hold the workpiece in a vice.
- File at 45° to the front of the workpiece. As you work, check regularly that you are filing evenly.
- Change the direction of the file by 90° every so often, so that you are 45° the other way from the front face of the workpiece.
- Check your workpiece is flat by holding a steel rule, straight edge or the blade of a tri-square against it.

### Drawfiling

Drawfiling is done to finish a component. The workpiece should be filed down until it is nearly completed. Then it can be drawfiled to provide an accurate and smooth finish. When drawfiling, the teeth are cutting 90° to the way they normally do, so a fine finish is produced.

- Grasp the file firmly at both ends.
- Move the file up and down the workpiece, rubbing with the file 90° to the way it is normally held. This way the teeth only take a very small cut in a similar way to how a carpenter uses a spoke shave.

Make sure the file is kept clean with a file card or wire brush to stop pins (clogging) in the file. Otherwise, you may scratch the workpiece and ruin the finish.

When drawfiling it is hard to keep the pressure even at the ends of the surface. Be careful not to make a hollow in the middle of the workpiece. To get an even better finish, hold a strip of emery paper flat along the file and then drawfile with the emery in contact with the workpiece.

## Filing an external curve or radius

The easiest way to file an external radius is to treat it as a multi-sided shape or polygon.

- Mark out the radius using either a radius gauge or dividers.
- Saw off as much waste material as you can, to save time.

- Start from a datum edge, if possible, to make the work easier to keep square.
- Clamp the workpiece in a vice using soft jaws.
- Straight file a flat until it touches the marked radius line, keep your filing flat as you go. You can use the datum as a reference by watching where the flat you are filing intersects the datum. If it is straight, then you are filing flat. If it turns to the left, you are filing a downward slope and to the right an upward one.
- Turn the workpiece in the vice and straight file another flat until it touches the marked radius.
- You will produce two corners or points for each flat you file. These corners need to be removed so should be straight filed down to the line as well.
- Blend the small flats into a curve once the radius is formed from the flats.
- Straight file in the direction of the curve. Allow the file to follow the radius, raising the handle as the file is pushed forward. A few strokes should sort this out.
- Drawfile the surface with a fine file to give it a good finish.

> **Did You Know**
>
> Using a long file when drawfiling makes it easier to keep the surface flat, as it is easy to see when the file is not level.

### Filing an internal curve or radius

To produce internal curves or radiuses, either use a half round file or round file. To file evenly, twist the file about 30° during the stroke. You will need to switch direction from clockwise to anticlockwise with every stroke of the file.

## Preparing the workpiece datums, using a file and marking out

| Checklist | | | |
|---|---|---|---|
| PPE | Tools and equipment | Consumables | Source information |
| • Safety boots<br>• Overalls<br>• Barrier cream | • Bench vice<br>• Engineer's tri-square<br>• Flat bastard file<br>• Flat second cut file<br>• Steel rule<br>• Surface plate table<br>• Angle plate<br>• Vernier height gauge | • Workshop tissue or rag | • Engineering drawing |

1 Clean and inspect the workpiece, checking it is suitable for use (the correct size and free of defects).

2 Deburr the mild steel bar using the straight filing technique, holding the workpiece in a bench vice.

3

Flat file to make the first datum edge using a steel rule to check for straightness, finish by draw filing.

4

Use an engineer's tri-square to check the second datum edge to see if it is square.

5

Flat file the second datum, checking with a square, and drawfile to finish.

6

Place the datum down on the surface table with the work against an angle plate and mark out using a Vernier height gauge.

## Chiselling

!  **Keep It Safe**

Safety glasses should always be worn when using chisels.

Cold chisels are effective cutting tools that can be used for a variety of work. They are made of high carbon steel, and hardened and tempered at the cutting edge. The end that is hit with a hammer is left soft to prevent it chipping when stuck by a hammer.

| Type of chisel | Use |
|---|---|
| **Flat chisel** | Used to cut and remove metal from a surface by chipping (which should always be done towards the centre of the workpiece). Choose a chisel that is slightly wider than the material you're cutting. Flat chisels can also be used to cut metal plate in a vice. They can also cut internal or external profiles in sheet metal on a cutting block |
| **Cross cut chisel** | Used for cutting grooves or slots, such as keyways. They can also cut grooves in the surface of a workpiece, allowing a flat chisel to cut wide areas |
| **Half round chisel** | Used for cutting circular grooves such as oil ways in bearings. They can be used to reposition a wrongly placed pilot hole |
| **Diamond point chisel** | Used to clean out the corners of recesses. Also used to correct the position of centre punch marks |

Table 8.06 Types of chisel and their uses

## Lapping

Lapping is a method used to produce a good surface finish or an accurate fit between two parts.

A rough (abrasive) paste or slurry called lapping (or grinding) paste is used in the lapping process. The grit size of the abrasive is chosen to suit the required finish.

The surfaces of the components to be lapped should be cleaned to achieve a good fit. Lapping grinding paste should be applied to one surface and the two components rubbed together carefully. The components should be moved over each other evenly. Check your work regularly. When you have an even finish, stop lapping.

## Engineer's hammers

Various hammers and mallets are used for hand fitting activities such as riveting, striking marking tools such as letter stamps and centre punches, helping with setting and assembly and chiselling.

| Type of hammer | Description | Use |
|---|---|---|
| **Ball pein hammer** | Has a hardened steel head fitted to a wooden handle. Comes in sizes ranging from 0.1 kg to 1.5 kg. Has a flat striking surface known as the face and a hemispherical striking surface known as the pein | Designed for riveting but make a good general purpose hammer |
| **Cross pein hammer** | Has a hardened steel head fitted to a wooden handle. Comes in sizes ranging from 0.1 kg to 1 kg. Has a flat striking surface known as the face and a thin chisel-like striking surface with a rounded top known as the cross pein | This is used for riveting against an edge or in a tight corner. A small component can also be hammered while it is held between finger and thumb as the cross pein slides between them. It is also known as the Warrington hammer |
| **Copper hide mallet** | It has a soft iron head that has replaceable faces of copper and leather. The soft faces are less likely to damage or mark the work | Used while setting and assembling equipment or workpieces |
| **Soft faced mallet** | It has a face made of rubber or tough polymers such as nylon | Used against soft metals such as aluminium to reduce the chance of bruising or marking components |
| **Dead blow mallet** | Very similar to a soft faced mallet but the head contains dense metal pieces that can move inside it. This prevents the head from bouncing and helps to deliver a stronger blow | Used whilst setting and assembling equipment or workpieces. The soft faces are less likely to damage or mark the work and is easier to use in small spaces |

**Table 8.07** Types of hammer and their uses

Misusing or being careless with a hammer can be very dangerous. Before using one, make sure:

- you have enough room for a clear swing
- no one is behind you
- the handle is clean and not oily or greasy
- the shaft is not split or damaged
- the head is secure and tight
- the head is not cracked or has chips missing.

A hammer with a hardened head should never be hit against another hammer or against a hardened component as it may burst or shatter with serious consequences.

## Drilling

When hand fitting, you will drill most of the holes you need with either a bench drill or a pillar drill.

A bench drill is a freestanding machine and can be used for:

- drilling
- reaming
- countersinking
- spot facing
- counterboring.

**Key terms**

**Chuck** – the special clamping device fitted to the spindle of a drill to hold twist drills and other tools

**Morse taper** – a taper on the end of tools such as drills and reamers that is used to hold the tool in place. It self-grips and can hold more firmly than a chuck

Normally cutting tools are held in the **chuck** but tools with a shank larger than 13 mm may have to be held directly in the machine spindle using a **Morse taper**.

Bench drills and pillar drills are known as sensitive drills. The drills have been designed using a rack and pinion system to lower the drill into the work. This allows a skilled operator to be able to judge when a drill is about to break through the work, when the drill needs to be cleared of swarf or when it needs to be sharpened.

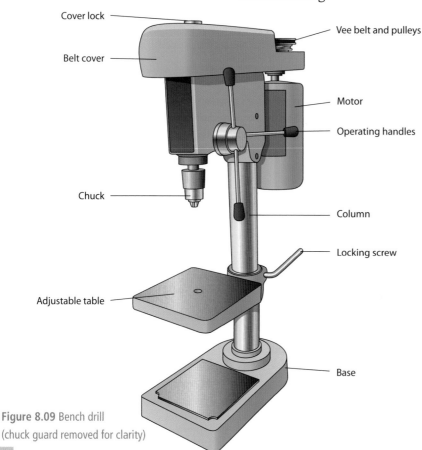

Cover lock
Belt cover
Chuck
Adjustable table
Vee belt and pulleys
Motor
Operating handles
Column
Locking screw
Base

**Figure 8.09** Bench drill (chuck guard removed for clarity)

Drilling machines have a table that can be raised or lowered. The work is clamped to the table, which can be swivelled to adjust the angle. Use an engineer's tri-square against the quill of the pillar drill to check the angle is correct before starting.

Bench drills have a range of different **spindle** speeds. The most common way of changing the speed is to move the position of the Vee belt on a pair of stepped pulleys. Some drilling machines also have a simple gearbox allowing high and low speed ranges.

The tools below are the cutting tools commonly used with a drilling machine.

| Tool | Description | Use |
|---|---|---|
| **Twist drill** | A standard drill with twisted flutes (grooves) used to drill holes. It may have a parallel shank held by a drill chuck or it may have a Morse tapered shank to hold it true | Used to drill holes. In small sizes come in 0.1 mm steps. Over 13 mm in diameter they normally have a Morse tapered shank |
| **Centre drill** | A short rigid drill that has a small diameter point that then tapers at 60° out to a larger diameter | Used to start holes, especially on circular work, as it does not wander from the centre of the workpiece |
| **Countersink drill** | A short ridged tool with an angle cutting edge of either 60° or 90°. They should be run at slow speeds to avoid chatter | Used to set flush countersunk screws and for countersinking before riveting |
| **Counterbore** | A tool with a flat bottom which can be used for **spot facing**. A counterbore is a short ridged tool with a location pin and a flat cutting face | Used to make a recess for cap-headed and cheese-headed screws |
| **Machine reamer** | This tool can either have a parallel shank or a Morse tapered shank. The body of a machine reamer is ground parallel with a short chamfer on the end. This chamfer forms the cutting lips on the ends of the blades (see pages 190–92 for more information) | Used for producing more accurate holes with a better surface finish than can be produced by a twist drill |

**Table 8.08** Types of cutting tools used with a drilling machine and their uses

**Key term**

**Chuck key** – a chuck key is a special tool that is used to open and close the jaws of the chuck to grip and change cutting tools such as twist drills

| | |
|---|---|
| **Drilling vice** <br>  | Must be positioned carefully and clamped down when drilling large holes (can be hand held for smaller ones). Drilling vices are the most useful clamping device on a drilling machine. They are easy to use and give a firm grip on the workpiece |
| **Angle plate** <br>  | Can be used to clamp large and irregular workpieces to the drilling table. The workpiece can be set upright using a tri-square |
| **Vee block** <br>  | Can be used with clamps to hold cylindrical components |
| **Clamping set** <br>  | A set of special nuts and bolts in different sizes. Used for clamping work directly to the drilling table or for clamping other workholding devices to the table (e.g. the drilling vice and the angle plate). The bolts are specially shaped to match the grooves in the drilling table |

**Table 8.09** Types of workholding devices used with drilling machines

## Setting up a drilling machine

| Checklist | | | |
|---|---|---|---|
| PPE | Tools and equipment | Consumables | Source information |
| • Safety boots<br>• Overalls<br>• Safety glasses<br>• Barrier cream | • Twist drills<br>• Small drill for pilot<br>• Drilling vice<br>• Parallels<br>• Centre punch<br>• Ball pein hammer<br>• Deburring tool | • Cutting oil | • Drilling speed table |

**1** Check the machine is isolated from the power.

**2** Set the correct spindle speed for the drilling operation. Check the machine table is true and free of swarf and dirt.

**3**

Set up the workholding device on the machine table. If using a small vice, these can be easier to set up and check on the bench first.

**4**

Set up the drill and be sure the machine spindle can cut to the required depth. Alter the table height if necessary. You may have to remove the vice before doing this as it may slide off or make the table too heavy to move.

**5**

Check all guards are secure and in place.

**6** Turn on the power and test emergency stop operation.

## Steps for successful drilling

| Checklist | | | |
| --- | --- | --- | --- |
| **PPE** | **Tools and equipment** | **Consumables** | **Source information** |
| • Safety boots<br>• Overalls<br>• Safety glasses<br>• Barrier cream | • Twist drills<br>• Small drill for pilot<br>• Drilling vice<br>• Parallels<br>• Centre punch<br>• Ball pein hammer<br>• Deburring tool | • Cutting oil | • Drilling speed table |

**1** Mark the hole position with a centre punch. The punch mark should be big enough for the central chisel edge of the drill point.

**2** Select a pilot drill that is just a little larger than the width of the chisel edge of the drill point.

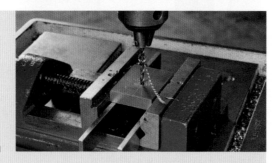

**3** Make a trial cut with the pilot drill, just spotting the centre punch mark. Check that the hole is in the correct position. A circle should be drawn to the same size as the hole and another a little smaller so that, before the drill has gone too far, it is easy to check its position for accuracy. If it needs correcting, the punch mark can be drawn over to the correct position with a large centre punch or half round chisel.

**4** Once the pilot hole has been drilled, isolate the power, then fit the right sized drill and change the spindle speed (see Table 8.10 on page 185 for guidance).

> **Key term**
>
> **Feed** – is the process of moving the rotating twist drill or cutting tool into the workpiece to drill a hole or remove material

**5**

Drill the required hole to the specification, relaxing the **feed** to allow swarf to escape and coolant (if used) to enter the hole.

**6** Check the hole and deburr.

The spindle speed you need will be decided by the type of drill and the type of material the workpiece is made from. You need to select a speed that will allow efficient cutting without overheating the workpiece. Using coolant allows you to work at faster speeds. However, coolant should generally be used to prolong tool life rather than speed work up. This is because it is often hard to get coolant to the cutting face, which makes it less effective at cooling down hot parts.

**Quick Tip**

You can use a large drill to deburr drilled holes by hand by rotating and pushing them at the edge of the hole.

| Drill diameter | Mild steel (revolutions per minute – rpm) | Aluminium | Brass | High carbon steel | Cast iron | Bronze | Stainless steel |
|---|---|---|---|---|---|---|---|
| < 3 mm | 2,500 rpm | 5,000 rpm | 4,800 rpm | 2,000 | 850 rpm | 3,000 rpm | 2,000 rpm |
| 4 – 8 mm | 1,250 rpm | 2,000 rpm | 2,400 rpm | 1,250 rpm | 450 rpm | 1,500 rpm | 1,250 rpm |
| 8 – 10 mm | 950 rpm | 1,600 rpm | 2,000 rpm | 880 rpm | 310 rpm | 1,200 rpm | 880 rpm |
| 10 – 14 mm | 650 rpm | 1,400 rpm | 1,250 rpm | 650 rpm | 220 rpm | 800 rpm | 650 rpm |
| 14 – 20 mm | 450 rpm | 800 rpm | 880 rpm | 325 rpm | 150 rpm | 550 rpm | 325 rpm |
| 20 – 30 mm | 325 rpm | 650 rpm | 640 rpm | 175 rpm | 96 rpm | 400 rpm | 175 rpm |
| 30 – 40 mm | 175 rpm | 325 rpm | 400 rpm | 96 rpm | 60 rpm | 245 rpm | 96 rpm |

**Table 8.10** A rough guide to drilling machine speeds

## Cutting fluids and compounds

When you are drilling, tapping and reaming, cutting fluids and compounds can be used to make the job easier.

There are many uses for cutting fluids and compounds.

**Hands On**

Practise changing the speeds on a pillar drill, remembering to turn off the power before removing the guards.

* Keeping the drill cool as heat can build up quickly in the cutting area causing it to fail.
* Preventing the workpiece from heating up, caused by friction with the drill. This can cause the work to expand which can lead to poor accuracy and finish.
* Allowing faster cutting speeds.
* Washing away chips and swarf.
* Giving a good finish.
* Working as a lubricant between the drill and the workpiece, helping the tool last longer.

There are three main types of cutting fluids and compounds: straight oils, soluble oils and greases.

### Straight oils

Straight oils are either vegetable, animal, synthetic or mineral oils. They can be used on their own or mixed. They are usually clear so you can see through them while you are machining. They act mainly as a lubricant, giving a good surface finish and extending tool life. They are expensive but are good for low speed operations where a good finish is needed.

### Soluble oils

Soluble oils – sometimes called suds – are oils that can be mixed into water. They are often milky white but can be other colours, such as green. They are very effective coolants that allow faster cutting speeds and are cost-effective. They do, however, make the work harder to see and they are not as good at lubricating as straight oils. Soluble oils are the most common lubricants used on machines.

### Greases

Greases or tapping compounds are a soft grease or paste used for tapping, reaming and other cutting operations where there is a need to significantly reduce friction. They give a good surface finish and reduce tool wear. They do not remove swarf as well as straight and soluble oils do. Greases are often applied with a brush. Never apply grease while the cutter is rotating.

Tapping grease should not be used with cast iron.

## Cutting screw threads

Screw threads are a very important method of fastening components together. They are self-locking and can be opened and closed as needed. They are used to take apart an assembly or maintain a piece of equipment.

There are many systems of screw threads, a lot of which are still in common use in the UK:

- metric (M)
- metric fine
- unified coarse (UNC)
- unified fine (UNF)
- Whitworth (BSW)
- British standard fine (BSF).

It is very important to always use the correct tap or die for the thread required. Some threads might appear to screw together but, if they're not the right match, their strength is severely reduced and they can easily fail.

## Tapping

A tool called a tap is used for cutting internal threads by hand. Taps are made of high speed steel (HSS) or high carbon steel (HCS). HSS is better but more expensive than HCS.

Taps are hard and brittle. They must be treated with care when in use otherwise they may break in the hole. This could scrap the workpiece as broken taps are almost impossible to remove even with specialist machinery.

Figure 8.10 A set of taps

Taps come in sets of three:

- **Taper tap** – is tapered for two-thirds of its length and is used to start the thread. The long taper helps it to line up with the hole and cut a true thread.
- **Second cut tap** or **intermediate tap** – has a taper for about a third of its length. It should be used after the taper tap to enlarge the tapped thread to the correct size. This is especially important with **blind holes**. Cheap tap sets often do not include this tap but if working on a budget you can make do with just a second cut tap (unless you are tapping a shallow blind hole).
- **Plug tap** or **bottoming tap** – cuts a parallel thread down its whole length. They have a slanted front to help cutting and should be used if a full depth thread is needed for a blind hole. Check the lead cutting edges for breakages as they are often damaged and can spoil a thread.

## Tapping internal threads

When tapping a thread, you first need to drill a hole into the workpiece to take the tap. The size of the hole needed for the tap will vary depending on the diameter of the thread and the **pitch** of the thread. It needs to be correct otherwise the tap could break or the thread could be weak making any fastening insecure.

To find the correct size of tapping drill, refer to a thread cutting table or a set of standards. Do not rely on using the core diameter of a thread. This will be too small and will cause the tap to jam or break. This is because the tap tends to slightly deform the metal it is cutting, forcing it into the thread form, as well as cutting it out from the workpiece.

To tap an M10 thread into the workpiece, follow the instructions below.

- Check the drawing specification and select the correct set of taps.
- Look up the tapping drill size in the thread table, for an M10 this will be 8.5 mm.
- Drill the correct size hole to depth. Remember not to include the length of the drill point when measuring the hole depth, as the thread needs the full diameter of the drill.
- Select the taper tap first and fit it to the correct size tap wrench. Apply some tapping compound or cutting oil to it. For an M10 thread the span of the wrench should be about 300 mm.
- Start tapping the hole. For a right-hand thread the tap should be turned clockwise. Once the tap has started to cut, check that it is square. If you are not sure, remove the wrench and use an engineer's tri-square to do this.

**Key term**

**Blind hole** – a hole drilled into a workpiece that does not go all the way through. When held up to the light, no light can be seen through the hole, i.e. it is a blind hole

**Pitch** – the distance between each peak of the thread. For *metric* threads, it is the distance between each peak. An M6 thread has a pitch of 1.00 mm and is often written as M6 x 1.00 mm. For *imperial* threads, the pitch is the number of peaks per inch so a ¼ inch diameter unified thread with a pitch of 20 threads per inch would be written as ¼ – 20 UNC.

**Figure 8.11** A tap wrench

- If the tap is not in line, continue to turn it and as you do move the wrench to bring the tap position back to square.

- Continue to cut the thread. For every clockwise turn of the tap, turn the tap anticlockwise for about a third of a turn to break the swarf. You will feel a little click. This stops the swarf from clogging the tap and damaging the thread. It also allows the swarf to drop clear if you are tapping a through hole.

- Repeat this with the second cut tap and then the plug tap. Start to screw the taps in by hand for a few turns so they do not get out of line with the thread that has already been cut.

- Check the thread you have cut using a bolt or screw to make sure it goes in to the specified depth.

## Cutting external threads

External threads are cut by a die. Dies are made of the same materials as taps, so if possible always use HSS dies because the HCS dies do not last as long or cut as well in tough materials.

The die is held in a die stock, adjusted to its widest setting and locked in place. The die has a split in it for adjusting the depth of cut. You do this by screwing the tapered centre screw in towards the die, spreading the die and making it cut a larger diameter. The die should then be locked in place using the two side locking screws.

All three screws must be present in the die stock and used correctly otherwise the die can shift and lock onto the work spoiling the thread. The die should be positioned in the die stock with the writing uppermost as this side is slanted, making it easier to start the cut.

A thread is then cut and checked either with a thread gauge or a suitable nut. If necessary the die is adjusted and another cut made until the correct size is reached.

In Figure 8.12 the die stock has been taken out so that the die and screws can be seen clearly.

The size of the thread denotes the size of the bar to use so an M10 thread uses 10 mm diameter bar and for a ½ inch UNC thread a bar of ½ inch diameter.

**Figure 8.12** Split button die

## Cutting an M10 thread on a piece of round bar

| Checklist | | | |
|---|---|---|---|
| **PPE** | **Tools and equipment** | **Consumables** | **Source information** |
| • Safety boots<br>• Overalls<br>• Barrier cream | • 10 mm split button die<br>• Die stock<br>• Screwdriver<br>• Engineer's tri-square<br>• M10 nut or thread ring gauge | • Workshop tissue or rag<br>• Tapping compound | • Drawing specification |

**1** Check drawing specification and select the correct die.

**2** Prepare the 10 mm diameter bar and file a chamfer (slanted side) to 45–50° on the end to be threaded.

**3** Mark the required distance to be cut and clamp the workpiece firmly in a vice. Then select the correct size die stock. For an M10 thread, the die stock span should be about 300 mm. Adjust the die to its widest setting and apply some tapping compound or cutting oil to the workpiece.

**4** Start cutting the thread. For a right-hand thread, the die should be turned clockwise. Once the die has started to cut, check that it is square. Use an engineer's tri-square to do this, checking the angle of the die stock against the bar. Remember to take two readings 90° apart. If the die is not in line, continue to turn it and, as you do, move the die stock to bring the die back to square.

**5**

Continue to cut the thread. For every clockwise turn of the die, turn the die anticlockwise for about a third of a turn to break the swarf. You will feel a little click. This stops the swarf clogging the die and damaging the thread. It also allows the swarf to drop clear.

**6**

Unscrew the die from the workpiece and check the thread with a nut or thread ring gauge. If needs be, adjust the die and make another cut.

## Problems when cutting threads

Problems you may come up against when cutting threads include:

- threads not cutting true – use a square and carefully check your work
- difficulty in starting a die – chamfer the work and make sure the die is the right way round
- overheating, or the tap or die getting stuck – apply tapping compound or coolant and make sure the tools are sharp
- broken taps – may be caused by careless bottoming out in blind holes.

## Reaming

Sometimes you may need a hole to be more accurately cut with a better standard of finish than can be achieved with a drill. This may be for setting pins or for bearings. If that is the case then you can drill a hole slightly smaller than needed then ream the hole to exactly the right size. Reamers cannot be used to correct any inaccuracy in the position or direction of a hole.

## Types of reamer

### Hand reamer

Hand reamers have parallel cutting edges (or shanks) with a square on the end for fitting a tap wrench as a handle. The body of a hand reamer has a slight taper on one end to guide it into the hole.

### Machine reamer

Machine reamers have a Morse tapered shank. They sometimes have a parallel shank for holding in the chuck of a drilling machine. The cutting edges are true to size along the whole length. The reamer has a chamfer at its bottom edge to help it line up straight in the hole as it reams.

### Adjustable reamer

Adjustable reamers have replaceable blades, which fit into tapered grooves on the body. The blades slide along the grooves and can be locked into any position by tightening screwed collars. By locking the blades in different positions the reamer can be adjusted to suit a range of sizes.

The adjustment is quick and accurate and variable within the range of the reamer. The wide range of adjustment also means you can allow for the blade shortening as it wears down with use. Blades can be reground and sharpened many times before replacements are needed.

## Using reamers

When a high degree of accuracy and finish is required, reaming is best done by hand. Machine reamers are very much faster but they aren't as accurate and don't finish as well as a hand reamer when operated by an experienced engineer.

## Reaming allowance

When making a reamed hole, the first step is to drill a hole slightly smaller than the size to be reamed. The amount that the drilled hole is under the finished size is called the reaming allowance.

The allowance required is different for hand reaming and machine reaming. It varies with the diameter of the hole and for different materials. There should be sufficient allowance for the reamer to cut at all times. If the allowance is too small, the reamer will rub, and the finish and accuracy will be poor.

When using a drilling machine to turn the reamer, the reaming allowance should be 3 % of the diameter of the reamer. So a 10 mm reamer would need a hole 9.7 mm in diameter – an allowance of 0.30 mm. For hand reaming an allowance of 1.5% to 2% of the diameter should be used. For a good-quality hole, tapping compound or oil should be used at all times. If using a machine reamer, then keep it to a slow speed of between 50 rpm to 100 rpm, depending on the size of the reamer.

## Hand reaming

Sometimes the hand reamer chatters and spoils the finish. This is caused by vibration between the workpiece and the tool, leaving a wavy unevenness to the hole.

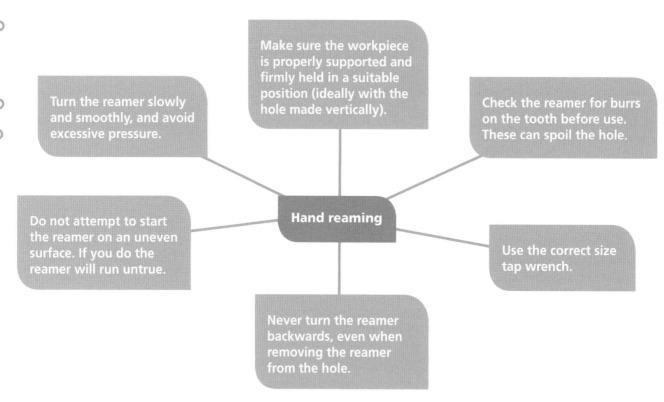

Make sure the workpiece is properly supported and firmly held in a suitable position (ideally with the hole made vertically).

Turn the reamer slowly and smoothly, and avoid excessive pressure.

Check the reamer for burrs on the tooth before use. These can spoil the hole.

Do not attempt to start the reamer on an uneven surface. If you do the reamer will run untrue.

Hand reaming

Use the correct size tap wrench.

Never turn the reamer backwards, even when removing the reamer from the hole.

**Figure 8.13** Tips for successful hand reaming

Some of the common causes of chatter are:

* lack of rigidity
* a blunt reamer
* poor workholding
* too much or too little cutting pressure
* too small or too large reaming allowance
* too little or wrong type of cutting fluid.

## Checking your work

Being able to check that your work is correct is a very important part of being a hand fitter. It is important to check the finish, form and dimensions of the workpiece as you work, so you can be sure that it meets the job specification.

Make sure no specified feature is left out of your checks as you cut and shape the workpiece. Every face and profile you produce should be checked. Be aware that making mistakes wastes time and money.

You will need to use some special skills and techniques to check your work to make sure it is to specification. Before you carry out these checks, make sure the workpiece is deburred correctly. If it isn't, your measurements may not be accurate.

Some of the ways of checking your work are as follows.

- **Linear dimensions** can be checked with a rule or micrometer. For close tolerance work (when your work needs a high degree of accuracy) you should always use a micrometer.
- **Squareness** should be checked using an engineer's tri-square. Hold the stock against the datum edge and use the blade to check against the surface. If you hold this up to the light, you will be able to see errors as small as 0.02 mm!
- **Flatness** should be checked with a straight edge or steel rule. Holding it against the surface and look for light shining through under the edge. You could also use the blade of a tri-square.
- **Angles** should be measured with a Vernier or plate protractor. Remember you will always need to measure from a datum edge to be sure the work is accurate.
- **Hole sizes** can be measured with a series of plug gauges. You can also use pieces of suitable round bar or the plain sides of drills as long as they are checked with a micrometer to make sure they are the correct size.
- **Profiles** can be measured using gauges and templates of the correct form by holding them against the workpiece.
- **Thread size and fit** can be measured using thread ring and plug gauges. For less precise work, or when the gauges are not available, standard nuts and bolts can be used.
- **Hole positions** can be checked by fitting a pin the correct size of the hole and measuring the distance from the pin to the datums. You will need to add the radius (half the diameter of the pin) to the measurement to get the centre position of the hole.

## Surface finish comparison gauges

The surface finish of the component will be specified. This should be checked as the workpiece is finished. You do this by looking at comparison gauges and comparing the feel.

Surface finish comparison gauges have samples of surface textures in differing degrees of roughness. Scratch the surface of a gauge with your fingernail in a direction 90° to the direction of cut, and you will be able to make a fairly accurate guess of the surface roughness of the finished work.

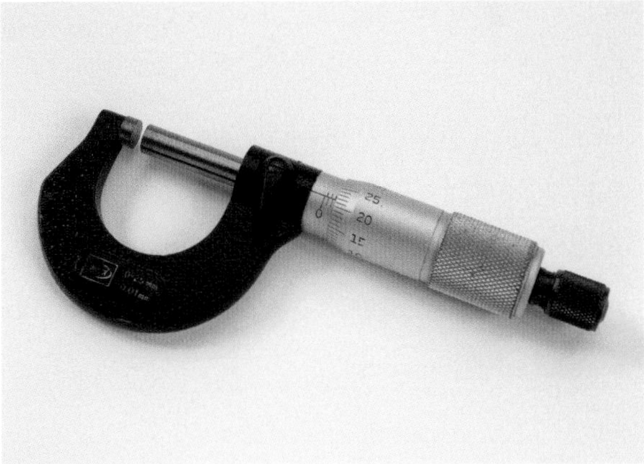

The roughness is measured by the roughness average number (Ra) and is measured in μm (micro metres).

Figure 8.14 A micrometer

## Micrometers

External micrometers are some of the most accurate measuring tools you will use as a bench fitter. They are not as versatile as other measuring tools but are very reliable, and easy to read and check.

External micrometers are used to measure thickness and diameters. They have a range of measurement of 25 mm for metric micrometers or 1" for imperial ones. This means to measure from 0 mm to 100 mm, four micrometers would be needed.

## Reading a metric micrometer

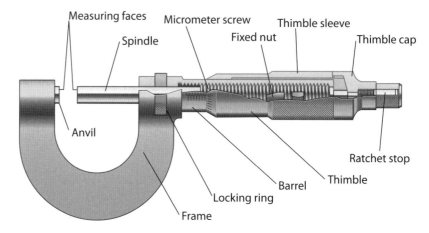

**Figure 8.15** A micrometer

The spindle of a metric micrometer has a pitch of 0.50 mm equivalent to two threads per 1 mm.

One revolution of the micrometer thimble moves the spindle through a distance of 0.50 mm. The thimble is divided into 50 equal parts (divisions), so that each part is 0.01 mm.

The barrel of the micrometer is split into 0.5 mm divisions so the turns of the thimble can be counted.

You can read the scale by following the steps in Table 8.11.

| | |
|---|---|
| Count the amount of graduations visible on the barrel of the micrometer – 10 | 10.00 mm |
| Add 0.5 mm if a half mm line is showing on the barrel | 00.50 mm |
| Add the number shown below the datum line  (e.g. 15 = 0.15 mm) | 00.15 mm |
| Add the amount of divisions between that number and the datum line (e.g. 1 = 0.01 mm) | 00.01 mm |
| Measured distance is | 10.66 mm |

**Table 8.11** How to read a micrometer scale

## QUICK CHECK

1  What should you make sure has been done to the workpiece before measuring it?
2  What piece of equipment do you need to measure an angle?
3  How many turns does a micrometer thimble make to measure 6 mm?

## Recording results

When you carry out quality control checks on the components you have made, be sure to record the results as part of the process. Remember to use the most suitable measuring tools for each operation.

All organisations have paper work or electronic documents that have to be filled out to prove the components you make meet the required specifications.

A typical quality control sheet or self-assessment sheet may look like the one shown in Figure 8.16.

| Component dimension | Tolerance | Measured size | Surface finish | Measuring equipment used | Meets specification |
|---|---|---|---|---|---|
| 35 mm dimension | 34.75 – 35.25 mm | 35.06 mm | 1.6 mm | Micrometer | Yes |
| Base and side face square to each other | 89.0° – 91.0° | 90° | 1.6 mm | Engineer's tri-square | Yes |

**Figure 8.16** Sample quality control sheet

# Dealing with problems

When you are bench fitting, sometimes things will go wrong or won't go as planned. If things don't look right, don't be afraid to ask. Your trainer or supervisor will have a lot of experience and you can learn a lot from them. They will be able to help you deal with problems and stop your work from being spoiled.

Make sure you always understand what your supervisor has said. If you are not sure, ask them to explain what they mean again before you do anything. It is better to ask for clarification before you start a job to avoid making mistakes and having to ask how to fix them.

As you gain more skill and experience you will be able to spot when things start to go wrong. You will then be able to work out what to do by yourself to sort out any problems.

If something does go wrong when using a power tool, *always* stop the machine and isolate it from the power supply. This will make the machine safe. After that you can try to find out what has happened and work out how to restart production safely. Remember, if in doubt, ask someone who knows what to do.

**Hands On**

Before starting a job, look critically at the tools you are about to use. Do they need sharpening or cleaning? If they do, ask someone to help you do this before you use them. It may avoid ruining your work.

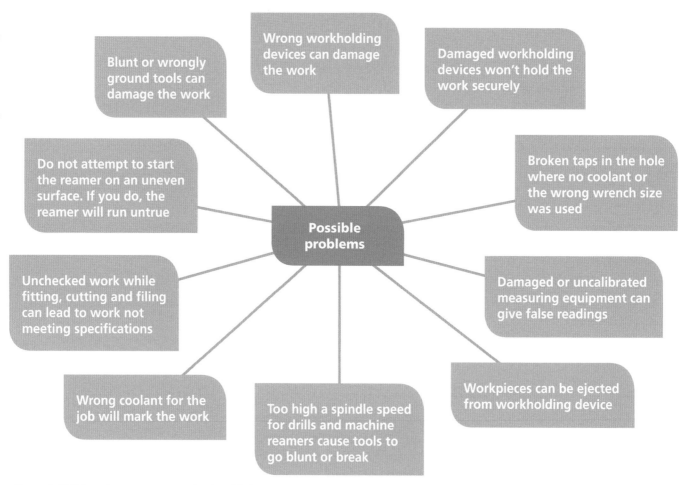

Figure 8.17 Things that can go wrong when hand fitting

1 When you have a problem with the tools and equipment you are using who should you go to for help?
2 Why is it important to check the calibration of measuring equipment before use?

## Making the work area safe and tidy

Tidying up when the job is done is an important part of the bench fitting process.

By tidying every day you will stop mess, tools and off-cuts building up in the work area and getting in the way as you work.

When you have finished work it is important to make the work area safe.

- Before you do anything else, always isolate any machines you have used from the power supply. This stops the machine accidentally starting while you are cleaning up.
- Check and rewind any extension leads or airlines before putting them away.

- Check any hand power tools for damage before putting them away. Clean any dirt, dust or grease from them.
- Clean any machines you have used. Swarf should go in the correct bin, skip or container.
- Check, clean and safely store any measuring equipment and gauges in the right places.
- Clean and sweep the bench and floor. Wipe up any spills.
- Clean and return every tool to the correct store or rack.
- Remove all waste and dispose of it safely.
- Return all PPE to the correct place. Check it for damage. Dirty PPE should be cleaned or replaced.

**Hands On**

Find out where scrap materials and tools belong in your workplace so you can tidy up quickly, safely and more efficiently, putting things back in the right order.

**QUICK CHECK**

1  Give three reasons why PPE should be carefully stored away at the end of the day?
2  Why is it important to put tools back in the correct place when you have finished using them?

## CHECK YOUR KNOWLEDGE

**1** What file can be used to produce flat surfaces and large internal curves?

  **a** round file

  **b** flat file

  **c** hand file

  **d** half round file

**2** Which of these tools should be used to cut metal?

  **a** hacksaw

  **b** tennon saw

  **c** rip saw

  **d** cross cut saw

**3** Which of these tools cannot be used to hold and support work when marking out?

  **a** a surface plate

  **b** an angle plate

  **c** a Vee block

  **d** plate protractor

**4** Flat filing is when you:

  **a** file across the block at 45° to the face then change the direction of filing by 90°

  **b** file towards you

  **c** hold the file sideways and move it back and forth across the surface of the work

  **d** file away from you in one direction only

**5** What is the correct sequence of operations for cutting and shaping materials?

  **a** datums, mark out, saw, file

  **b** saw, mark out, file, datums

  **c** file, datums, saw, mark out

  **d** mark out, file, saw, datums

**6** What pitch of hacksaw should be used for cutting 1.5 mm thick steel?

  **a** 14 TPI

  **b** 24 TPI

  **c** 32 TPI

  **d** 18 TPI

**7** When using taps to make an internal thread, what order should they be used in?

  **a** taper, intermediate, plug

  **b** plug, intermediate, taper

  **c** intermediate, plug, taper

  **d** taper, plug, intermediate

**8** What cut of file is best for roughing out mild steel?

  **a** dead smooth

  **b** smooth

  **c** second cut

  **d** bastard

**9** What tool cannot be held in a tap wrench?

  **a** countersink

  **b** hand reamer

  **c** taper tap

  **d** plug tap

**10** Which measuring tool can measure the diameter of a 20 mm bar most accurately?

  **a** Vernier calliper

  **b** engineer's tri-square

  **c** steel rule

  **d** micrometer

# 9 Using lathes for turning operations

This chapter is all about the lathe. The lathe is a machine tool that is used for shaping metals and other materials. It works by spinning the workpiece allowing the operator to then bring a cutting tool into contact with it to machine it down to the correct shape.

This process is called turning. Lathes can also be used to machine flat surfaces on the ends of the workpiece.

In this chapter, you will learn about:

- health and safety
- the lathe
- making your first cuts
- turning skills
- producing holes

- cutting techniques
- checking your work
- dealing with problems
- shutting down

# KITTING UP

## Keeping Safe

Health and safety is very important when you are using lathes. Even with guards in place, swarf and coolant can fly off the lathe and hit you and others around you. So before you start to use the lathe it is important to think carefully about what you are about to do and about what might go wrong.

When working with a lathe, there are several hazards you might come across:

- flying **swarf** and coolant
- hot swarf
- rotating machinery
- dust and noise
- sharp tools and edges on components.

Remember when working on the lathe other people may be working around you and they may be hurt if something goes wrong.

Before working check:

- Is the work area tidy and safe?
- Are the machine guards in place and in the right place?
- Do you know how to stop the machine normally and in an emergency?
- Is the workpiece held tight but not so tight that it is damaged?
- Have you been told about working safely on the job you are about to start?
- Are the tools sharp and undamaged?
- Are the feeds disengaged?
- Is there anything loose in the headstock or chuck that may fly out when the machine is turned on?

*Safety glasses* – protect your eyes from flying swarf and coolant while using lathes for turning

*Overalls* – protect your skin and clothes from contamination by oils, swarf and coolant. They also stop loose or baggy clothing from getting caught in the lathe while it is working

*Long hair* – tie back, put it in a hair net or under a cap

*Rings and jewellery* – should be removed in case they catch on the lathe

*Barrier cream* – protects your hands from dirt and oil and makes them easier to wash

*Safety boots or shoes* – protect your feet from falling objects, tools and swarf

# The lathe

A lathe is a complex machine tool and has lots of different parts. Figure 9.01 shows a centre lathe as these lathes are the most commonly used. However you may also use a capstan or turret lathe.

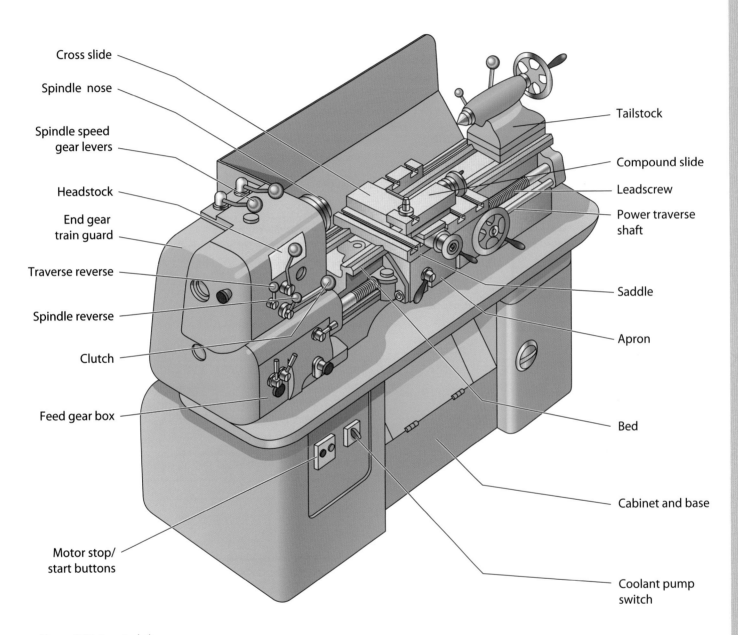

- Cross slide
- Spindle nose
- Spindle speed gear levers
- Headstock
- End gear train guard
- Traverse reverse
- Spindle reverse
- Clutch
- Feed gear box
- Motor stop/ start buttons

- Tailstock
- Compound slide
- Leadscrew
- Power traverse shaft
- Saddle
- Apron
- Bed
- Cabinet and base
- Coolant pump switch

**Figure 9.01** A centre lathe

| Component | Description |
|---|---|
| Headstock | Contains the gears or pulleys that allow the operator to change the speed of the spindle |
| Spindle | The rotating shaft that runs through the headstock. It is often hollow to allow the bar to be fed through the headstock. The workholding devices are held on to the spindle |
| Lathe bed and slideway | The backbone of the machine that the saddle runs on. It is parallel to the spindle axis. It can engage with the leadscrew to cut threads and often also has a power feed |
| Saddle | Supports the cross slide and allows the cutting tool to move along the spindle axis |
| Cross slide | Mounted on the saddle and moves 90° to the spindle axis. It is used for facing off or for changing the depth of cut. This often has a power feed |
| Compound slide | Fitted to the cross slide and supports the toolpost. It can also be swivelled to different angles to cut **tapers** and **chamfers** |
| Toolpost | Holds the cutting tool at the correct height firmly to allow machining to take place |
| Tailstock | Runs on the lathe bed slideway and is in line with the spindle axis. It has a barrel that can be moved in and out by the handwheel. It can be used to hold drills, drill chucks, dead centres and live centres. These are held in a tapered hole bored down the centre of the barrel called a **Morse taper** |
| Leadscrew | An accurate screw thread that is geared to the spindle and allows threads to be cut with a single point tool |

Table 9.01 Components of a lathe

## Workholding devices

When machining a component on a lathe, the workpiece must be held safely and securely without damaging your work. Table 9.02 describes some of the workholding devices used on the lathe with some of their uses and advantages/disadvantages.

| Workholding device | Description | Uses | Advantages/disadvantages |
|---|---|---|---|
| **Three jaw chuck** | Has three jaws that move at the same time when the chuck is tightened or loosened, making sure that the work is centred on the machine axis | Can be used to hold smooth round bar (**cold rolled**) or bar with sides divisible by three (e.g. a hexagonal bar) | Can be used in lots of different places and easy to set up but it does not grip very well. Large unsupported lengths are likely to fly out during heavy cuts. If the work is removed, it often loses **concentricity** |
| **Four jaw chuck** | Has four jaws that are each tightened individually to secure the work on the machine axis | Can be used to hold round, square and other irregular shaped materials with sides divisible by four. It also should be used for holding **hot rolled** material | It takes longer to make sure the work is aligned correctly but has greater accuracy than the three jaw chuck. Has a very strong grip and can hold components off centre for making concentrics. Some are made of cast iron and have a maximum speed rating so check carefully before use |
| **Between centres** | A catch plate is locked to the nose of the spindle and a dead centre fitted to the bore of the spindle to hold the work at the headstock. A live or dead centre is fitted to the tailstock to support the work at this end. Once the workpiece has a centre drill hole at each end, it can be fitted to the machine. Power is transmitted to the work via a lathe carrier, sometimes called a driving dog | Often used for long shafts but can be used for other components | Can be used to take heavy cuts and is useful where a lot of material has to be removed. It is also quick and easy to check work when using it as it realigns on the centres. Both ends of the component have centre drill holes which might get in the way of the work |
| **Collet chuck** | A slitted sleeve designed to be locked firmly around a piece of bar | Can only be used to hold the size and shape of workpiece the collet has been designed for. More than 0.1 mm deviation from this will cause problems | This method of workholding has a very strong grip and high accuracy but cannot be used in all situations |

**Table 9.02** Lathe workholding devices

## Using a three jaw chuck safely

When you use a three jaw chuck to hold your workpiece, it is very important that you check everything as you work.

- Remove all **burrs** and clean the bar so the jaws can grip.
- Check that the chuck jaws are clean and free from swarf.
- Check that the chuck is mounted correctly on the machine spindle.
- Make sure you have the right size chuck key so it will not slip.
- Turn off the machine's power and put your foot on the brake so the chuck will not move as you work causing you to slip.
- Put the bar in the chuck without too much sticking out (about 30 mm).
- Tighten the chuck up but if using brass or aluminium make sure you do not damage the metal.
- Spin the chuck by hand and make sure the work is in line and free from obstruction.

If the workpiece you are clamping is only held by a small part of the jaws, then the work can distort and become loose in the chuck, eventually flying out. If you also do not tighten the chuck up enough or if there is too much of the workpiece sticking out, then the work can bend as you turn, damaging and bruising it as it loosens in the chuck. For the best finish the workpiece should only stick out from the chuck a short way unless supported by a tailstock centre.

Figure 9.02 Cleaning and deburring mild steel bar

Figure 9.03 Mounting the bar in a chuck with 30 mm sticking out

## QUICK CHECK

1 What workholding method would you use for square bar?
2 How are the chucks mounted on the lathe that you use?

## Cutting tools

There are lots of different cutting tools that you can use on the lathe. You will need to choose the correct tool for the job you are doing. A lot of the tools are made for particular jobs. Table 9.03 describes the main types you may come across.

**Keep It Safe**

To avoid injury, always remove the tool from the toolpost before reaching into the machine.

| Tool | Description | Use |
|---|---|---|
| **Right-hand turning tool** | The standard general purpose tool used on the centre lathe | Can turn diameters and face off surfaces. It can cut from right to left and toward the centre of the work |
| **Left-hand turning tool** | The same as the right-hand turning tool but cuts from left to right | Used for turning diameters but can still face off in the normal direction |
| **Boring tool** | Often a long thin tool that can be put inside a hole to machine internal surfaces. It is not as rigid as turning tools. Lighter cuts have to be made to avoid **chatter** and a poor finish | Used to cut internal diameters and faces. Can also be used to cut internal tapers. Can produce high-quality, accurate holes or bores |
| **Parting off tool** | Long and thin with a tip that is often slightly wider than the shank, giving clearance as it cuts. Must be set 90° to the spindle axis (using an engineer's tri-square to help you do this) | Used to separate the finished workpiece from the material held in the chuck. Can only be used to cut toward the spindle axis of the machine |
| **Screw cutting tool** | Has a tip shaped to match the form of the thread being cut – normally 60° for metric threads and 55° for Whitworth threads. Other points are available or can be ground depending on the thread form required | Used to cut external threads on a lathe working with the correct leadscrew settings. An internal tool similar to a boring tool is used to cut female threads |
| **Form tools** | Ground to the shape required for the finished shape and usually plunged into the work. Often cuts over a large area and is prone to chatter. Must be used with care to avoid breakages | Can be used to form complex shapes, radiuses, tapers and chamfers |
| **Grooving tool** | Shaped like a smaller version of the parting tool | Can be used to produce accurate grooves in the workpiece. An example could be for **circlips** or **O rings** |
| **Knurling tool** | There are two types:<br>• calliper – clamps around the workpiece to form knurls<br>• pivot – pushes into the workpiece to form knurls<br>They are not really cutting tools but work by forming the metal into the required shape | Can produce straight knurls and diamond knurls to plain diameters. Must be run at slow rotational speeds of about 40 rpm to stop the rollers overheating. Must run at high feed rates otherwise the machining time is very slow |

**Table 9.03** Lathe cutting tools

Check you have set the lathe tool at the right height by making a trial facing cut. Inspect the end of the workpiece to make sure the tool is correct. If the tool is too low, a fine wire will be present at the end of the bar and if it is too high, there will be a smooth bump. If the tool is set just right, the faced end will be flat.

**Quick Tip**

When you use a knurling tool always make sure you use lots of coolant. This washes away any small bits of swarf that have broken off and makes the finish better.

## Tailstock tools

You need to make sure you have the right tools and equipment for the tailstock. Getting this right is just as important as setting up the workholding equipment and cutting tools. The tailstock can be used to hold cutting tools but it can also be used to help support the work being turned.

The types of cutting tools commonly held in the tailstock are drills, reamers, taps and dies. These are tools used to cut threads. Often tools used in a tailstock are held in a chuck but they may locate and be held in the tailstock using a Morse tapered shank.

**Key term**

**Play** – looseness between parts that may lead to loss of accuracy

| Tool | Description | Use |
|------|-------------|-----|
| Centre or dead centre | A hardened bit of steel with a 60° taper on one end and a Morse taper on the other | Can be used to support work but must be lubricated and only run at low speeds otherwise it may melt. Very useful for setting tool height |
| Live centre or rotating centre | A hardened 60° angled point that rotates on precision bearings (unlike the dead centre which is fixed) | Used to support high speed turning operations but may not be as accurate as a dead centre due to **play** in the bearings. The live centre is more bulky and may get in the way while turning small diameters |
| Half centre | A dead centre with part of the taper cut away | The cut-away must be positioned towards the tool then more space is available for tools to get in and machine small diameters |
| Drill chuck | A standard drilling chuck that has a Morse taper to suit the tailstock barrel | Used to hold centre drills and small twist drills normally up to 13 mm diameter |
| Centre drill | A short rigid drill that has a small diameter point that then tapers to a larger diameter | Used to start holes as it does not wander from the centre of the workpiece. It also makes a hole that will support the taper of a live or dead centre for workholding |
| Twist drill | A standard drill with twisted flutes used to drill holes. May have a parallel shank that is held by a drill chuck or a Morse tapered shank to hold it true in position | Used to drill holes. Come in small sizes of 0.1 mm steps. When over 13 mm in diameter they normally have a Morse tapered shank |
| Tailstock die holder | Holds a thread cutting die true to the axis of the machine in the tailstock. Allows the die to be drawn forward but not turn | A very useful tool for cutting male or external threads on the outside of barstock |
| Tailstock tap holder | Holds the tap in the tailstock barrel ready for cutting a thread. The tap can slip in the holder preventing the brittle tap from breaking. When the machine is reversed to remove the tap, it is held still allowing the tap to wind out of the thread | A useful tool for holding thread-cutting taps in a lathe to cut female or internal threads |

**Table 9.04** Tailstock tools

## Quick change and four way toolpost

A quick change toolpost or a four way toolpost is used to hold the lathe tool in position ready for cutting. The tool is fitted to the quick change toolpost and the tool height changed by the adjusting screw, then locked on the cam lock.

On a four way toolpost, the tool height is set by using packing pieces and shims under the tool to ensure it is set to the correct height when it is tightened. This takes longer to set up but the advantage is that four tools can be set at the same time. This makes the time between tool changes quicker as the post just has to be rotated.

Always check that any drill you are about to use is sharp and undamaged to reduce the chance of breakage but also check the condition of the shank as damage to this may cause the drill not to be held centrally.

Figure 9.04 A toolpost on a lathe

## Setting and adjusting tool speeds and feeds

For lathe tools to work effectively and efficiently while turning they have to work in the correct conditions. Factors that determine the correct speed to set are:

- the workpiece diameter
- the type of material the workpiece is made from
- the material the cutting tool is made from
- whether there is coolant and what type.

Tool manufacturers recommend cutting speeds that give the best finish and longest life for their tools. So before you start work check the spindle speeds that need to be set. Either ask your supervisor what speeds you will need to use or look them up in a tool catalogue or data book.

If the steel swarf looks blue or dark brown and is hot, it is likely you are machining too fast. Slow the machine down and recheck that every thing is okay. Both the spindle speed and the feed rate will affect this.

**Keep It Safe**

Always remove the drill chuck from the tailstock before mounting and tightening a twist drill or centre drill. This is in case the chuck slips in the barrel causing you to cut your hand on the flutes of the drill.

## Changing the feed rate

The feed rate is the distance the tool moves for every revolution of the workpiece. It is normally described as mm per revolution (mm/rev).

| Feed rate on lathe | Suggested use |
| --- | --- |
| 0.03 mm/rev | Fine finishing cuts used to finish accurate work |
| 0.05 mm/rev | A good general purpose turned finish |
| 0.1 – 0.15 mm/rev | Quickly remove material for rough cuts |
| 0.5 – 1.0 mm/rev | Good for knurling where a fast rate is needed, not all machines will be able to travel at 1.0 mm/rev easily |

Table 9.05 Table of suggested feed rates for machining on a lathe

These feed rates are just a guide for you. Depending on the machine, cutting tool and workpiece you are using, slightly different settings may have to be made. Always make some trial cuts to check to see that the tool does not rub or rip the workpiece.

Use the steps below to help you set the feed rates.

- If the machine you are using has a gearbox for cutting speeds, turn the lathe spindle either under power or by hand. Never do this with the feed engaged.
- Using the chart on the machine or in the machine handbook set the dials and levers to the correct position for the feed rate you want to use.
- If you try to set the feed rate without the spindle turning, it can be very difficult to get the feed gears to mesh. The feed will not work or will move at the wrong speed.

## Changing the tool speed

The spindle speed on a lathe needs to be changed depending on what materials are being cut, what tools are being used and the diameter of the workpiece. Table 9.06 gives you a rough guide to the speeds you should be using. But always check with your work planning sheet or your trainer before starting, as the speeds they give will be more accurate.

Table 9.06 outlines the speeds for mild steel. If turning high carbon steel, use half the speed shown and for aluminium double it.

| Diameter of workpiece | High speed steel tool | Insert tip tool |
| --- | --- | --- |
| 5 mm | 1,900 rpm | 15,500 rpm |
| 10 mm | 950 rpm | 8,000 rpm |
| 15 mm | 640 rpm | 5,300 rpm |
| 20 mm | 480 rpm | 4,000 rpm |
| 25 mm | 380 rpm | 3,100 rpm |
| 30 mm | 320 rpm | 2,500 rpm |
| 35 mm | 270 rpm | 2,200 rpm |
| 40 mm | 240 rpm | 2,000 rpm |

**Table 9.06** A rough guide to cutting speeds on a lathe

This is intended as a guide and tool manufacturers' data sheets should be checked.

To change the spindle speed on lathes with a gearbox in the headstock:

- stop the machine and make sure the spindle is not moving
- turn off the power to the machine
- wiggle the spindle with your right hand while operating the speed change levers with your left, allowing the gears to mesh
- once in gear, rotate the spindle by hand to check it has engaged correctly
- continue machining.

**Keep It Safe**

Never try to change the lathe speed gears while the chuck is still moving, unless the machine instruction manual says to do so.

## Coolants and cutting fluids

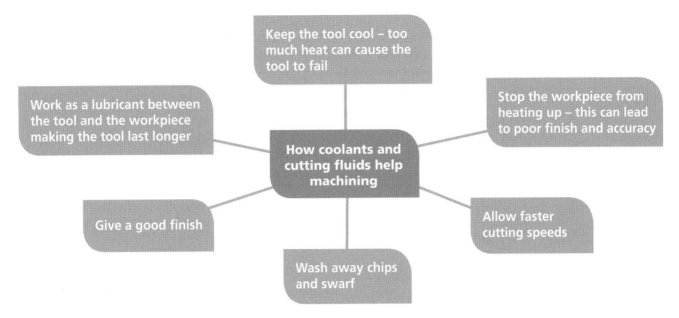

Keep the tool cool – too much heat can cause the tool to fail

Work as a lubricant between the tool and the workpiece making the tool last longer

Stop the workpiece from heating up – this can lead to poor finish and accuracy

**How coolants and cutting fluids help machining**

Give a good finish

Allow faster cutting speeds

Wash away chips and swarf

**Figure 9.05** How coolants and cutting fluids help machining

Cutting fluids are often recycled by the machine using a pump fitted inside. The tray that the lathe bed sits on drains into the tank ensuring a constant supply of coolant.

There are three main types of cutting fluids and compounds:

- **Straight oils** – usually clear so you can see what is going on while turning. They act mainly as a lubricant giving a good surface finish and long tool life.
- **Soluble oils** – mixed with water. They are often a milky white colour and are very effective coolants that allow faster cutting speeds. They are the most common lubricants used on machines.
- **Greases** or **tapping compounds** – soft grease or paste used for tapping, reaming and other cutting operations. Good at slow speeds. They give a good surface finish.

Tapping compounds and greases should always be cleaned from tools after use with rag. This is because swarf is often mixed in with it and can cause damage to tools as they are stored.

**Keep It Safe**

Never apply coolant or tapping compounds to moving workpieces with a brush or rag as they may get caught in the machine causing injury and damaging your work.

**Did You Know**

Not all materials need coolant and can machine better without them. Grey cast iron and brass break into little chips when machined making coolant unnecessary.

**Keep It Safe**

Wash off any coolant splashed on your skin as soon as possible. It can cause serious skin problems if left on the skin too long. Be careful not to get coolant soaked into your overalls.

**Hands On**

Try cutting with different coolants and tapping greases. Then cut without any. Make a note of the difference. This will help you to achieve the finish you require when you are working on important jobs.

# Making your first cuts

You are now ready to use a lathe to cut metal for the first time. For this exercise you will be turning a piece of 25 mm diameter, 100 mm long bar down to 23 mm diameter for a length of 25 mm, similar to that shown in Figure 9.06.

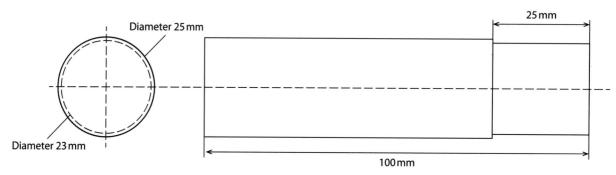

**Figure 9.06** Round bar with a turned step

## Safety

First things first, you need to be safe:

✓ Isolate the machine from the mains power supply using the wall isolator or the isolator on the rear of the machine. Do not rely on the push-in stops on the machine.

✓ Make sure the working area around the machine is safe and clear of obstructions, and the floor is clear of slip and trip hazards.

✓ You are going to use a self-centring three jaw chuck. If it's already fitted, make sure it is secure and in the fully locked position. If you have to fit the chuck yourself, follow the manufacturer's instructions. Make sure all the joining surfaces with the spindle are clean, free from swarf and dry so the chuck lines up correctly with the machine axis. Check the chuck jaws do up and line up in the centre. Never leave the chuck key in the chuck.

✓ Check that there is no swarf or other material inside the spindle tube in the headstock as this could fly out once the machine starts.

✓ Check that the saddle and the cross slide move. If they don't, it either means that the feed has been left engaged, so disengage it, or that a bed or slide locking bolt has been tightened, so slack that off.

✓ Check that all the guards are in place and secure.

✓ Make sure that nothing has been left on the headstock that could fall into the rotating chuck.

✓ Check the oil sight glasses to make sure enough oil is in the machine.

✓ Select the correct spindle speed and feed rate. Set the feed rate to 0.05 mm/rev.

✓ Ensure that the coolant pump is turned off and the pipe facing down into the bottom of the bed.

✓ Make sure you have your safety glasses on (try to get into the habit of wearing them all the time in the workshop not just when you are machining).

✓ Turn on the machine at the wall and start it. Watch it run to make sure all is okay. Check the operation of the feeds, the stop buttons and brake.

✓ Lift the chuck guard and check the safety interlock works (if fitted) and the machine stops.

Now you know the lathe is safe to use.

## What you need

Once you have selected the correct workholding device and safety checked the lathe you are about to use, you need to gather your tools together. You will need:

- a live or dead centre
- a right hand turning tool
- bright mild steel bar 25 mm diameter and 100 mm long
- a second cut flat file
- rag to clean
- 0 mm – 25 mm micrometer
- steel rule
- odd leg callipers.

If the lathe you are using has no scale for length measurements you will need the steel rule and odd leg callipers to set the length.

Remember that only the part of the cutting tool that actually cuts should be in contact with the workpiece otherwise the tool will rub. Ceramic carbide insert tip tools can normally be set at 90° to the spindle axis to do this. Most are designed to face off and turn down diameters without being repositioned.

**Keep It Safe**

Make sure that tools and scrap cannot fall onto the chuck when the machine is running as they could fly from the machine causing serious injury.

# How to set the tool on a centre lathe

| Checklist | | | |
|---|---|---|---|
| **PPE** | **Tools and equipment** | **Consumables** | **Source information** |
| • Safety boots<br>• Overalls<br>• Safety glasses<br>• Barrier cream | • Flat file<br>• Steel rule<br>• Right-hand cutting tool<br>• Live centre<br>• Odd leg callipers | • Cutting oil or coolant<br>• Rag | • Tool manufacturer's data sheet for surfacing speed |

**1**

Clean and deburr the mild steel bar using the file and rag.

**2**

Mount the bar in the three jaw chuck with 30 mm of bar protruding (check with a steel rule).

**3**

Fit and secure the right-hand cutting tool in the holder.

**4**

Adjust the tool to centre height and check against centre in the tailstock.

**5**

Make a trial facing cut and check that there is side clearance and that the tool cuts to the centre of the bar. Adjust the tool height if necessary.

**6**

Once the bar has been faced off, reset the tool and turn down the diameter to 23 mm for 25 mm long.

## Machining down to the correct size

After setting the tool and facing the bar off true (step 5) the faced edge can be used as the first machine **datum**.

If the machine you are using has a scale on the bed for turning lengths (this is called the **z axis**), you can set the dial to zero, face off and then you will know the position of your tool in relation to that faced edge. If the lathe does not have this scale, then you can set the odd leg callipers to 25 mm using the steel rule and mark the bar at 25 mm.

It is very important you do not remove the workpiece from the chuck until you have finished machining that stage. This is because every time the work is removed from the chuck more inaccuracies are introduced as the work never goes back in exactly the same place. Exceptions to this would be when using the four jaw chuck or turning between centres.

<table>
<tr><td>Key term</td></tr>
<tr><td>Datum – a reference position from which dimensions are taken or measurements made</td></tr>
</table>

## Machining down to the correct size

| Checklist | | | |
| --- | --- | --- | --- |
| **PPE** | **Tools and equipment** | **Consumables** | **Source information** |
| • Safety boots<br>• Overalls<br>• Safety glasses<br>• Barrier cream | • Flat file<br>• Steel rule<br>• Right-hand cutting tool<br>• Live centre<br>• Odd leg callipers | • Cutting oil or coolant<br>• Rag | • Tool manufacturer's data sheet for surfacing speed |

**1** Before turning the lathe on, position the tool ready for turning diameters, making sure there is clearance on the front face to the right of the cutting tip.

**2**

Get the cutting tip close to the bar but not touching.

**3** Turn on the machine and then slowly bring the tool tip into contact with the rotating bar using the cross slide until it touches. You may hear this happen before you see the little curl of swarf form on the tool tip.

**4**

Without touching the cross feed, move the tool to the right using the saddle (z axis).

**5**

Now put on a cut using the reading on the cross feed dial of between 0.3 mm and 0.5 mm if you can. Remember to check if the machine reads diameters or radiuses on this dial.

**6**

Engage the automatic feed and start the cut, watching all the time and listening – a change in sound is often the first warning of something going wrong.

**7**

Stop the automatic feed just before the 25 mm mark either on the saddle dial or on the bar. Finish the final feed gently by hand.

**8**

Without touching the cross slide dial and handle, remove the tool away from the workpiece by turning the saddle handle or wheel. The tool should move toward the right on the z axis.

**9**

Stop the machine and measure the diameter of the bar with the micrometer. You now have two datums – one for length and one for diameter. You will probably find at this point you have taken off more than you thought.

**10** Put on another cut. Try not to take off more than 1 mm of the diameter at this stage but measure at the end of each cut. If you accidentally turn the cross feed dial the wrong way or too far, then you will have to make a trial cut again to establish your diameter reference with the tool tip. Try to make your finishing cut about 0.3 mm.

It is not good practice to use the compound slide for general turning operations as it is not true to the axis of the machine and will often produce shallow tapers that will be out of tolerance.

**Keep It Safe**

When measuring your work, or tightening or loosening the chuck, keep your foot on the brake. This stops the machine starting accidentally and prevents injury.

## Cleaning down and making safe

An important part of preparing and using lathes for turning operations is cleaning down and making the machine safe.

Slide ways stay in good condition, keeping their accuracy

Coolant lasts longer and you are not affected by old oil and swarf

**A clean lathe is a healthy lathe because**

They are easier to set up than dirty ones

**Figure 9.07** Why it is important to keep your lathe clean

Follow these steps to keep a lathe clean and in good condition.

✓ Isolate the machine from the supply, turning off the main switch on the wall.

✓ Remove the cutting tool and centre, cleaning them and putting them away. This reduces the chance of cutting yourself as you clean down.

✓ Remove the workpiece if you have not already done so.

✓ Put all the other tools used away, making sure they are clean first.

✓ Sweep down the machine starting with the sides and bed, sweeping the swarf into the base of the machine.

✓ Empty the swarf out of the machine, disposing of it in the correct bin or skip, recycling it if possible.

✓ Dry the bed and slides with a rag, moving the slides and tailstock to make sure they are dry.

✓ Clean and sweep your working area, mopping up any spills and removing any waste.

Well done! You have just successfully used the lathe safely and turned your first bit of metal.

**Keep It Safe**

Never handle swarf with your hands – use a rake or shovel to lift it out of the machine.

**Keep It Safe**

If you notice anything wrong with the lathe and are not sure how to put it right, let your supervisor know before continuing with your work.

## Working with lathes – a summary

In summary, here is what you have to do to make a lathe ready to start machining:

- isolate the machine from the power supply
- make sure all guards are present and in good condition
- fit the correct workholding device for the job to be undertaken
- make sure there is no unsecured bar or material inside the headstock spindle
- make sure no automatic feeds have been left engaged and disconnect the leadscrew unless needed
- check that the correct levels of lubricant and coolant are in the machine, checking sight glasses and coolant tank
- make sure the coolant is not turned on and the coolant nozzle is pointing down toward the machine
- check that there is not excessive **backlash** on any of the machine slides.

And at the end of the session you must *always*:

- isolate the machine from the power supply
- put the tools away, cleaned
- clean the lathe and work area.

> **Key term**
>
> **Backlash** – the name given to play in the threads that move the slides on a centre lathe. Too much backlash may make the toolpost move suddenly towards the work, ruining it. Backlash also causes problems when you change direction as you then get a false reading – the dial moves but the slide does not.

**Figure 9.08** Facing on a lathe

**Figure 9.09** Turning on a lathe

# Turning skills

Turning on a lathe uses many skills, the most important are looked at below.

## Facing

Facing is normally the first turning operation you do. It produces a flat end that can be used to measure from and to check that the tool is centred. Facing involves using a right-hand cutting tool and moving it from the edge of the workpiece towards the centre.

## Turning

Turning is used to produce accurate diameters on the lathe. When a number of different diameters have to be turned on a component, try to arrange your turning activity so that the smallest diameter is on your right pointing toward the tailstock. This way, long cuts can be made along the length of the component, removing the waste above the smaller diameters near the tailstock as you go. Always turn the largest diameter down to size first if possible.

## Grooves

The methods used to produce grooves, undercuts and **parting off** are the same. A cross slide is used to feed a thin tool into the work gently, to the required depth of the groove. Usually the tool tip is the same width as the groove or undercut but is tapered slightly on each side to give clearance for the cutting edge. Be careful not to turn the tool sideways as it has no sideways strength and will snap if you try to turn normally with it.

# Producing holes

Making or enlarging a hole using a lathe tool is called boring. Some of the ways of creating and finishing holes on a lathe are as follows.

- **Boring** – boring tools can be used to make accurate holes that would be hard to drill or ream. Boring tools lack strength and rigidity as they have to go inside the workpiece and may chatter. To avoid this, take only very light cuts at slow feed rates.

- **Drilling** – drills can either be held in the drilling chuck or in the Morse taper bored in the barrel of the tailstock. Set the correct speed for the drill using a data table or ask your trainer. As drills are harder to keep cool than external cutting tools, the cutting speeds are slightly slower. Remember to use lots of coolant and clear the swarf by moving the drill in and out as you work.

- **Reaming** – machine reamers are not able to cut a hole on their own and must only be used to open out a hole to the correct size. A hole should be drilled with a twist drill first, to a slightly smaller diameter than the finished hole size (3% smaller often works well). A reamer can then be used to produce a more accurate hole. They produce a good internal surface finish if used with care.

**Figure 9.10** Grooving on a lathe

## Drilling

Try different machining techniques on the lathe. You can use the piece of mild steel you have already practised on when you turned the 23 mm diameter step.

## Drilling a 10 mm diameter hole down the centre of the workpiece

| Checklist | | | |
|---|---|---|---|
| **PPE** | **Tools and equipment** | **Consumables** | **Source information** |
| • Safety boots<br>• Overalls<br>• Safety glasses<br>• Barrier cream | • Centre drill<br>• 10 mm drill<br>• Drill chuck | • Cutting oil or coolant<br>• Rag | • Tool manufacturer's data sheet for surfacing speed |

**1** Mount the centre drill in the drill chuck, checking it is sharp and not broken. A good size drill is one with a 3 mm diameter tip.

**2** Check that the Morse taper on the drill chuck and tailstock barrel are clean. Mount the drill chuck in the tailstock. Check it is secure.

**3** Set the spindle speed to about 750 rpm.

**4** Move the tailstock so that the drill point is just clear of the faced off end of the workpiece. Move the toolpost and cross slide out of the way if necessary.

**5** Check that the workholding device can be rotated without touching the tool or toolpost.

**6** Start the machine and slowly turn the hand wheel to start drilling. Remember to use coolant and go gently, pulling the tip out regularly to allow coolant in and to clear swarf.

**7** Drill until the centre drill starts to cut on the tapered cutting surface.

**8** Stop the lathe and extract the drill chuck by winding the hand wheel the other way until the Morse taper is freed.

**9** Remove the centre drill and replace with the 10 mm drill. Then mount the drill chuck back in the tailstock barrel.

**10** Start the machine and note the position on the scale on the barrel where the drill starts to cut. Then cut – with lots of coolant and clearing swarf as before – until the full depth has been cut.

## Large drills

When using larger drills remember that a pilot hole should be drilled to give the **web** of the drill clearance before the large drill is fitted and used. If you look at the cutting edge of the drill, you will see an angled chisel face between the two cutting edges. This is normally between 3 mm and 6 mm long. Do not worry if the pilot drill is not as long as the intended hole – the flutes (grooves) of the drill will support it and keep it true.

To drill a large hole 30 mm in diameter:

- centre drill the end of the bar as before
- drill the right size pilot hole, using a drilling chuck (about 5 mm diameter for this size hole)
- fit the 30 mm drill and select the correct speed – for mild steel the calculated speed is 263 rpm but be prepared to go slower
- start drilling, using lots of coolant and retracting regularly to clear swarf
- check the swarf as it comes out of the hole as both coils should look the same – if they do not, the tool may have been incorrectly sharpened and the hole maybe oversized.

Always check a drill before use to make sure it is not blunt or damaged. There should be no chips out of the cutting edges and both cutting edges should be the same length and angle. The drill must be straight. You can check this by rolling the drill on a surface table.

If you are unsure about the condition of the drill you are about to use, ask your supervisor or get a new one.

## Boring

Boring tools need to be treated with care on a lathe. Here are some handy tips to help you when using a boring tool:

- use slow feed rates such as 0.03 mm/rev

> **Key term**
>
> **Web** – the thick central part of the drill that does not have a cutting edge

> **Quick Tip**
>
> Be careful when drilling with a centre drill. They are very hard and brittle and can break easily, scrapping your work. Make sure you select the right speed and clear the swarf as you go.

> **Quick Tip**
>
> When drilling a hole to take a live or dead centre, drill with the centre drill three-quarters of the way up the tapered part of the cutting face. This ensures the correct profile hole to mate with the centre and support the workpiece correctly.

**Figure 9.11** Boring tool

- use only light cuts – 0.3 mm to 0.5 mm at a time
- remember to turn the cross slide handle the other way – to remove metal you are coming out not going in (jotting down the measurements on a scrap of paper may help)
- if the tool does chatter, try sticking a small weight near the tip of the tool with a bit of modelling clay
- it can be hard to set centre height accurately, so use a Vernier height gauge or scribing block to transfer the height from the centre to the tool tip, running the base of the Vernier on the cross slide.

## Reaming

Reamers are not the same as drills and need to be used differently. They rely on the machine keeping them straight and true as they accurately open out a hole that has already been created in the workpiece by a drill. The pre-drilled hole should be about 3% smaller than the finished reamed hole.

Reamers are held in the tailstock, usually by a Morse taper. Some smaller machine reamers have a parallel shank that can be held in a drill chuck. Reamers are run at slow speeds – about 80 rpm is a good speed for reaming into most types of steel. Tapping grease and straight oils work well with reamers, giving a better finish.

 **Keep It Safe**

Only use machine reamers under power. Hand reamers used under power in a machine may grab in the hole and smash.

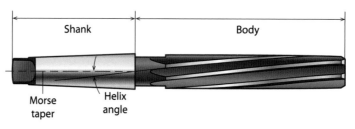

**Figure 9.12** A machine reamer

### QUICK CHECK

1. What is the difference between a pilot drill and a centre drill?
2. How are reamers held in the tailstock of a lathe?

## Cutting techniques

When you are working on a lathe different types of cuts have to be used as you progress with the job. Some different types of cuts include:

- roughing cuts
- finishing cuts
- grooving and parting
- form tools
- knurling
- turning tapers.

## Roughing cuts

Roughing cuts are used to rapidly remove material while turning. It's not a very accurate method of turning because the tool, workpiece and machine can bend under load. The correct cutting speed is crucial as the tool is working very hard while roughing. Special roughing tools are available that are designed to take the extra loading but you can use the normal right- and left-hand cutting tools if you use them carefully.

Follow the steps below for efficient roughing.

- Make sure your workholding is secure. It is good practice to use a live centre to support the other end of the bar.
- Use lots of coolant. Soluble oil is best for this as it keeps the work and tool cool, and stops the work expanding and loading the tailstock.
- Use feed rates from 0.1 mm/rev to 0.3 mm/rev.
- Depending on the diameter of the bar, you can make deep cuts of up to about 5 mm off the diameter in one go. Be sure to build up to this depth, checking as you go. Be aware of the limits of your machine.
- Watch the live centre carefully to see if it stops rotating. If the work is pushed into the chuck, the workholding will then no longer be effective.
- Remember to change the spindle speed after nearly every cut as the diameter of the bar reduces quickly.
- Be prepared to stop the machine at any time. Remove swarf if it builds up so much that it could interfere with the workholding device.

## Finishing cuts

Finishing cuts are used to achieve the required finish and accuracy specified in the component drawing. Feed rates are set to fine and much smaller cuts are taken. It is a good idea to make trial cuts on parts of the bar that will be machined off later.

Follow the steps below for efficient finishing.

- Use fine feed rates such as 0.03 mm/rev or 0.05 mm/rev.
- Set the correct spindle speed for the material and the tool.
- Make sure your tool is sharp or select a fresh insert tip.
- Use a finishing grade insert tip if available.
- Use coolant. Straight oils can be even better but will ruin soluble coolant if mixed in the machine.
- Check your measurements carefully.
- Make sure the workpiece is cool (room temperature) before making the final finishing cuts. Otherwise when it cools, it will shrink sometimes by a surprising amount.
- Take small cuts and try to make the final cut about 0.3 mm.

Remember to always check your work before removing it from the machine.

**Quick Tip**

If the swarf starts to come off in a long ribbon turn the automatic feed off and then on again. This breaks the swarf and stops it jamming around the work or machine.

**Keep It Safe**

Always stop the machine and use pliers to clear swarf. Do not be tempted to use your hands.

## Grooving and parting

Grooving and parting tools can be thin and may break easily so more gentle control of the lathe is needed than for normal turning.

When using grooving and parting tools:

- use a slower speed than calculated – a reduction of up to 50% will make a big difference
- lock the saddle to stop sideways movement
- use a slow automatic feed rate if possible – often when feeding by hand the movement is not very smooth and the tool will dig in
- check the tool is on centre height as this is critical – if higher or lower it will put extra strain on the tool
- listen as the tool cuts – a change of noise often warns you when something is going wrong.

If you are unable to part off your component safely because there is not enough room for the tool or it will rub on the workholding device used then remove the bar from the lathe and saw it off with a hacksaw with the bar stock held in a vice.

Do not be tempted to saw while the workpiece is still in the lathe as you may slip and damage the lathe bed or hurt yourself.

## Form tools

Form tools are used for turning components such as acorn nuts, knobs, handles, Vee belt grooves and studs, that have short tapers, radiuses and complex shapes.

Form tools are ground to the required profile and then gently fed into the workpiece until the required shape or depth is reached. Form tools are not easy tools to use, as there is often a wide cutting edge in contact with the workpiece that can cause the tool to be overloaded.

Use low lathe speeds with form tools to prevent heat building up and tools being snatched. Straight cutting oils and tapping greases will help prevent this. It is a good idea to make some practice cuts on a bit of scrap taken from the same material as your workpiece. This will help you gauge how to handle the cutting process because often different profiles react in different ways.

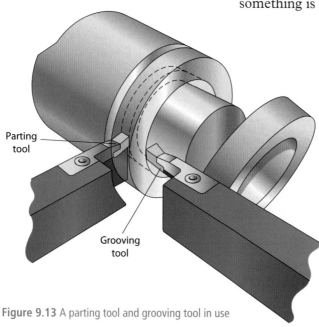

Parting tool

Grooving tool

Figure 9.13 A parting tool and grooving tool in use

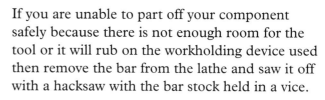

External radius tool

Internal radius tool

Figure 9.14 Simple form tools

## Knurling

Knurling is not a cutting process as it does not remove any metal. Instead it is used to create a pattern (an indent) in a metal. A pattern is indented into the work to provide a grip on the surface. Knurls are often put on components to give finger or hand grip.

There are two types of knurls:

- **straight knurls** put a series of lines or ridges running lengthways along the axis of the work around the circumference of the workpiece
- **diamond knurls** form a diamond pattern on the workpiece.

There are two types of knurling tools: a **calliper type** and a **plunge type**. The calliper type is easier to use but only has one type of roller fitted. The plunge type often has a rotating head so different grades of knurl can be selected quickly.

When using a knurling tool:

- set a slow spindle speed such as 40 rpm
- set as fast a feed rate as you can – approximately 0.5 mm/rev to 1 mm/rev
- make sure the knurling tool is set dead square and on centre height
- make sure the tool overhangs by the smallest amount to keep it firmly in place
- make sure the workpiece is securely held and use a centre to give additional support if necessary
- use a lot of coolant to keep the rollers cool and wash any metal fragments away
- always bring the knurling tool into contact with the workpiece once it is spinning
- use a wire brush to clean a finished knurl and remove metal filings.

## Turning tapers

There are four ways of producing a taper on a centre lathe, as shown in Table 9.07 on page 224.

**Figure 9.15** Calliper type of knurling tool

**Figure 9.16** Plunge type of knurling tool

**Keep It Safe**

If you knurl to the end of the workpiece make sure you remove the burr formed with a small chamfer as it is often very sharp.

| Method | Description |
|---|---|
| Form tool | Cutting short tapers with a form tool can be done by turning the lathe tool to the required angle and gently plunging, cutting the taper. Or you can use a tool with the correct angle ground in the tip |
| Compound slide | Can be used to cut longer tapers. Swivel the compound slide to the required angle and clamp it down. Then feed it by hand using the compound slide hand wheel. Before you start to cut, make sure you have enough travel on the compound slide to achieve the taper you want. Internal tapers and chamfers can be cut using a boring tool |
| Taper turning attachment | Can be used to cut tapers of up to about 250 mm long. You normally fit the taper turning attachment to the rear of the cross slide and adjust it to only 20° each way. You will achieve a much more accurate taper this way. Automatic feed can be used to obtain a better surface finish but setting times are longer |
| Offsetting the tailstock | Setting the tailstock out of line with the machine axis can produce long shallow tapers. But this method is not often used because it takes a long time to set and reset. To turn tapers using this method, the workpiece must be held between centres. Quite often the degree of taper is limited to the distance the headstock can be moved out of alignment. It is also limited by the fact that the centre becomes out of alignment with the centre hole. This does not work well with short workpieces |

Table 9.07 Four different methods for turning tapers

**Hands On**

Practise turning tapers using the compound slide using two hands to slowly feed the tool. This will improve the surface finish on your workpiece.

## Thread cutting

There are a number of different techniques for producing threads on a lathe, but one of the simpler ways is to use taps and dies.

Using taps and dies on a lathe is a good way of producing internal and external screw threads. They can be produced in two ways. You cut an **internal thread** with a tap in a process called tapping. You cut an **external thread** with a die in a process called threading.

The tap and die can be held in special tool holders in the tailstock allowing threads to be made.

## Cutting an external thread under power on a lathe

| Checklist | | | |
|---|---|---|---|
| **PPE** | **Tools and equipment** | **Consumables** | **Source information** |
| • Safety boots<br>• Overalls<br>• Safety glasses<br>• Barrier cream | • Right-hand cutting tool<br>• Micrometer<br>• M12 split button die<br>• Tailstock dieholder<br>• M12 nut or ring gauge | • Cutting oil or coolant<br>• Rag<br>• Tapping compound | • Thread tables |

1 Turn the outside diameter of the workpiece to the required outside diameter of a thread. (An M12 thread would be 12 mm diameter.)

2 Set the die in the tailstock dieholder, opening it up to its **maximum metal condition**.

3 Insert the dieholder firmly in the tailstock ensuring it has been gripped tightly, then check that the sliding part moves freely.

4 Apply tapping compound to the workpiece.

5 Start the spindle on a slow speed (e.g. 40 rpm) and wind the tailstock hand wheel until the die starts to cut.
Be ready to use the brake to stop the machine promptly once the die has travelled to the required position.

6 Turn the hand wheel in reverse giving enough clearance for the die to pull back fully.

7 Engage reverse until the die is clear of the thread.

**Key term**

**Maximum metal condition** – the largest possible size a component can be without being out of tolerance. In the case of a hole this means it is the smallest it can be

8 Check the thread with a nut or ring gauge and re-cut if necessary.

## Cutting an internal thread under power on a lathe

To tap a hole and make an internal thread on a lathe using a tailstock tap head or taping chuck, follow the instructions below.

1. Centre drill, then drill a tapping hole into the workpiece to the correct depth.
2. Set the spindle speed to a slow speed.
3. Fit the tap to the tapping head then put the tapping head into the tailstock.
4. Apply tapping compound to the tap.
5. Start the machine and run the tap into the hole.
6. Once the tap has reached the bottom of the hole, reverse the spindle and the tap will come out.

**Figure 9.17** Work being checked on a lathe using a micrometer

## Checking your work

Checking your work is covered in Chapter 8, pages 192–196. Many of the checks and information you will need for working with lathes is similar to that for hand fitting.

As you turn a component you have to check the finish, shape and sizes regularly to make sure that it meets the job specification. All the dimensions should be checked as you progress because a wrongly sized feature could turn the work to scrap. If the mistake goes unnoticed, it will waste time and money.

The surface finish should be specified for the workpiece and this must be checked as the workpiece is machined. The second to last cut should be checked on the machine by using surface comparison gauges using a visual inspection and by comparing the feel by scratching with your fingernail.

When checking your work, remember to use the most suitable measuring tools for each operation available.

## Dealing with problems

When you are using a lathe, sometimes things go wrong or do not happen as you expect. You need to deal promptly and effectively with these problems by seeking help and guidance from the relevant people. It is important to be honest with yourself and, if you're not sure, ask for help.

If something does go wrong, stop the machine, isolate it from the power supply and make the machine safe. Find out what has happened and ask for help so you can continue to work safely. If you are not sure what to do once you have asked for help, do not be afraid to ask again.

Possible problems

- Excessive spindle speeds causing the tool to wear or break
- Poor or inadequate planning
- Incorrect feed rate giving the wrong surface finish and maybe damaging the tool
- Excessive backlash causing errors
- Blunt or incorrectly ground tools giving a poor finish
- Failure to check work as machining progresses
- Damaged or uncalibrated measuring equipment giving false readings
- Incorrect coolant marking the work
- Misused or incorrectly set workholding equipment causing damage to the workpiece/machine
- Worn or damaged lathe
- Unsuitable lathe used for the task, e.g. too big or too small

**Figure 9.18** Possible problems when using a lathe

## Shutting down

When you have finished work, it is important to make the work area safe and clean.

- Before you do anything, isolate the machine from the power supply. This prevents the machine accidentally starting while you are cleaning it.
- Remove the cutting tools to prevent you from injuring yourself while reaching into the machine to clean it.
- Clear your work area.
- Remove all waste.

## CHECK YOUR KNOWLEDGE

**1** What is the name of the tool used in the tailstock to support your workpiece?

a countersinking tool
b live centre
c tap
d reamer

**2** What is the most common workholding method found on a lathe?

a three jaw chuck
b four jaw chuck
c a collet
d between centres

**3** What speed would be the best for reaming or knurling on the lathe?

a 3,000 rpm
b 1,500 rpm
c 450 rpm
d 90 rpm

**4** Screw threads are cut on a lathe using taps and what other tool?

a counter sink
b dies
c twist drill
d reamers

**5** When making roughing cuts on a lathe, the quickest way to remove metal is by setting the machine to a:

a slow feed rate and shallow cut
b slow feed rate and a deep cut
c fast feed rate and a deep cut
d fast feed rate and a shallow cut

**6** When cleaning a lathe at the end of a session the first thing you should do is:

a turn off the power and take out the tool
b remove the guards
c sweep off the lathe bed
d mop up spilt coolant

**7** Which metal can be cut on a lathe without coolant?

a cast iron
b aluminium
c steel
d stainless steel

**8** Which of the following is a common method of holding tools in the tailstock barrel?

a four jaw chuck
b morse taper
c collet
d face plate

**9** When the diameter of the workpiece gets smaller, to keep the tool cutting well, the spindle speed should be made:

a to stay the same
b slower
c faster
d unchanged as it makes no difference

**10** Which of the following tools cannot make a hole in the workpiece using a lathe?

a twist drill
b boring tool
c centre drill
d knife edge cutting tool

# 10 Carrying out sheet metal cutting, forming and assembly activities

This chapter introduces you to the skills you will need to cut and form sheet metal into different shapes for different uses. You will also explore all the tools and equipment you will need for safe and effective working. Gaining skills and knowledge about sheet metal work will allow you to make many different products that can be used in lots of engineering sectors. You will gain the expertise, skills and experience that can be used in many jobs, not just engineering.

In this chapter you will learn about:

- tools and equipment needed
- marking out
- cutting and shaping materials
- forming equipment
- shrinking and stretching techniques

- joining and assembling sheet metal components
- checking your work
- dealing with problems
- making the work area safe and tidy

# KITTING UP

## Keeping safe

Health and safety is very important when you are working with sheet metal. It can be heavy, hard to move and often has sharp edges. You need to be careful as you handle it. The personal protective equipment (PPE) you need to wear may vary depending on what you are doing. If you are unsure ask your trainer or supervisor, as it is important that you use the correct equipment for the job you are doing.

When you are making large or heavy components, follow any instructions carefully to make sure you support and move sheet metal correctly. This will help avoid the sheet metal being kinked, stretched or damaged while you work.

Before carrying out any activities in the workshop, a risk assessment should be completed. Make sure you read this document carefully and check with your supervisor if there is anything you are not sure about. You need to work with the relevant health and safety legislation covered in Chapter 1 pages 2–6.

Always keep your work area tidy and clean up at the end of the day, putting your tools and equipment back in the correct places. This makes you work more efficiently and safely. Sheet metal can take up a lot of space so keeping your tools tidy and in one place will help to make your work more efficient.

**Safety glasses** – protect your eyes from flying objects when using power tools, and from splashes when using maintenance sprays, oils and sealants. Wear safety goggles when using grinders

**Ear defenders or ear plugs** – should be worn when using noisy power tools or hammering metal

**Overalls** – protect your skin and clothes from contamination by oils, metal particles and sealants. They can also keep loose or baggy clothing from getting caught in equipment or machinery

**Gloves** – leather and canvas gloves may also need to be worn depending on the activity. Chain mail gloves can be useful for handling sheet metal

**Dust mask** – protects your lungs while carrying out activities that create dust, e.g. grinding

**Safety boots or shoes** – protect your feet from falling objects or tools

**Barrier cream** – protects your hands from dirt and oil, and makes them easier to wash

# Tools and equipment needed

Before you start working with sheet metal you need to make sure you have all the tools, materials, equipment and safety equipment you need. These will usually be kept in a storeroom. Make sure you tidy everything away carefully after use. The checks you will need to make for materials, tools and equipment you will use are covered in Chapter 8, pages 166–67.

The checks you will need to make for materials, tools and equipment you will use are covered in Chapter 8, pages 166–67.

**Quick Tip**

If you use the last of something in the store, such as some nuts and bolts or tapping compound, make sure you let someone know so that they can order some more.

**Did You Know**

Some materials and tools may need to be ordered before you can start a new job, so be sure to allow time for this.

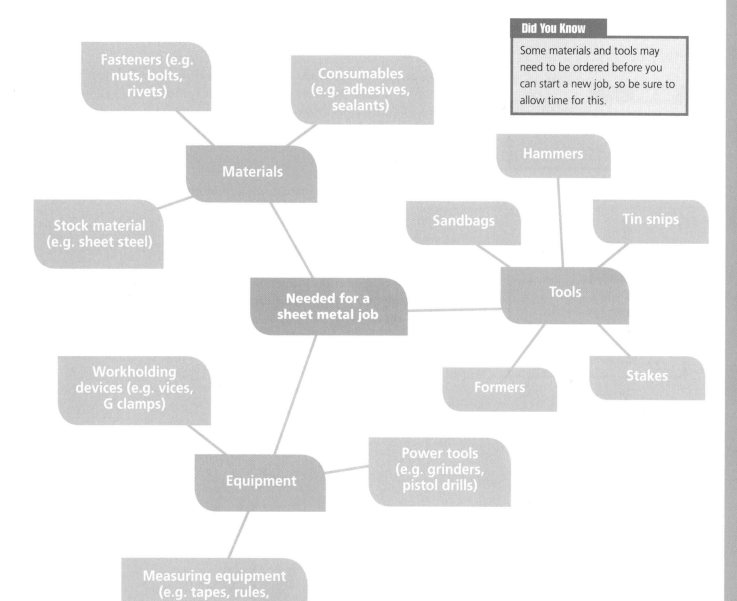

**Figure 10.01** What you will need to get the job done

**Hands On**

Find out where the job instructions, drawings and other information that you may need for a job can be found.

# Marking out

Before marking out sheet metal, you need to prepare it so that the surface you mark up is free from dirt, grease and swarf.

## Preparing sheet metal for marking out

To prepare for marking out, first you need to clean off any protective oils and greases from the sheet. Any films put on to sheet metal to protect a special surface should be left on and can be marked on while measuring up.

Use a rag or industrial tissue to wipe and clean the metal. If it is very dirty or oily you may need to use a degreasant. Make sure you wear the appropriate PPE, as degreasants can be irritating to the skin and harmful. You may also need to remove any swarf or metal particles using a wire brush or steel wool. Once the workpiece has been cleaned, you can **deburr** it.

Tools you can use to deburr sheet metal include:

- deburring tools
- a smooth file
- sheet metal edge deburring tools.

To mark out components to the correct specification you need to use lots of marking and measuring equipment. You should look after and take care of these tools, storing them carefully when not in use. Many of the marking out tools you will need are shown in Chapter 8 pages 168–70. Table 10.01 shows some additional tools you may need for metal work.

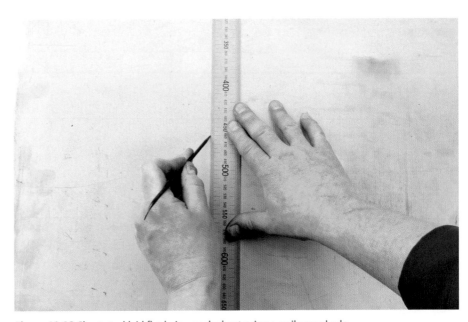
Figure 10.02 Sheet steel laid flat being marked out using a scriber and rule

| Tool | Use |
|---|---|
| **Centre punch** | Used to make an indent in materials that can be used to position a drill or mark a pivot point for dividers or trammels |
| **Straight edge** | Used for marking longer lines on components where the measurements are made with a rule |
| **Engineer's marking blue and paint** | Used to mark out some metals as they enable the marking to be seen more easily. Only use where marks need to be made |
| **Chalk line** | Used for marking out long lines on materials. Fix the string at both ends of the workpiece and stand a small square, touching the line, in the middle of its length. Lift and release the string to leave a chalk mark on the material. The square helps to keep the string line straight as you pull it up |

**Table 10.01** Additional tools used for marking out

## Using datums and templates

Once the workpiece is cleaned and deburred you are ready to establish your **datum** edges or positions. Check your drawing to see if there are any datum points specified. Remember, datums are your reference points when working so they must be correct.

More information on datums can be found in Chapter 8, page 171.

You can use templates to help you mark out complex components, or any shapes that would be hard to mark out by hand. Templates can be made from paper or card, but will last longer if they are made from a hard plastic or metal.

More information on templates can be found in Chapter 8, page 171.

More information on datums can be found in Chapter 8, page 171.

More information on templates can be found in Chapter 8, page 171.

### Hands On

Practise marking out on sheets of paper using a sharp pencil instead of a scriber. These samples can be used as checking aids when you mark out components for real.

### Quick Tip

Use typists' correction fluid instead of marking blue to help mark out dark coloured sheet where marking blue would be difficult to see.

### Keep It Safe

Marking blue contains methanol, which is highly flammable and toxic. It must be used in a well-ventilated place, away from any possible fire hazards.

### Key term

**Datum** – a point, face or line that you measure from as you mark out your work. As your work continues you then use these datums to check that you are working to size.

### Quick Tip

Sometimes you will need to mark large radiuses or have development marks outside the component. To do this, clamp scrap to the side of your workpiece to mark up, rather than waste sheet metal.

### Keep It Safe

Be careful lifting sheet materials onto a work surface for marking out as they may bend and slide off, injuring you as you handle them. Do not struggle – ask someone to help.

# Cutting and shaping materials

There are many different ways of cutting and shaping materials. Some of the tools you can use are covered in this section.

## Tin snips

Tin snips are one of the most useful and versatile hand cutting tools for cutting thin sheet metal. They come in many sizes – the most common is up to 400 mm long. The main types of snips are shown in Table 10.02.

| Type of tin snip | Use |
|---|---|
| **Tin snips (or tinman's shears)** | Used for making straight accurate cuts in thin plate and for large external curves. They are also made with left or right curved blades for cutting internal and external radiuses in thin sheet |
| **Universal combination snips (or gilbows)** | Designed for universal cutting, or internal or external cutting of radiuses and contours. They can cut thicker material than tin snips but cannot be used for close trimming because the blade is too wide. They are available in right- or left-handed versions |
| **Compound action snips (or aviation snips)** | Designed to cut aluminium for the aviation industry but they are popular for general use as they are smaller than tin snips but still able to cut the same thickness of metal. The compound action makes the effort of cutting easier with a series of levers. They are available in straight, left or right cut |

**Table 10.02** Types of tin snip

When using tin snips:

- always hold the sheet you are cutting firmly in your free hand.
- with your free hand push down against the sheet metal, as it will rise as you are cutting.
- if you cut off the line or don't use the snips correctly this can sometimes make a small pin of sheet (sliver) rise from the cutting area. Gently hammer this flat before continuing as it may effectively double the thickness of metal you are trying to cut. This could cause the snips to jam.

## Bench shears

Bench shears are mounted to a bench and are operated by a lever or handle. They can cut thicker metal than hand shears, typically up to 3 mm thick.

They are used to cut straight cuts and outside (external) curves in sheet metal. The metal can be fed through the machine so cuts longer than the length of the blade can be made.

You must always check that there is no one standing behind you as you use a bench shear, as you could easily hit them with the handle as you cut.

Make sure you keep your fingers away from the cutting area – always use the adjustable finger (a piece of metal bolted to the bench shear) to stop the sheet metal from rising up and jamming in the blade.

### Throatless bench shears

Throatless bench shears are used to cut internal and external curves. This is done by moving the sheet as it is fed into the cutting edge. This type of shear is less common and needs a lot of skill to use it.

## Guillotines

There are two types of guillotine:

- foot operated treadle guillotines
- power operated guillotine.

Guillotines are set up and used in the same way. The only difference is that the power guillotine has a trigger that causes electrical or pneumatic (air) power to make the cut. The foot operated guillotine has a foot treadle which is pushed down to cut the sheet metal.

When cutting large sheets on a guillotine, use left and right gilbows or aviation snips to start the cut on the cut line. This makes a small tab of metal that drops down so the sheet can be pulled against the blade before cutting to ensure it is on line.

Figure 10.03 A bench shear

 **Keep It Safe**

Take care as you are loading the sheet on to a guillotine or flat bench as the sheet may bow and slide from your grip, slicing into you or others around you.

 **Keep It Safe**

Ear defenders should be worn when operating a power guillotine.

**Quick Tip**

When using a treadle guillotine for long cuts on thicker sheet material, two operators may be needed. Once the sheet metal has been positioned correctly one operator should place their weight on the left-hand treadle without making a cut, then the other operator should push quickly on the right. The weight of the other operator allows a smooth cut to be made.

Figure 10.04 Power operated guillotine

The guillotine has several stops or gauges to set the material in the correct place ready for cutting.

| Gauge | Use |
|---|---|
| **Fixed side gauge or squaring gauge** | Fitted to the left side of the guillotine table or bed and set square to the bottom blade of the guillotine. Guides the metal and allows square cuts 90° to another face to be made. This allows datums to be cut and prepared |
| **Front gauge** | Bolted to the bed of the guillotine, between the operator and the blade. Work can be lifted over the gauge and pulled back towards it, allowing cuts to be made, with waste falling away at the back. Can be set at an angle and the metal sheet rested against the side gauge for more precise angle cuts |
| **Back gauge** | Slides on arms above the surface of the sheet metal after it has passed through the blades. Mounted on the opposite side of the blade to the operator, it cannot be seen during use so must be checked to make sure it is in contact with the metal. Easiest gauge to use and the most accurate |
| **Bevel plate** | An L-shaped plate bolted in the front gauge position and used to align sheet metal in position for cutting angled surfaces and faces |

**Table 10.03** Types of gauge used on guillotines

**Figure 10.05** Bevel plate

## Safety points

Safety is very important when using guillotines as they are powerful machines and can easily trap and crush or cut off fingers. Always follow these safety tips when working with guillotines.

1. Always isolate a powered guillotine from its power supply before setting up or cleaning down.

2. Check the condition of the blade by looking down the sighting hole above the bottom blade.

3. Make sure your fingers are not between the guillotine bed and the sheet metal or they may get crushed as the machine operates.

4. Make sure all guards are in place before using the guillotine.

5. If two of you are using a treadle guillotine, make sure your partner is clear of the treadles as you set up.

6. Never try to cut thicker material than specified on the machine – remember that if the blade is starting to wear the guillotine may not be able to cut as thick a material as specified.

## Cutting on a guillotine

| Checklist | | | |
|---|---|---|---|
| **PPE** | **Tools and equipment** | **Consumables** | **Source information** |
| • Safety boots<br>• Overalls<br>• Barrier cream<br>• Safety glasses<br>• Ear defenders | • Steel rule<br>• Engineer's tri-square | • Workshop tissue or rag | • Workshop specification |

**1**

Check the sheet metal is large enough to make the required blank size and find the best side to start to work from.

**2**

Load the sheet metal onto the guillotine bed with its best side running on the fixed side gauge. It may not be true (straight) but check – looking down the sighting hole – that a roughly even strip about 6 mm wide is over the bottom blade.

**3**

Check its position again to be sure it is positioned correctly then make the cut.

**4**

Now position this fresh edge (your first datum) against the side gauge. With about 6 mm over the bottom blade, make the second cut 90° from the first cut edge.

**5**

Set the back gauge to the correct distance, using a steel rule, checking the distance at both ends of the bottom blade.

**6**

Cut the sheet steel and check the dimension and squareness of the sheet metal before making the final cut.

## Circle cutting machine or trepanning machine

Handwheel

Stop screw

Cutting head

Operating handle

Lower cutter adjuster screw

Lower cutter bearing
adjustment nuts

Pallet adjustment wheel

Bow

Clamping pallets

Handwheel
(circle diameter control)

Bar

Clamping handle bow

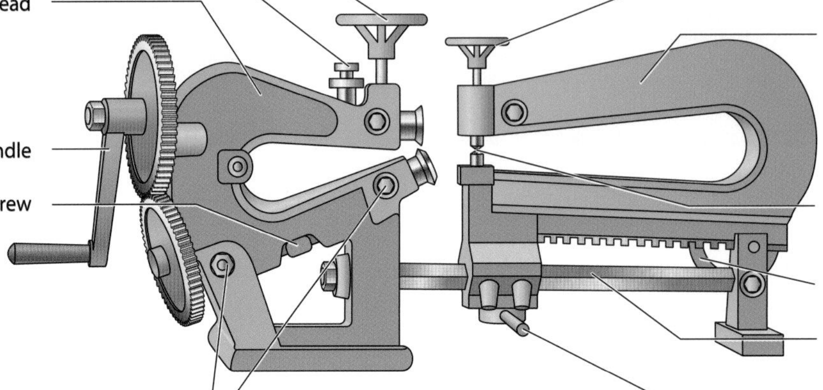

**Figure 10.06** Circle cutting machine

A circle cutting machine or trepanning machine is a rotary cutter. Imagine an oversized tin opener and you will have a good idea about how it works.

It can be used to cut sheets that need to be rolled into cones or used for funnels. It can make complete or partial circles. The instructions below show how a circle cutting machine works.

- Grip the flat metal sheet in the central clamping pallet. This has a raised bump and a hollow that will make a centre punched mark on the sheet metal.
- Adjust the bow to the radius you want. If the diameter of the circle has been marked by dividers or trammels, it should be easy to set the top cutting wheel to this line to set the diameter.
- Make sure you lock the bow in position using the clamping handle. You then need to turn the workpiece fully by hand. This is so you can make sure it will pass through the machine.
- Turn the operating handle and apply a gentle cut with the hand wheel.

Remember when you are using the machine to take your time and just put a small amount of cut on for every revolution. The sheet is only being held in place by the centre punch mark in the middle and it may deform, spoiling the circle, if you try to make to bigger a cut.

Remember to cut the outer diameter first. If you are cutting a partial cut, always increase the cut in the middle of the sheet and not the edge. This makes it easier when the cutting edge comes off the sheet metal.

## Hacksaws and files

Hacksaws and files are covered in Chapter 8, pages 172–78. Look back at this section for more information on the different types and their uses.

### Hacksaws

Hacksaws can be used for sheet metal work but are far slower than tin snips, hand shears and guillotines. When you use hacksaws with thin sheet, try to keep three teeth in contact with the sheet metal. You might have to hold the saw at a shallow angle to the surface of the sheet metal to make the cut. Hacksaws are useful for cutting fine detail in sheet metalwork when snips or hand shears are hard to use.

You can't use a hacksaw for large sheets of material, because the depth of the frame limits its reach. A sheet saw has a hacksaw blade fitted to a flat metal blade. This can pass through the material like a hand saw allowing you to cut large sheets. The sheet saw can be used on corrugated materials that cannot be cut using a guillotine.

### Files

Files can be useful for deburring sheet metal and making slight adjustments to finished work. When using a file to deburr thin sheet materials, be careful not to remove too much material from the edge as this might make it hard to weld or join.

The best file for deburring sheet metal is a single cut hand smooth file. The single cut teeth make it easy to control on thin edges.

## Hand power tools

Hand power tools are a very useful addition to a sheet metal worker's toolbox. They are powered by electricity (240 V, 110 V or battery operated) or by air (pneumatic tools).

When working on large components they can be easily transported to where they are needed. This means heavy or awkward workpieces can be left where they are and work carried on around them rather than working around fixed machines. Table 10.04, shows the most common power tools you will use.

**Keep It Safe**

Always check power tools and equipment before you use them for frayed leads, damaged plugs or cases. Always wear the correct PPE before you start.

| Power tool | Use |
|---|---|
| **Portable shear** | A useful tool for rapidly cutting straight lines and curves. Fitted with a set of fine blades to make small cuts about 3 mm long. The blades move at over 1000 cuts a minute and can cut thin sheet at nearly 10 m per minute leaving a clean edge |
| **Portable nibbler** | Has a punch and die and rapidly creates a series of small overlapping holes. It can be placed through a drilled hole and used to cut internal profiles that otherwise could only be cut by expensive press tools. Can cut straight and curved lines and leaves less distortion than a portable shear but leaves a slightly serrated edge due to the punching action of the cutter |
| **Pistol drill** | Very useful for drilling holes in hard to reach places for riveting or for screws and bolts. A pilot drill of about 3 mm should be used first for larger holes to make drilling the component easier |
| **Angle grinder** | Very useful for removing burrs, cleaning surfaces and flattening welds and tacks. Can be used with cutting discs, grinding wheels, sanding discs and flap wheels. When using on components that may need to be welded, do not grind too deeply as this will make the material weak and thin |

Table 10.04 Common power tools and their uses

## Bench drills

A bench drill is a freestanding machine and can be used for:

- drilling
- countersinking
- trepanning.

More information about bench drills can be found in Chapter 8, pages 180–86.

When using a bench drill for sheet metal work, keeping your workpiece secure is very important. This is because sheet metal can be grabbed by the cutting tool and spun, causing nasty injuries. The sheet should be bolted or clamped directly to the machine table and never held by hand.

Portable drilling machines can be held onto sheet steel with built-in magnets and have all the advantages of a drilling machine as well as being portable. Its only disadvantage is that it cannot grip non-ferrous sheet materials.

Drilling tool bits useful for sheet metal work are shown in Table 10.05.

| Tool | Description | Uses |
|---|---|---|
| **Twist drill** | A standard drill with twisted flutes (grooves) used to drill holes. It may have a parallel shank held by a drill chuck or it may have a Morse tapered shank to hold it true | Used to drill holes. In small sizes come in 0.1 mm steps. Over 13 mm in diameter they normally have a Morse tapered shank |
| **Countersink drill** | A short ridged tool with an included angle cutting edge of either 60° or 90°. Should be run at slow speeds to avoid chatter | Used to set flush countersunk screws and for countersinking prior to riveting |
| **Trepanning tool** | Has a central drill or pin and a single point cutting tool on an adjustable arm | Used to cut large diameter holes. Must be guarded carefully before use and run at slow speeds |
| **Cone drill** | A cone shaped drill which is either stepped or tapered. If the drill is stepped, each step corresponds to a specific size | Very useful for cutting holes in sheet up to about 40 mm in diameter |
| **Hole saw** | A central guide drill with a circular saw blade used for cutting holes | Better at cutting large diameter holes in thicker plate. If used correctly, it leaves an almost burr-free hole |

**Table 10.05** Drilling tool bits used in sheet metal work

## Forming equipment

Once metal has been cut to size it then needs to be bent and fashioned into the correct shape. This is called forming. For sheet metal, forming can involve folding, rolling and hammering into shape.

## Rolling machines

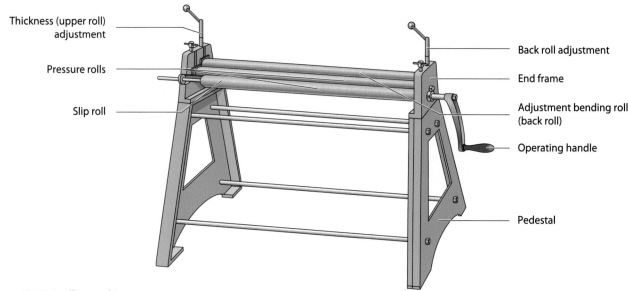

Thickness (upper roll) adjustment

Pressure rolls

Slip roll

Back roll adjustment

End frame

Adjustment bending roll (back roll)

Operating handle

Pedestal

**Figure 10.07** A rolling machine

Many products made of sheet metal need circular bends – for example tubes, pipes and curves. These bends are made with a rolling machine.

Rolling machines for thin sheet (up to 3 mm thick) have three rollers:

- The **front two rollers** lie one on top of the other. They are used to lightly pinch the sheet metal and grip it allowing it to be drawn through the machine against the back roller.

- The **back roller** puts the set on the sheet to form a curve.

- One of the front two rollers is called the **slip roll**. This can be removed and loosened at one end to slide the tube that has been rolled from the machine.

As a rule the smallest roll that can be produced on a rolling machine is about 1.5 to 2 times the diameter of the roller used.

You must know what type of rolling machine you are using. Try looking at the grooves for wired edges in the rollers to help you identify the type of machine.

- A **roll up machine** has a slip roll at the top of the pinch roll set and grooves in the bottom pinch roller.

- A **roll down machine** has the slip roll at the bottom and grooves in the top pinch roller. Large diameter curves cannot be rolled on this, as the sheet metal hits either the floor or machine.

**Quick Tip**

You can also produce radiuses on a sheet but you will need to take more care as the metal cannot be removed easily from the machine between passes.

## Rolling a curve on a rolling machine

| Checklist | | | |
|---|---|---|---|
| **PPE** | **Tools and equipment** | **Consumables** | **Source information** |
| • Safety boots<br>• Overalls<br>• Barrier cream<br>• Safety glasses | • Steel rule<br>• Engineer's tri-square<br>• Radius template | • Workshop tissue or rag | • Work specification<br>• Drawings |

**1**

Gently grip the sheet metal between the pinch rollers. This grip must be light or the metal will be deformed and stretched causing a larger diameter than needed. It is a good idea to make a feeler gauge out of a bit of scrap the same thickness as the workpiece metal to set the pinch at either end of the rollers correctly.

**2**

Wind the sheet through to check that it tracks okay and does not veer to one side. If it does, this could be caused by incorrect pressure on one of the thickness adjusters on the pinch roll.

**3**

Wind the back roll into position until it is just touching the sheet metal evenly across the sheet.

**4**

Wind the metal back until its front edge is just on the centre of the back roller. Adjust it for a slight set or bend in the sheet.

**5**

If you are rolling a tube, roll the metal all the way through. Then reverse and roll through again on the same setting to remove the kink put in the sheet by the first roll as it started.

**6**

Slowly and evenly adjust the back roller, rolling the sheet through until the desired curve has been formed. Remove the sheet from the rolls.

## Bending machines

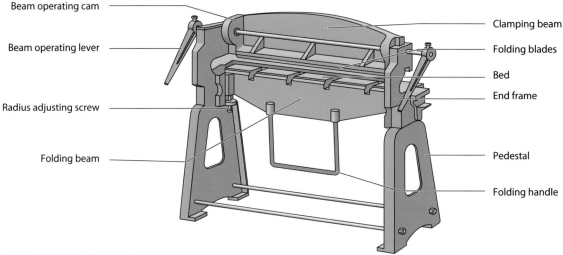

Beam operating cam

Beam operating lever

Radius adjusting screw

Folding beam

Clamping beam

Folding blades

Bed

End frame

Pedestal

Folding handle

**Figure 10.08** A bending machine

Bending or folding machines are designed to produce straight bends or folds in sheet metal. They can be hand powered or electrical. It is important to plan carefully before carrying out this kind of work as it often has to be done in a correct order to meet the specification. The three main steps in bending work are:

- **Clamping** – check if the workpiece can be clamped using the clamps on the machine. If not you may need to use special clamps.
- **Folding** – check the folding beam clears the work. This becomes more and more important as more folds are put into the workpiece as sometimes the work can be damaged by the next fold.
- **Work removal** – you need to be able to remove the workpiece after you have finished the final bend.

Figure 10.09 shows some examples of the variety of bends and combination of bends you can create on a bending/folding machine.

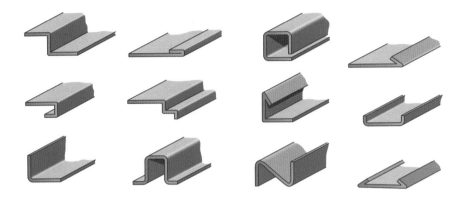

Figure 10.09 Folds from a bending machine

## Wheeling machines

The wheeling machine forms compound (double curvature) curves from flat sheets of metal and can smooth mallet marks from a curved or dished sheet. This is known as wheeling. Because wheeling machines require a lot of skill and labour, they are expensive machines to use. However, the machine can produce many different sheet metal forms.

It is used wherever low volumes of compound curved panels are required, such as guards, curved ends of tanks and bowls. Aluminum is easier to shape than steel, because it is softer. For one-off pieces or small batches the wheeling machine is a useful tool.

## Jennying machines

A jenny is a hand operated tool designed to prepare and finish the edges of sheet metal. It has matched pairs of rollers that can be fitted onto the machine to perform many different tasks. It can be used to bend a **flange**, **swage**, **close**, **joggle** and wire an edge. All of these processes are designed to stiffen the edge and make it safer when the product is used.

A jenny can also be used to help join metal together, such as producing a flange on a disk of metal ready to be joined to the base of a tube of rolled sheet. A jenny can also be fitted with rotary cutting blades to cut long lengths of strip or irregular profiles.

### Safety points

A jenny is a useful tool as it can produce shapes and forms on straight, irregular and circular edges. When using a jenny, the following points should be noted.

- Never overtighten the rolls on a jenny. Only grip the material lightly otherwise the jenny may act as a circular cutter, shearing off the edge.

### Key terms

**Swage** – a shape or form pushed into cold metal, often as a groove or radiused channel. Used to strengthen sheet material. Corrugated iron could be considered a series of swaged grooves

**Joggle** – an offset bend or kink in the sheet like a step which will allow one flat sheet to be placed above the other for joining. It will also strengthen the sheet

**Flange** – an external or internal ridge, or rim (lip) that can make an edge more rigid and strong. Can be used to attach to another object such as a base to an open tube

**Close** – rolling or folding an edge over on itself to make it rounded and stiffer. Often used to finish sheet metalwork

Figure 10.10 Jennying machine

- Use flanging rolls to tuck in a wired edge.
- Use the gauge to set the correct edge distance and try out on a piece of scrap first.
- When flanging a disc use a small piece of folded metal to protect your hand and thoroughly deburr the workpiece first.

## Stakes and formers

Stakes and formers are a very important part of sheet metal hand work. They are mainly used with soft hammers such as box wood mallets so that the sheet metal or stake is not bruised and damaged. Table 10.06 describes the main sheet metal stakes used for shaping sheet metal

| Type of stake | Use |
|---|---|
| **Bick iron** | Used with a wooden mallet for making circular and angular bends. It is finely tapered and useful for simple curves and fine cones, e.g. funnels |
| **Funnel stake** | Used to bend larger cylindrical and conical shapes. Often sheet metal is bent just by hand pressure with the imagined apex of the cone lined up with the point of the funnel stake |
| **Hatchet stake** | Used for turning edges past 90°. Can be used to fold edges and form the start of wired edges. They are also useful when folding small boxes |
| **Half moon stake** | Used to raise flanges on circular work or curves, e.g. bowls and radiused corners |
| **Creasing iron** | Used to make straight angular bends, help with wiring, closing edges and making grooves |
| **Round bottom stake** | Used to finish the bases of cylindrical work. Made in various diameters |
| **Raising stake** | Used with a raising hammer or raising mallet to form deep hollow shapes |
| **Bench mandrel** | Used with a mallet to fold or gently curve sheet metal. They can also hold a stake in the square socket |
| **Wooden former** | Used to shape curves and forms in sheet metal |
| **Sandbag** | Used with bossing mallets for hollowing and forming sheet metal. Made of tough buffalo hide |

**Table 10.06** The main types of stakes used for shaping sheet metal

A wide range of special hammers and mallets are also used for sheet metal work, the most common ones are described in Table 10.07.

| Type of mallet or hammer | Description | Use |
|---|---|---|
| **Tinman's mallet** | All of these have a head made of a very hard, dense wood such as box wood or lignum vitae | Used for bending sheet metal or hammering sheet flat without stretching or bruising |
| **Bossing mallet** | | Used to shape internal curves in sheet metal either with a sandbag or hollow wooden former |
| **Raising mallet** | | Wedge-shaped face is used to shrink metal with a round headed stake or raising stake. Also used to raise a bowl shape in sheet material |
| **Planishing hammer** | Has a highly polished hardened face, often with one flat and one curved | Used for finishing marks out of sheet metal work, often from work that has been hammered into shape |
| **Flattening hammer** | Similar to planishing hammer but has two flat surfaces, one round and one square for reaching into tight corners | Used to produce a flat surface for car body and panel work. Similar in use to the planishing hammer |
| **Blocking hammer** | Has a long hammer head with polished radiused ends | Used for shaping curves, bowls and indentations in sheet metal |
| **Raising hammer or stretching hammer** | A steel version of the raising mallet having a wedge-shaped end and a flat end | Wedge-shaped face is used with a round headed stake or raising stake to shrink metal. Also used to raise a bowl shape in sheet material |
| **Shrinking hammer** | Has a chequered or corrugated face | Used to shrink stretched sheet metal. The sheet is heated to red heat and hit with a shrinking hammer to reduce its size |
| **Tucking hammer** | Has straight peins with sharp edges | Used for finishing off wired edges or hammering sharp corners in sheet metal. The outer edge of the hammer is radiused to allow close hammering to a vertical face |

**Table 10.07** Types of mallet or hammer

**Raising** a bowl or dome contracts and thickens the metal, whereas **hollowing** stretches and thins the metal. Raising always start from the centre of the blank working out, whereas hollowing always starts from the edge working in.

## Wired edges

Wired edges are used to strengthen and finish off an edge of sheet metal, making it rigid and giving it a curved top to make it safer to handle.

# How to wire a simple edge

| Checklist | | | |
|---|---|---|---|
| **PPE** | **Tools and equipment** | **Consumables** | **Source information** |
| • Safety boots<br>• Overalls<br>• Barrier cream<br>• Safety glasses | • Steel rule<br>• Engineer's tri-square<br>• Tinman's mallet<br>• Hatchet stake<br>• Bending machine<br>• Planishing hammer<br>• Bick iron<br>• Pliers<br>• Creasing iron | • Workshop tissue or rag<br>• Edging wire | • Work specification<br>• Drawings |

1 Measure the wire and then add 2.5 times the diameter of the wire to the edge of the sheet metal –  this is the wiring allowance. If the wire is 3 mm in diameter then add 7.5 mm (i.e. 2.5 x 3 mm = 7.5 mm) to the edge.

2 Mark out the wiring allowance along the edge of the sheet metal.

3 Using a bending machine or a hatchet stake and tinman's mallet, bend the edge of the  sheet metal over ready to take the wire.

4 Hold the wire in position and, with the sheet laid on a flat surface such as a bick iron, gently hammer  the folded sheet over the wire. Start in the middle using the tinman's mallet.

5 Once the wire is trapped, use a planishing hammer to gently tuck the edge of the sheet metal into the gap  between the wire and sheet, sealing the wire in place. A hatchet stake can also be used to do this.

6 Finally, lay the wired edge face down in the right sized groove in the creasing iron and gently  hammer with the tinman's mallet to smooth the edge and tighten the sheet metal on the wire.

# Shrinking and stretching techniques

When forming sheet metal by hand some of the metal will be shrunk and made thicker and some will be stretched and made thinner. It is the **malleable** properties of metals that allow them to be shaped by hand and machine.

When shaping and forming it is important to understand the properties of the material you are working with. A skilled sheet metal worker needs to know how metals behave and how they will flow as they are worked and shaped. You need to learn how much force is needed to shape the metal when working with hammers and mallets, and in what direction force should be applied.

Table 10.08 shows the three types of blow or hammering technique used in sheet metal work.

**Key term**

**Malleable** – can be shaped or formed by bending or hammering into shape without splitting or cracking

**Quick Tip**

If bending machines or hammering is likely to mark your work, use some thin sheet or a block of wood to protect the workpiece as you shape it.

| Blow | Description | Example shown |
|---|---|---|
| **Solid blow** | When metal is struck firmly over a solid steel head or anvil. A solid blow stretches the metal and can be used to bend or hollow the work | A solid blow being used on a bent angle form to make it curve |
| **Elastic blow** | An elastic blow will form sheet metal, barely stretching it and can be used to thicken the metal by shrinking it. Either the mallet head or the tool is made of a resilient material such as wood | An elastic blow being used to shape a bowl using a bossing mallet and the edges being shrunk to remove wrinkles |
| **Floating blow** | A floating blow controls the direction the metal flows in when forming. The workpiece is held over a suitable stake and hit off solid, forming a dent at the point of impact. Used for raising an edge, the head of the anvil or stake is not directly under the hammer | A flange being raised on a sheet using floating blows |

**Table 10.08** Types of blow

**QUICK CHECK**

1  What piece of equipment can be used to form a cylinder of sheet metal?
2  Name the different tools that are in the workshop that can be used to cut sheet metal.
3  Name three different stakes used in sheet metal work and state what they are designed to do.

**Hands On**

Practise cutting, marking and bending on off-cuts and scraps using all the necessary equipment in the workshop. This will help you get familiar with the equipment and how the material reacts to each process.

# Joining and assembling sheet metal components

There are many ways of joining and assembling sheet metal components. Some of the most common methods are described in this section.

---

**Making a grooved seam**

Self-securing joints such as a grooved seam are an effective method of joining two sheets together or two edges to form a tube. There is no heat involved so there is no distortion and a sound joint can be easily made.

1. Mark out joining allowances and bend up each edge of the sheet to be joined.

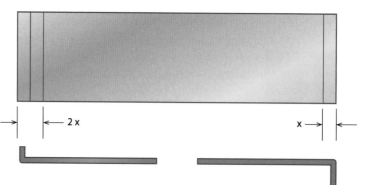

2. Using a tinman's mallet, fold both laps over a strip of scrap the same thickness as the sheet material being used.

3. Hook the two parts together and hammer the edge gently to lock together.

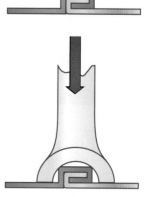

4. Close down the joint with a grooving tool to lock and finish the edge.

---

## Soldered joints

A soldered joint can be made by **tinning** a simple lap or joggled joint and then sweating the edges together with a hot soldering iron. More information about soldering can be found in Chapter 7, pages 158-61.

For successful soldering with metals, follow the steps below.

1. Select a soldering iron with a high enough wattage to easily heat the metal you are using.

2. Clean with wire wool the joint areas to be soldered until the metal is bright. Do not use emery as this will leave grains in the metal which may spoil the joint.

3. Use a good-quality paste flux and wipe it along the joint area with a scrap of metal. Do not use your finger as the flux is harmful.

4. Slowly wipe the soldering iron down the joint area, applying extra solder to each part of the joint area leaving a thin film of bright solder.

5. Apply the cleaned soldering iron again to the tinned area. Smoothing it down should thin any bumps or thick patches of solder that may move the joint out of line.

6. Apply a small amount of flux to the tinned faces and bring the two parts of the joint together.

7. Slowly run a cleaned soldering iron down the outside of the joint, watching the tinned joint area for signs of fusing, only moving on once this has happened.

## Riveting

Riveting is a fast, simple, reliable and cost-effective form of fastening. Light rivets, used for sheet metal work, are usually permanent fasteners and are for assemblies that do not have to be taken apart. They can also be used as hinges, pivots and spacers.

Rivets are available in steel, brass, aluminium and copper. Most types of rivet have to be passed through an aligned hole before forming the end of a rivet (clinching), with the exception of the self-piercing rivets. The most common types are described below.

> **Quick Tip**
>
> To keep a soldering iron tip clean, wipe it regularly with a bit of flux paste on a rag or paper towel as you work.

> **Keep It Safe**
>
> Solder flux is an irritant and should be kept off your clothing and skin. Follow the manufacturer's safety guidelines when using it.

| Type of rivet | Description |
| --- | --- |
| **Solid rivets** | Strong but require more work to clinch than other rivets. Can have a range of head shapes. The end of the rivet is clinched with a ball pein hammer |
| **Tubular rivets** | Have some of the advantages of solid rivets but are easier to clinch. There are three types of tubular rivet:<br>• **short hole rivets** are used in the same way as solid rivets but with easier clinching<br>• **double tapered hole rivets** do not expand in the hole when clinched and are useful for brittle materials<br>• **bull nose rivets** are used for maximum strength and have a shank that swells as it is clinched |
| **Self-piercing rivets** | Specially designed to pierce and clinch at the same time and can be very quick to use. More suited to applications in soft materials such as aluminium |
| **Blind or pop rivets** | Can be used where access can only be gained on one side, but often used where access can be gained on both sides. The rivet is clinched by a pop rivet gun which grips the central mandrel and pulls. When the rivet is clinched the mandrel snaps with a popping sound leaving the rivet in place |

**Table 10.09** Types of rivet

**Quick Tip**

When drilling holes for blind rivets for sheet metal assemblies, if possible, support the sheet with a length of scrap wood to stop the sheets distorting.

To assemble sheet metal components using blind rivets, follow the steps below.

1. Check the specification and select the correct size and type of blind rivet for the task.

2. Select the correct drill size for the rivet.

3. Fit the right size nozzle to the blind rivet clinching tool to match the mandrel of the blind rivets being used.

4. Trial fit the components together to make sure they fit correctly.

5. Drill the correct holes in the outer sheet and deburr them carefully.

6. Line up the sheet on the assembly, checking its position and clamp in place if possible. Drill the first hole through using the hole in the outer sheet to guide the drill.

7. Use a correct size rivet clamp or put a rivet in the hole and check again before clinching the first rivet.

8. Check alignment of the component and drill a second hole, then rivet and check again.

9. Drill and finish all the specified rivets one at a time to reduce the chance of error.

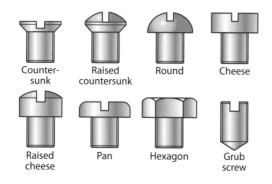

Counter-sunk    Raised countersunk    Round    Cheese

Raised cheese    Pan    Hexagon    Grub screw

**Figure 10.11** Types of screw

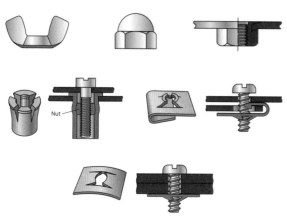

**Figure 10.12** Types of nut

## Mechanical fasteners

Mechanical fasteners such as nuts, bolts and screws can be used to join sheet metal components and assemblies together. Their main advantage is that they can easily be taken apart again for maintenance or service reasons (see Figure 10.11).

**Self-tapping screws** are used for fast assembly work and don't loosen when vibrated. There are two types:

- **thread forming** screws moves the work material to produce its thread. These are used in soft materials
- **thread cutting** screws for cutting a thread into hard brittle materials in a similar way to a tap.

Standard hexagonal **nuts** are used with screws to fasten parts together (see Figure 10.12).

When access can only be gained from one side, **rivet bushes** or **rivet nuts** can be used to provide a good thread in thin sheet.

**Bolts** are screws that do not have a thread all the way to the head of the screw. The plain area is stronger than the threaded part and can be aligned in a hole more easily.

# Checking your work

Some of the methods you will need to check your work with sheet metal are covered in Chapter 8, pages 192–96.

Are all parts put together correctly with secure and firm joints?

Have all the burrs and sharp edges been removed?

Are the edges square?

Are there any cracks or dents from hammering?

**Checks for sheet metal work**

Are there any twists or distorted parts?

Is it the right size and within tolerance?

Is it the correct shape and does it match the drawing?

**Figure 10.13** Checks for working with sheet metal

# Dealing with problems

If something does go wrong while using a power tool *always* stop the machine and isolate it from the power supply before you investigate. This will make the machine safe.

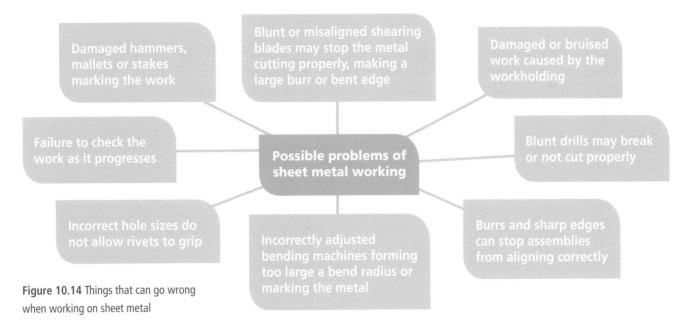

Damaged hammers, mallets or stakes marking the work

Blunt or misaligned shearing blades may stop the metal cutting properly, making a large burr or bent edge

Damaged or bruised work caused by the workholding

Failure to check the work as it progresses

**Possible problems of sheet metal working**

Blunt drills may break or not cut properly

Incorrect hole sizes do not allow rivets to grip

Incorrectly adjusted bending machines forming too large a bend radius or marking the metal

Burrs and sharp edges can stop assemblies from aligning correctly

**Figure 10.14** Things that can go wrong when working on sheet metal

# Making the work area safe and tidy

Information about making the work area safe and tidy after work can be found in Chapter 8, page 196. You will need to make sure that hammers, mallets and stakes are in good condition after use. You will also need to re-tin and clean any flux from soldering iron tips before storing them to prevent the soldering tip corroding.

## CHECK YOUR KNOWLEDGE

1 What piece of extra PPE should be worn when handling sheet metal other than safety boots and overalls?

  **a** strong leather gloves
  **b** safety glasses
  **c** ear defenders
  **d** hard hat

2 Which sheet metal cutter could be powered?

  **a** hand shear
  **b** guillotine
  **c** bench shear
  **d** tinman's snips

3 Burrs and slivers should always be removed while you are working with sheet metal. Where can they be found?

  **a** on the surface of sheet metal
  **b** on the working faces of new tools
  **c** on the surface of the inside of a bend as it is formed
  **d** on the edges of unfinished sheet metal

4 Blind rivets are best used to join

  **a** assemblies where a flush, snag-free surface is required both sides of the join
  **b** hard brittle materials
  **c** components together where you can only reach one side
  **d** assemblies that need to be taken apart often

5 Which mallet or hammer should be used with a sandbag to form a curve?

  **a** bossing mallet
  **b** tinman's mallet
  **c** planishing hammer
  **d** raising mallet

6 Which of these is used to cut datum edges on a guillotine?

  **a** front gauge
  **b** back gauge
  **c** side gauge
  **d** bevel plate

7 What tool used for cutting sheet metal was originally designed for cutting aluminium?

  **a** tinman's snips
  **b** gilbows
  **c** hand shear
  **d** aviators snips

8 What stake can be used to prepare sheet metal ready to wire a straight edge?

  **a** raising stake
  **b** funnel stake
  **c** half moon stake
  **d** hatchet stake

9 When raising a bowl you should start to hammer

  **a** in the centre of the blank
  **b** at the edge of the blank
  **c** at the edge of the planned base of the bowl
  **d** halfway between the edge of the bowl and the planned base

10 Swaged, panned down, knocked up and joggled are all types of

  **a** self-securing joints
  **b** rivets
  **c** screw
  **d** fastener

# 11 Using manual oxy-fuel gas and manual metal arc welding equipment

We have used heat to form and join metals for hundreds of years. Along the way, we have discovered that these processes can create immensely strong structures and tools. Welding is crucial to so much of the world's engineering and construction achievements. From ships to tower blocks, cars to aircraft, welding literally provides the glue that holds these constructions together.

Welding is a highly skilled task. It can only be mastered through patient practice and attention to detail. Because it involves heat, light and potentially toxic and explosive chemicals, welding is also extremely dangerous so enormous care has to be taken. A careless attitude or lack of knowledge could be lethal. Welding health and safety should never be taken for granted.

Welding is, however, a skill that is rewarding, highly regarded and in much demand in our modern world.

In this chapter you will learn:

- what welding is
- welding health and safety
- manual oxy-fuel gas welding
- manual arc welding
- stop and starts
- welding joints, materials, forms and positions
- welding different forms

# KITTING UP

Although most welding work is carried out in workshops and the factory environment, some welding is done on construction sites. The following items of PPE are compulsory on most construction sites and need to be worn in addition to welding PPE:

- **welder's hat** to protect hair from sparks
- **fume masks** to protect breathing – air supply helmets can also be worn
- **protective footwear**
- **ear defenders** – in noisy work areas and when using noisy machinery (e.g welders often use grinding tools to prepare metal for welding or to smooth down the bead after welding is finished)
- **dust masks** – in work areas where there is a lot of dust
- **spark-proof overalls**

Before carrying out any activities in the workshop, a risk assessment should be completed. They describe the risks and how they should be controlled. The Provision and Use of Work Equipment Regulations 1998 covers the use of equipment to ensure it is suitable for the intended use, safe, used only by those with training and with suitable safety measures.

*Welding goggles and helmets* with dark face plates – much darker than those in sunglasses

*Auto-darkening welding hood* – newer versions automatically self-darken

*Oxy-fuel goggles*

*Heavy leather gloves* – hot metal such as electrode stubs and workpieces should never be handled without gloves

*Protective long-sleeved jackets* – avoid oily greasy clothing. A spark may ignite them

*Hard hats* – protect hair from sparks

*Protective footwear* – protect your feet from falling objects or tools

# Paperwork

| Document | What it tells you |
|---|---|
| Control of Substances Harmful to Health (COSHH) Regulations | The main set of regulations that makes sure all workers are not harmed by chemicals and fumes of any sort. These are particularly important to welders because welding causes harmful gas to form around the workpiece |
| Health and Safety Executive (HSE) WL8: COSHH essentials for welding, hot work and allied processes | A document that applies COSHH regulations to welding and talks about providing and maintaining good ventilation in areas where welding takes place |
| HSE HSG139 The safe use of compressed gases in welding, flame cutting and allied processes | A guide explaining how to safely handle gas equipment used for oxy-fuel gas welding |
| British Compressed Gas Association (BCGA) | An organisation made up of welding companies and equipment suppliers. The BGCA produces publications dealing with welding safety |
| ISO 15614-1:2004 | This standard applies to the arc and gas welding of steels. It is the standard for all welding testing. There are other standards for different types of welding |
| The Confined Spaces Regulations 1997 | Although no one should work in confined spaces, there are times when it is necessary. The Confined Spaces Regulations shows how this can be done as safely as possible |
| The Work at Height Regulations 2005 | Describes how to work safely on scaffolding and ladders |

# Toolkit

Welding equipment is described in more detail later in this chapter. An oxy-fuel gas kit is made up of:

- gas cylinders
- regulators
- hoses
- a torch
- flash back arrestors.

An arc welding kit is made up of:

- a welding machine
- cables
- electrodes
- clamps.

Other welding equipment required is listed in the table below.

| | | | | |
|---|---|---|---|---|
| **Tape measure** | Available in various sizes and lengths. Used to measure positions of equipment, saw cuts and drilled holes | | **Slag or chipping hammer or pick** | For chipping away welding waste products called slag | |
| **Grinding tool** | For preparing the surfaces prior to welding or for smoothing-off after welding is finished | | **Jigs, clamps and weights** | For securing the workpiece for welding | |

## QUICK CHECK

1 Name one type of eye protection worn by welders.
2 What sort of clothing must be avoided when welding?
3 Who are the BCGA?

**Figure 11.01** Welding is a method of joining metals together using heat

# What is welding?

There are three main ways to join metal together using heat.

**Soldering** – the method of joining two metals by melting a third metal onto them, which acts as an adhesive. Soldering is generally used for smaller joints such as cable terminations. This is done below the melting point of the parent materials.

**Brazing** – similar to soldering but carried out at a higher temperature. Brazing is used where some level of mechanical strength is required. This is done below the melting point of the parent materials.

**Welding** – uses heat to melt the two pieces of metal together. A 'filler' is often added into the joint to help with the binding process. Welding provides an extremely strong joint and is used for major engineering jobs, such as construction, steelwork, pipework and shipbuilding. This is known as fusion welding.

## QUICK CHECK

1  What is soldering used for?
2  How does welding create a joint between two pieces of metal?
3  List three types of engineering job that welding is used in.

# Welding health and safety

Welding is a hazardous job. It can involve the use of an exposed flame, extreme heat and volatile gases as well as the use of electrical equipment. It is often carried out on construction or heavy manufacturing sites, which are already dangerous work areas.

First aid facilities and a qualified first aid person should be available for each shift for immediate treatment of flash burns to the eyes as well as skin burns.

The HSE publication COSHH WL8 has a useful checklist for welders.

- Learn to use the controls properly.
- Make sure that extraction equipment is in the correct position and is working properly.
- Always use, store and maintain protective equipment as instructed.
- Check for leaks, wear and damage to welding equipment.
- Tell your supervisor if you find any problems. Never carry on working.
- Put out the oxy-fuel gas welding torch or switch off the arc welding machine when you stop for a rest or a break.
- Always co-operate with anyone carrying out health checks.
- Always wash your hands before you eat, drink or go to the toilet.
- You must never clean your hands with solvents or concentrated cleaning products.
- Use the barrier creams provided to protect your skin and keep to the instructions.

## Risk assessment

Before any work takes place a risk assessment must be drawn up. A welding workshop should already have a general risk assessment covering the work carried out there. For small jobs this does not need to be written down but is a general check that it is safe to begin work. For larger jobs this will be documented. Risk assessment forms should contain the following:

- the tasks that make up the job
- what the hazards are for each of these tasks
- what safety measures are being taken to reduce the risk, for example, eye protection, gloves
- who the hazard could affect, for example, a member of the public who is walking past or other people working nearby.

Some risk assessment forms also have columns for the likelihood of an accident taking place and how serious it would be.

For more information on risk assessments, see Chapter 1, pages 7–8.

## Welding at height

Some welding takes place at height. In such situations, the welder must:

- put into practice the safety measures outlined in the Work at Height Regulations
- make sure the work area is safe
- make sure there are barriers both to prevent falls and to stop heavy tools and equipment from dropping onto anyone working below.

Precautions must also be taken to protect others from sparks and hot slag which may drop from the weld.

## Welding in confined spaces

Welding can also be carried out in **confined spaces**. When such work is necessary, the following precautions must be taken.

- Ensure a Permit to Work has been issued before work starts (see Chapter 1).
- Open and secure all access covers and doors so that they can't close and trap you inside. You must be sure you could get an unconscious person out.
- Test that there is:
  o enough oxygen
  o no flammable gas
  o no toxic gas or chemical.

These tests require specialist equipment and an expert may need to be called in to carry them out.

- Ensure there is a way of turning off power and gas supplies from outside the confined space.
- Remove any materials that may catch fire or become a hazard if exposed to heat or gases from welding.

**Key term**

**Confined space** – a work area where a welder can actually enter and work but movement and space are limited. For example, a container, tank, trench or duct

**Hands On**

What are the main headings for a welding risk assessment?

259

## Heat and sparks

Fire and burns are the main welding hazards. As well as the flame or **arc**, welding produces:

- sparks – formed from small fragments of hot metal
- spatter – larger pieces of molten metal.

Sparks, spatter and molten **slag** can pass through cracks, along pipes and through wall or floor openings. They can cause burn injuries and start fires without the welder knowing.

To prevent fires and explosions:

- keep equipment free of oil and grease because they are flammable, which means that they will easily catch fire.
- do not weld near flammable materials
- avoid welding in or near:
  - paint spray rooms - the fumes in spray rooms can ignite suddenly and cause an explosion
  - degreasing tanks – contain fumes even if they are empty and might also contain the remains of flammable liquids and chemicals that are used in them
  - storage areas – may contain flammable material, including cardboard and paper packaging
  - ventilators – could draw in welding fumes and spread them round the building
- make sure a 'fire watcher', equipped with an extinguisher, is present if welding is being carried out where there is a risk of fire
- check the area for signs of fire when finished.

## Eye injury

The electric arcs used in arc welding are not only extremely hot, but are so bright they can cause eye damage. The most common form of this is 'arc eye', which is an inflammation of the **cornea**. In very bad cases it can burn the **retina** of the eyes. It is vital to wear the eye protection listed at the start of the chapter. Tinted anti-flash glasses are often worn by welders.

Transparent welding curtains should also be put up around the welding area to protect other people from the arc.

## Inhaled matter and particles

Welders are also often exposed to dangerous gases and tiny, airborne particles. Arc welding smoke and fumes contain **oxide** particles which can find their way into your lungs and cause damage to tissue. It is important to use extractors to remove these fumes from the area you are working in.

## Gas

The most common gases created by welding are **carbon dioxide** and **ozone**, which are both harmful when inhaled. Welding areas must be ventilated so that these gases are removed and fresh air drawn in. The arc also creates carbon monoxide and nitrogen dioxide. These gases are toxic.

# Manual oxy-fuel gas welding

Oxy-fuel gas welding is one many types of welding, that exists today. Oxy-fuel gas welding is carried out using bottled gas and a flame. There are two gases used. One of these is always oxygen, the other can be acetylene or occasionally hydrogen, which can be used for welding low melting point metals like aluminium or magnesium. Acetylene is the only fuel gas which can be used to weld steel.

Using flammable gas and a flame is extremely dangerous so a strict safety procedure must be followed and the equipment always handled correctly and with respect.

## How manual oxy-fuel gas welding works

Oxy-fuel gas welding uses fuel gas and oxygen to weld metals. Both of these are flammable when ignited and burn at temperatures high enough to melt metal. The most common combination is oxygen and acetylene.

### Oxygen

Oxygen is used to increase the flame temperature. Although it is part of the air we breathe, it is highly flammable and must be treated with respect.

### Acetylene

Acetylene is a fuel gas and can burn at about 3,500°C when combined with oxygen. It is explosive and has to be handled very carefully.

## Equipment

### Cylinders

Acetylene gas is contained in special cylinders which help to store the acetylene in a safe manner. Acetylene is highly reactive and is dissolved in acetone and contained within a porous mass inside the cylinder.

Acetylene cylinders also have a safety plug fitted at the bottom of the cylinder. If the cylinder is heated to above approximately 100°C the safety or fusible plug will melt and allow the acetylene to escape before dangerous pressures are developed.

Cylinders of all types should not be exposed to heat or shock and should always be stored upright. Never allow oil or grease to come into contact with fittings as they can become highly flammable and explosive.

**Keep It Safe**

Both the fuel and oxygen cylinders should be kept upright and securely fastened to a wall, post or a portable cart. An oxygen cylinder is especially dangerous because its contents are stored at pressure. If the cylinder falls over and its valve is knocked off, the cylinder will become a dangerous missile, with enough force to smash through a brick wall. For this reason, an oxygen cylinder should never be moved around without its valve cap screwed in place.

**Figure 11.02** An oxy-fuel gas welding set on a trolley

**Figure 11.03** Pressure gauges and adjustment knob

## Pressure regulator

The regulator is used to control the pressure at which the gas is released from the cylinders. Most regulators have two stages:

1. **fixed pressure** – as the gas is used, the cylinder gas pressure falls, this part of the regulator keeps the cylinder gas release at a constant pressure

2. **adjustable pressure** – this controls the pressure reduction from the intermediate pressure to the low outlet pressure.

The regulator has two gauges:

- cylinder contents pressure
- outlet/hose pressure.

An adjustment knob is used to set the required pressure.

## Gas hoses

Only use hoses that are specifically designed for welding. They are usually two hoses run side by side, i.e. a double-hose design. Color-coding makes them easy to identify:

- oxygen – blue
- acetylene – red.

Oxygen and fuel gas hose connectors are threaded in opposite directions to make sure the right hose is connected to the correct outlets and so that oxygen and acytylene cannot be interchanged.

- Oxygen – right-handed as normal.
- Fuel gases – left-handed thread with an identification groove cut into the nut.

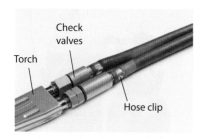

**Figure 11.04** Crimped hose-clips

Connections between flexible hoses and fittings must be made by crimped hose-clips fitted over a barbed spigot. Worm-drive or Jubilee clips must not be used. The hoses should also be taped together at 1 m intervals.

## Flashback arrestor

Flashback arrestors must be fitted between the regulator outlet and the hose. This is to stop the flame or the oxygen-fuel mixture being pushed back into the cylinders in the event of an explosion at the torch end.

## Non return or check valve

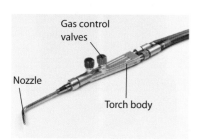

**Figure 11.05** A welding torch

A check valve allows gas to flow in only one direction. The valve is a chamber containing a spring-loaded ball that is pressed against one end of the chamber. It will allow gas to flow towards the torch but blocks any gas flowing back towards the cylinder.

Non return valves are fitted between the flashback arrestor and hoses and are also fitted at the torch end of the hoses. They are used on both gas lines.

### Welding torch

The torch is held by the welder and used to heat the weld area in order to make the weld. There is a mixing chamber inside the torch body where the fuel gas and the oxygen are combined before the gases reach the nozzle. The mixture is adjusted using the valve knobs. The oxygen valve is coloured blue and the Acetylene valve is red.

Welding nozzles screw into the end of the mixing chamber and are interchangeable. The size used will depend on the thickness of the parent metal and the type of joint being welded.

**Figure 11.06** Welding electrodes

### Welding rods

Welding rods provide the filler for the weld. Many also contain material that will form a shield around the arc and stop the build-up of gases that cool the welding area.

## Preparing to carry out oxy-fuel gas welding

### The materials

The materials to be welded need to be prepared.

- Clean joint faces – they must be free from oil, grease, moisture, paint and rust.
- Prepare weld edges – either grind a bevel or flat edge, depending on the type of weld needed.
- Set up the joint – make sure the edges are level and secured so that there is no movement while welding takes place. Use weights to hold sheet metal flat and prevent bending caused by the heat. Small pipes can be laid in a length of angle iron to stop them rolling. A series of small spot welds also help secure the joint.

**Figure 11.07** Metals prepared for welding (cleaned and bevelled)

### The equipment

Before carrying out oxy-fuel gas welding, you must carry out all the following checks and jobs in the order shown.

1. Check regulators, hoses and check connections for leaks and damage.
2. Fit the correct gas nozzle to the torch.
3. Check that a flashback arrestor is fitted.
4. Set gas pressures.

### Leak detection

Oxy-fuel gas equipment, including joints, hoses and valves should always be tested for leaks when full cylinders are fitted. Daub all the welding equipment with the correct leak detector spray around all joints. If there is a leak, bubbles will appear and show you exactly where the leak is found. Never use equipment that is leaking fuel gas or oxygen.

 **Keep It Safe**

Backfire is a common problem for beginner welders. This is when a flame burns back into a torch. When this happens there is a loud bang. It is caused by holding the torch too close to the workpiece. A partly blocked torch nozzle can also cause backfire.

If a backfire happens:

1. Shut off the torch valves, first the oxygen then the fuel gas.
2. Shut off the oxygen and fuel gas cylinder valves.
3. Cool the blowpipe with water.
4. Check the equipment for damage or faults.

## Basic oxy-acetylene welding

| Checklist | | | |
| --- | --- | --- | --- |
| PPE | Tools and equipment | Consumables | Source information |
| • Welding goggles or helmets with face plates<br>• Heavy leather gloves<br>• Protective long-sleeved jacket or overalls<br>• Protective footwear | • Oxy-acetylene welding set<br>• Clamps and jigs<br>• Slag hammer<br>• Grinding tool | • Metal plate<br>• Welding rods | • HSE HSG139<br>• COSHH<br>• HSE WL8: COSHH essentials for welding, flame cutting and allied processes<br>• ISO 15614-1:2004 |

**1**

Open the torch acetylene valve and ignite. Make sure you purge the system before lighting.

**2**

Set the flame by adjusting the acetylene valve until the flame sits on the torch tip and the smoke disappears.

**3**

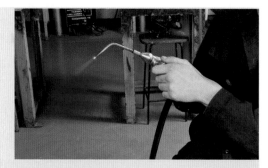

Open the oxygen torch valve slowly until you have the flame type that you need.

**4**

Apply the flame to the base metal and hold until a small puddle of molten metal is formed.

**5**

Move the puddle along the path where you want the weld bead to form.

 **Safe working**

Ignite the welding flame using a specialist welding friction lighter. Never use a match or flammable lighter.

## Neutral Flame

A neutral flame is used for most oxy-gas welding. It causes the molten metal puddle to be clear. The metal flows easily and will not boil or spark. A neutral flame doesn't normally have any harmful chemical effect, such as oxidation or increased carbon, on the metal being welded. Neutral flames are normally used to weld mild and stainless steel, cast iron, copper and aluminium.

A neutral flame has two areas, or zones. The inner zone is where the acetylene and the oxygen combine and should be a bright bluish-white colour. There should be a light blue flame around the inner zone.

To create a neutral flame:

1. Set and light the torch according the step-by-step instructions on page 284.
2. Increase acetylene until the flame is like a white feather.
3. Gradually open the oxygen valve to shorten the acetylene flame.
4. When the flow of acetylene is decreased or the flow of oxygen is increased the feather will fade.
5. The neutral flame begins when the feather disappears.
6. Look for a clear inner cone to the flame.
7. Make sure no whitish streamers or feathers are present at the end of the cone.

## The bead

The bead is the joining line between the two workpieces. A regular bead is the mark of a good-quality welder. Controlling the speed of welding will help you form an even, smooth bead. For example, if the bead gets too wide, you need to increase the **welding travel speed**.

## The rod

When welding, the filler rod must be added to the molten puddle. When not adding it to the puddle, the filler must be kept out of the flame to protect filler metal from **oxidisation**.

Do not let the welding flame burn off the filler metal. If this happens, the filler will not wet into the base metal properly and the weld will be weak. A sign of this is a series of cold dots on the base metal.

## Closing down the equipment

To avoid fire or explosion, oxy-fuel gas welding equipment must be closed down in the correct sequence.

**Figure 11.08** A rod and a weld puddle

> **Key term**
>
> **Welding travel speed** – the speed at which you move the welding puddle along the join between the two metals

> **Key term**
>
> **Oxidisation** – a reaction between oxygen and any other substances it comes into contact with. In some metals this takes the form of rust. In other metals this causes discolouration. In welding, oxidisation can take place if flames are not set up correctly or if metals are not dry and free from oil and grease

# Closing down oxy-fuel gas welding equipment

| Checklist | | | |
|---|---|---|---|
| **PPE** | **Tools and equipment** | **Consumables** | **Source information** |
| • Welding goggles or helmets with face plates<br>• Protective long-sleeved jacket or overalls<br>• Protective footwear | • Oxy-acetylene welding set | None needed for closing down | • HSE HSG139<br>• COSHH<br>• HSE WL8: COSHH essentials for welding, flame cutting and allied processes<br>• ISO 15614-1:2004 |

**1**

Close the acetylene torch valve first to prevent unburned fuel gas escaping.

**2**

Close the oxygen valve.

**3**

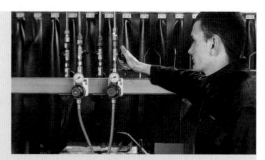

Close both cylinder valves.

**4**

Open the acetylene and oxygen valves on the torch body one at a time to allow gas in each line to escape. Watch for the regulator gauge until the line pressures are at zero.

**5**

Close the acetylene and oxygen torch valves. This stops the reverse flow of gas into an opposite line.

**6**

Release the line pressure-adjusting screws on the acetylene and oxygen regulators.

# Manual arc welding

Arc welding uses electricity instead of gas to provide the heat for welding. Electricity needs a complete circuit to be made before current can flow. In arc welding the electricity is provided by the welding machine. It flows along the welding leads, through the electrode, the metal workpiece then back to the welding machine.

Although this type of welding does not use gas and a naked flame it still generates tremendous heat. There is also the danger of electric shock. This means that arc welding safety procedures must be followed strictly. Remember that the light from an arc is extremely bright. It will not only damage the welder's eyes but also the eyes of anyone nearby.

## How manual arc welding works

Arc welding uses heat generated by an **electric current** to melt the workpiece metal. Both **a.c.** and **d.c.** current can be used for arc welding.

### The arc

The arc consists of an electric current flowing between a **positive** and a **negative** electrode. A high **current** is needed to ignite the arc. One method for starting the arc is to touch the electrode to the piece of metal being worked on, and then pull away slightly. The arc is hot enough to melt most metals.

### The arc welding circuit

An **electric circuit** is needed for electric current to flow. An arc welding circuit is made up of:

- an electrode – usually a length of wire
- a cable – connected to the metal itself using a return clamp.

Both these components are connected to the welding machine. The welding machine is a **transformer**. This machine produces a low voltage (e.g. 40 V) and a high current (e.g. 130 A).

This current flows to the electrode and is strong enough to pass through the gap between the electrode and the metal. As it passes through the air, the current forms a very hot and very bright arc.

Figure 11.09 A welding arc

**QUICK CHECK**

1 What is oxygen used for in oxy-fuel gas welding?
2 What colour is an acetylene hose?
3 What is a flashback arrestor?

**Key term**

**Electric current** – a flow of electricity, measured in amps (A) (see Chapter 4)

**a.c.** – stands for alternating current. It is an electrical supply that constantly reverses direction. Our mains electrical supply is a.c. but for welding a transformer is used to increase the current

**d.c.** – stands for direct current. It is an electrical supply that always flows in the same direction. A battery supplies d.c.

**Voltage** – a measurement of electrical pressure. It is this pressure that causes the current to flow around a circuit

**Electrical circuit** – a closed loop around which electricity flows. It is made up of a power supply, a conductor and a load (see Chapter 4)

**Transformer** – an electrical machine that can either increase or decrease the supply voltage and current.

**Did You Know**

Electric current flows from **positive** (+) to **negative** (-). Look at a battery and you will see these clearly marked on the battery case (see Chapter 4).

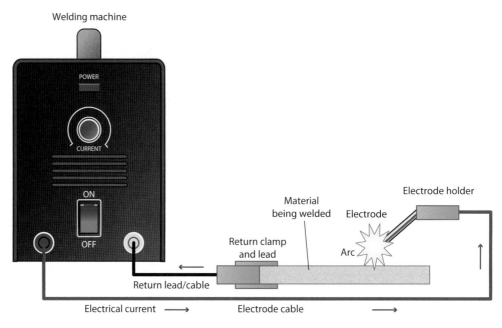

**Figure 11.10** An arc welding circuit

## *Shielding*

Because arc welding is carried out at high temperature, metals can react with chemicals in the air, such as oxygen and nitrogen. This reaction weakens the weld.

Special electrodes are used to help protect against this. These have a covering, called a flux, which forms a gas or vapour shield around the arc as the electrode burns.

## The difference between d.c. and a.c. arc welding

The type of current used in arc welding plays an important role.

### *d.c. welding*

The current can be set to flow in either direction.

* **Positively charged electrode** – when the electrode cable is attached to the positive terminal and the earth clamp is attached to the negative terminal the electrode will melt quickly. A positively charged electrode causes shallow welds.

* **Negatively charged electrode** – when the electrode cable is attached to the negative terminal and the earth cable is attached to the positive terminal. The polarity is called direct current electrode negative (DCEN) or straight polarity. A negatively charged electrode makes deeper welds.

### *a.c. welding*

This is when the current alternates rapidly back and forth between the electrode and the return clamp and metal. This results in medium-penetration welds.

## Arc blow

Arc blow sometimes occurs when using d.c. to weld. The electrical current sets up a magnetic field around the electrode. This magnetic field can be strong enough to pull the arc from its path, which can create a poor weld and excessive spatter. Arc blow is often worse at the ends of a joint, for example at the top part of Vee joint or in the corners of a Tee joint.

Using a.c. can reduce arc blow. The constantly changing current means that the magnetic field does have time to strengthen enough to distort the arc.

Arc blow does not occur when welding with a.c., so if it isn't possible to change to a.c., try the following.

- Forward blow – move the return connection to the edge of the welded joint.
- Backward blow – move the return connection to the start of the joint.
- Move the earth connection as far from the joint as possible.
- Add a second connection to the return clamp and connect one clamp to opposite end of the section.
- Wrap a short length of the earth cable around the workpiece to set up a second, magnetic field that counteracts the first.

## Manual arc welding equipment

### Welding machine

The welding machine is the main part of the welding set and contains the power supply. A transformer is used to convert mains voltage to a lower voltage and produce a high current in an a.c. welding machine.

Usually **d.c. welding machines** can change the direction of current flow (polarity) in the welding circuit by using a change-over switch on the machine or by swapping the electrode and clamp connections.

Many arc welding machines are fitted with a warning lamp that will come on if the transformer is overheating. The machine itself will also cut out. The transformer must cool down and the warning light go out before welding can continue.

### Welding leads

Welding leads are flexible and designed for use in harsh conditions. The **conductors** are stranded, which means they are made up of dozens of smaller wires, making the cable flexible. The **insulation** is usually flame and smoke resistant. Welding cables are large because they are designed to carry high current. The smallest are usually 16.0 mm² and the larger versions can be up to 50 mm². Welding leads should be checked to see that they haven't been damaged and are free from cuts or burned insulation.

### Electrodes

The electrode is a length of conductor through which current flows to or from the weld. It has a metal core, which is either the same or **compatible** with, the metal being welded. The core is covered by a substance called flux. Flux contains chemicals. These make the joints stronger.

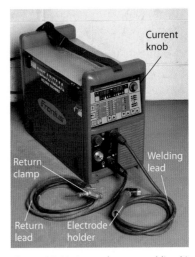

**Figure 11.11** A complete arc welding kit

**Key terms**

**Conductor** – the part of a cable which carries electrical current, for example the copper core

**Insulation** – a material that will not carry electrical current, for example PVC covering

**Compatible** – when two materials fit or work together

The electrode is held in a clamp with an insulated handle. Arc welding electrodes are available in various diameters and lengths, each designed for various joint positions and thicknesses.

| Electrode diameter | Thickness of metal | Current setting |
|---|---|---|
| 1.6 mm | 1.50 mm | 40 A–55 A |
| 2.00 mm | 2.00 to 2.5 mm | 50 A–70 A |
| 2.50 mm | 3.00 to 6.00 mm | 75 A–95 A |
| 3.20 mm | 4.00 to 10.00 mm | 10 A–140 A |
| 4.00 mm | 8.00 to 25.00 mm | 140 A–180 A |
| 5.00 mm | 12.00 to 50.00 mm | 100 A–240 A |
| 6.00 mm | 20.00 to 100.00 mm | 240 A–350 A |

Table 11.01 Welding rod size and current needed for various thicknesses of metal

| Electrode type | Use |
|---|---|
| **Rutile** (titanium dioxide) | Creates a stable arc with low spatter and is the common general purpose type |
| **Basic** (calcium carbonate and fluoride) | Has a moisture-resistant flux coating, low spatter, good arc striking and is used on carbon steels |
| **Cellulosic** (cellulose) | Penetrates deeply, produces only a light slag covering and is used for high-speed pipe welding |
| **Iron powder** | Added to the flux and results in deep penetrating welds. It is very efficient and used for flat or horizontal-vertical weld on structural steels |
| **Surfacing and non-ferrous alloy** | Used for special applications, e.g. building-up of worn surfaces and providing a wear-resistant finish |

Table 11.02 The five main types of electrode and their uses

## Care and storage of electrodes

The condition of the electrodes will affect the quality of the welded joint. Damaged electrode coating results in poor arc stability and can also reduce the shielding effect. Most electrode coatings absorb water.

To keep electrodes in good condition:

- only open new packets of electrodes when they are needed
- store electrodes in clearly marked groups
- keep different types of electrode separate
- do not store in a warm, dry place
- rotate stock so that electrodes are not stored for long periods
- discard damaged electrodes.

## Electrical safety

Because arc welding relies on an electrical supply to work, there is the added hazard of electric shock.

**Keep It Safe**

Switching off the welding machine using its own on-off switch is not enough. There will still be a live supply flowing into the equipment even if it is not operating the welder.

## Isolation of electrical supplies

Never carry out any checks or servicing on welding equipment if it is connected to the electrical supply. If it is plugged into a socket, whether a 13 A or an industrial one, pull out the plug. If it is permanently connected to an electrical supply, switch off its **isolator**.

| Electrical component | Precautions |
| --- | --- |
| **Welding leads** | • Check for damage to the insulation<br>• Make sure the lead is not cut or otherwise damaged<br>• Keep cable dry, free of oil and grease, and protected from hot metal and sparks<br>• Make sure the terminations are tight and secure<br>• Join welding cable using fully insulated lock-type connectors |
| **Earthing** | • Ensure the welding machine itself is connected to earth. This should be carried out via the supply to the machine<br>• Ensure the workpiece is connected to earth. The welder should be insulated from the workpiece while the welding is taking place because there is a risk of shock |
| **Electrode and electrode holder** | • Use fully insulated electrode holders<br>• Do not use damaged holders or any with protruding screws<br>• Never touch the electrode unless the welding power source is off because the electrode is electrically live |

Table 11.03 Checks to be carried out on arc welding equipment

## Interference with pacemakers

Some welding machines use a **high-frequency** a.c. current which can affect pacemakers of people with heart problems. Anyone with a pacemaker must stay at least 2 m from the welding and 1 m from the actual weld site.

## Preparing to carry out manual arc welding

Welders will be issued with specifications for the welding job. These will help you choose the correct electrode type and welding method.

### The welding area

Prepare the work area for the welding job. Place welding screens in the correct position to protect others.

- Make sure the fume extraction works correctly.
- Make sure there is a supply of fresh air if the welding job is on site.

### The materials

For information on materials needed in arc welding, see page 257.

### Connecting up

1. Attach the leads attached to the machine.
2. Make sure the return clamp is firmly attached to the workpiece on clean, solid metal.
3. Place the return clamp as close to the proposed weld as possible.
4. Set the correct current for the job.
5. Connect the welder to the mains supply.
6. Switch the machine on.

### *Striking the arc*

- Put the face mask in place.
- Bring the electrode to the work surface at an angle of approximately 70°. Strike an arc by briefly touching the work surface with the tip of the electrode then snatching it back to a distance of approximately 1.5 mm.
- If the electrode is not pulled away quickly enough it may weld itself to the workpiece. If this happens, give it a sharp tug to free it, and try again.
- If this doesn't free the electrode, turn the welding machine off straight away because the electrode will overheat.
- If you withdraw the electrode too far once the arc is struck, the arc will be lost. In this case try again.

# Basic arc welding technique

## Shutting down an oxy-acetylene weld unit

| Checklist | | | |
|---|---|---|---|
| PPE | Tools and equipment | Consumables | Source information |
| • Welding goggles or helmets with face plates<br>• Heavy leather gloves<br>• Protective long-sleeved jacket or overalls<br>• Protective footwear | • Arc welding set<br>• Clamps and jigs<br>• Slag hammer<br>• Grinding tool | • Metal plate<br>• Electrodes | • HSE HSG139<br>• COSHH<br>• HSE WL8: COSHH essentials for welding, flame cutting and allied processes<br>• ISO 15614-1:2004<br>• Electricity at Work Regulations |

**1**

Set the required current.

**2**

Connect the return clamp to the workpiece as close to the weld as possible.

**3**

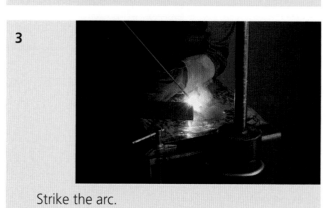

Strike the arc.

**4**

Move the electrode along the joint between the two metals. A pool of molten metal will form, keep the tip in this molten pool at all times. If you hear an even crackling noise, this is an indication of a good weld.

**5**

The area of weld should be a complete fusion of the electrode and workpiece metal.

**6**

Chip or grind away any slag that forms on the surface of the weld.

## QUICK CHECK

**1**  What is a rutile electrode used for?

**2**  What checks should be carried out on welding leads?

**3**  What are the two types of electricity supply used for arc welding?

### Hands On

Practise striking an arc. There may a tendency to jump and overreact when an arc is struck for the first few times, so practice is important.

## Stops and Starts

When welding using the manual metal arc welding process, the weld often has to stopped and re-started in mid run. This is the because the welding electrode is often used up before the weld has been completed or the amperage setting needs to be changed due to the work heating up too much or because of a change in material section (thickness). When the weld is stopped it leaves a small dimple or crater at the end of the run you have just completed. If the weld is not re-started properly this will cause a poor weld that will not meet the specification. Craters can be a stress raiser and an area of weakness in a welded joint, so it is very important that they are filled.

To stop and restart the weld a few simple steps need to be followed:

* Use a slag or chipping hammer and wire brush to clean up the small crater and weld area removing all traces of slag. Use an angle grinder to remove any stubborn slag.

* Fit a new electrode or make sure there is no ball of metal fused to the end of the electrode you are using.

* Start the weld just ahead of the small crater left during your last run, in the same direction you were welding before you stopped, on an un-welded part of the joint.

* Run the electrode over the crater to fill it in by going the opposite direction to normal. Then continue to weld in the correct direction.

When you come to the end of a weld where there is a crater, you can pause at the end by holding the electrode still or by going slightly back on the weld to fill the crater and leave an even finish.

When you start a weld on the edge of a plate, move the electrode back towards the edge to fill the starting crater that can be created. Be careful – if overdone the weld can melt through the material and leave a hole.

### Quick Tip

Unless you are certain that you have selected the correct amperage setting for your weld, it is a good idea to first burn an electrode on a piece of material the same thickness as the job. This will help you to get a good start first time when it really matters.

### Quick Tip

Try to avoid striking your electrodes on parts of the fabrication that are not going to be welded over. Arc strikes are stress raisers and also cause craters. When restarting a weld it is a good idea to strike the arc ahead of the start point on an area that will form part of the weld.

# Welding joints, materials, forms and positions

## Types of welded joints

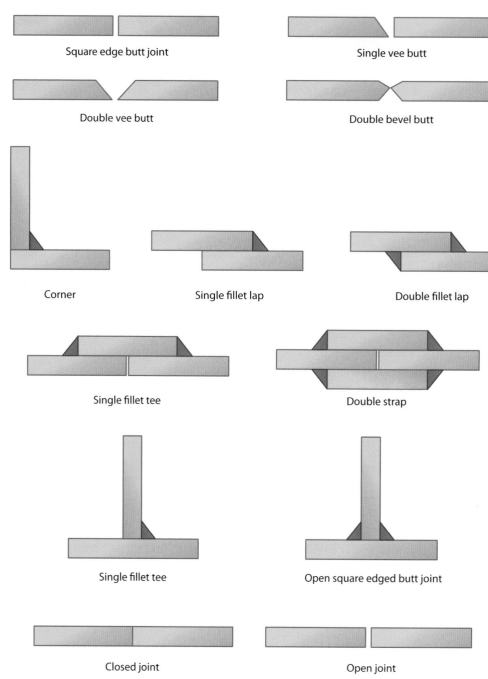

Figure 11.12 A set of joints

# Welding different forms of material supply

There are many different shapes and forms of material that a welder will need to weld. Some of the common forms are shown below.

## Plate

When plates are welded together the welding area will need to be prepared correctly. You may need to prepare the edges of the plate. For a butt joint the most common form of preparation is a double vee butt, but a single bee or double bevel butt joint may also be used depending on the material thickness. A gap can be left in a square edge butt joint (see Figure 11.12) to help the welder to achieve full penetration. This type of joint is the easiest to prepare but is limited to thinner plate thicknesses of approx. 4 mm and below.

When a vee butt joint is used, a root run should be made using a smaller diameter electrode to enable full penetration to be achieved. Don't worry about filling the vee completely as, once the root has been cleaned of slag and checked for inclusions, a capping run can be made using a larger diameter electrode. Welds on thick metal may need more than ten runs to be completed.

Corner, tee, fillet, strap and lap welds naturally form their own preparation and will often not need to be worked on unless they have a thick oxide layer or paint coating that needs removing.

## Sections

When these are welded together, treat each welded face as a single weld, e.g. a box section being welded end-to-end would be four butt welds. The thickness will help you to decide the preparation needed for the join.

The weld becomes more complex when two box sections are joined at 90° to each other to form a tee shape. In this case there may be two single fillet tee welds and two butt joints.

Be very careful with the butt joints. One side will be the open end of a tube and the other will be the full section of the outside corner of the box section. Heat will be taken away by the full section of the outside corner so, to allow the correct fusion of the joint, the welding electrode must be angled towards this side of the weld. This will also prevent the cut end of the tube from melting.

Remember to always weld tack assemblies into position and check dimensions with a square and rule before welding up completely.

## Pipe

The ends of each section of pipe should be bevelled using a grinder. Securing the sections of pipe is important. One method is to lay the sections in a length of angle iron. There are tools available to clamp the sections of pipe together. Because the surface is curved, the welding angle constantly changes. It is best to practise on a pipe with a large diameter.

**Key term**

**Sheet metal** and **plate** – these terms refer to the same material but when sheet metal is thicker than 6 mm it is often referred to as plate

**Quick Tip**

When fabricating assemblies before welding it is a good idea to keep tack welds as small as possible but strong enough to hold the structure in place. Small tack welds can often be welded over. This will help you to avoid the need for grinding them out as the welding moves along the joint.

## EN ISO 6947 Welding positions

Welding often involves large structures that cannot be turned and different welding positions have to be used. These positions are often specified in the written welding instructions to make sure that the welds meet the standard needed. The main welding positions are:

- **Flat (PA)** – flat on the ground or table top. This is the easiest weld as the molten pool is easier to control. Examples include a simple butt weld or a tee weld angled at 45° so that both faces form a natural trough for the weld.
- **Horizontal vertical (PB)** – one part of the weld is horizontal and one part is vertical. Examples include a fillet tee weld with the bottom of the tee horizontal and the upright vertical when the bottom plate is flat on the bench.
- **Horizontal (PC)** – this weld is like welding a horizontal line on a wall. For example, joining two upright tubes with a butt joint or joining two plates one above the other.
- **Vertical upwards (PF)** – weld straight up starting at the bottom. It is quite difficult as the weld pool needs to be controlled by waving the electrode from side-to-side so the correct angle is kept and to make sure the molten metal does not roll off the plate as it is being welded. It can however produce very strong welds.
- **Vertical downward (PG)** – this weld starts at the top of the joint and goes straight down the join line. It is easy to run off the joint line because it can be difficult to see, so it must be completed quickly. It is not as strong as a vertical upwards weld but it is useful for outside corners on thin plate or square edge butt welds in sheet metal.

## Requirements for welds

The following checks must be carried out once a welding job has been completed.

- Are the workpiece dimensions accurate?
- Are the pieces of metal aligned correctly?
- Is the welding bead neat and regular?

### BS4872 Part 1 Weld test requirements

The BS 4872 standards state that the weld test requirements are that:

- the welds are fused and that there is no:
  - undercut
  - overlap
  - surface inclusions
- joins at the stop and start positions are merged together smoothly with no humps or craters in the weld surface
- tack welds are blended in and form part of the finished weld
- there are no cracks.

**Figure 11.13** A good weld

**Figure 11.14** A bad weld

## CHECK YOUR KNOWLEDGE

1 COSHH WL8 suggests the following with regard to welding:

   a Learn to use the controls properly. Tell your supervisor if you find any problems.

   b Take regular breaks. Eat and drink every four hours.

   c Adjust acetylene flame until it is touching the torch tip. Apply flame to the base metal and hold until a small puddle of molten metal is formed.

   d Add a second connection to the earth clamp and connect one clamp to the opposite end of the section. Wrap a short length of the earth cable around the workpiece to set up a second, counteracting the magnetic field.

2 Slag is:

   a used welding electrodes

   b the iron power added to iron powder electrodes

   c tiny particles of hot metal

   d waste material caused by welding

3 Checking for leaks in oxy-fuel gas equipment is carried out using:

   a grease

   b leak detector fluid

   c acetone

   d oil

4 The colour codes for oxy-acetylene hoses are:

   a oxygen – green, acetylene – red

   b oxygen – blue, acetylene – red

   c oxygen – red, acetylene – green

   d oxygen – red, acetylene – blue

5 Taking good care of arc welding electrodes involves:

   a keeping them in plastic containers and always wearing gloves to handle them

   b storing them in clearly marked groups, keeping different types of electrodes separate

   c using damaged ones first and keeping them in damp conditions

   d storing different types in one place and opening their packets as soon as they are purchased

6 Before checking or servicing an arc welding machine:

   a switch off the machine using its own on-off switch

   b leave it on so you can see what the fault is

   c pull out the plug if it is a plug-in type

   d switch off electrical supply to the whole work area

7 The line of fused metal that runs along the join between two welded sections is called the:

   a line

   b junction

   c splice

   d bead

8 The threads on oxy-fuel gas hose connectors have which of the following thread directions?

   a oxygen – right-handed, fuel gas – right-handed

   b oxygen – left-handed, fuel gas – right-handed

   c oxygen – left-handed, fuel gas – left-handed

   d oxygen – right-handed, fuel gas – left-handed

9 Joins at stop and start positions should:

   a form separation points between sections of the weld

   b merge together smoothly with no humps or craters in the weld surface

   c protrude higher than the rest of the weld

   d be clearly marked

10 When igniting a welding torch, which one of the following sequences should be carried out?

   a open oxygen valve and light the oxygen first

   b open both valves, and light the oxygen and acetylene at the same time

   c open acetylene valve and light the acetylene first

   d open either valve and light either gas first

# Index